LEADERSHIP IN SOCIAL ADMINISTRATION
Perspectives for the 1980's

LEADERSHIP
IN
SOCIAL
ADMINISTRATION
PERSPECTIVES FOR THE 1980's

Edited by
Felice Davidson Perlmutter
and
Simon Slavin

Temple University Press, Philadelphia

Temple University Press, Philadelphia 19122
© 1980 by Temple University. All rights reserved
Published 1980
Printed in the United States of America

Library of Congress Cataloging in Publication Data
Main entry under title:
Leadership in social administration.
  Bibliography: p.
  Includes index.
  1. Social work administration.
I. Perlmutter, Felice Davidson, 1931–
II. Slavin, Simon.
HV41.L35   361.3'068   80-12946
ISBN 0-87722-172-3 cloth; 0-87722-201-0 paper

To Jean and Dan
our Partners and Friends

CONTENTS

viii   Contents

PART IV:
HUMAN RESOURCES AND SOCIAL ADMINISTRATION

CONTRIBUTORS

Leslie B. Alexander, Ph.D.
Assistant Professor, Graduate School of Social Work and Social Research, Bryn Mawr College

Burton Gummer, Ph.D.
Associate Professor, School of Social Welfare, State University of New York at Albany

Larry Hirschhorn, Ph.D.
Assistant Professor, Department of City and Regional Planning, and Senior Research Analyst, Management Behavioral Sciences Center University of Pennsylvania

Toba Schwaber Kerson, D.S.W., Ph.D.
Assistant Professor, Graduate School of Social Work and Social Research, Bryn Mawr College

Roger A. Lohmann, Ph.D.
Associate Professor, University of West Virginia

Felice Davidson Perlmutter, Ph.D.
Professor, School of Social Administration, Temple University

Willard C. Richan, D.S.W.
Professor, School of Social Administration, Temple University

Seymour Rosenthal, M.S.W.
Associate Professor and Director, Center for Social Policy and Community Development, Temple University

Simon Slavin, Ed.D.
Professor, School of Social Administration, Temple University

Ione D. Vargus, Ph.D.
Dean, School of Social Administration, Temple University

Harvey Weiner, D.S.W.
Director of Addictive Behavioral Programs, Hahnemann Community Mental
Health Center, Philadelphia

Thomas W. Weirich, Ph.D.
Associate Director of Research and Evaluation, Hahnemann Community Mental
Health Center, Philadelphia

Albert E. Wilkerson, D.S.W.
Professor, School of Social Administration, Temple University

Scott Muir Wilson, Ph.D.
Assistant Professor School of Social Administration, Temple University

James D. Young, J.D.
Associate Professor, Center for Social Policy and Community Development,
Temple University

PREFACE

Interest in the administration of the social services has increased in the 1970's. Sarri and Hasenfeld (1978) interpret this development as a reaction to the ideological and social reform decade of the 1960's. Whatever the cause, it is clear that the social services are being critically assessed by a variety of constituencies including government, taxpayers, consumers, as well as professionals. In earlier decades social administration was a function of the private sector, and meeting clients' needs was the dominant concern of the social work executive; the current emphasis, reflective of the temper of the times, is with efficiency rather than with effectiveness.

Consequently, social administrators are turning rather consistently to business administration and management for their technical expertise. While this may be appropriate if done on a selective basis, the danger exists that social work, the core profession with the longest experience in the social services, will be swallowed up in the process and lose its professional integrity, its concern for people, their problems, and the problems of our society which affect the lives of the consumers of our services.

We have prepared this volume because we believe that executive leadership in social administration must be grounded in the fundamental values and historical concerns of the social work profession. Recent literature on administration does not shape the technical content in such a way that it reflects the distinctive characteristics of social welfare organizations. Central to our view point is the notion that social administration must simultaneously be concerned with ideological commitment and technological competence. Although social administration is a technical activity, it is not a neutral activity: the executive is always involved in decision-making which reflects an ideological orientation. The concern with ethics and values, fundamental to the social work profession (Levy, 1976), not only provides the baseline for executive behavior but also sets the stage for the administrative advocacy which we view as a core function of administration. In varying degrees all the essays are linked in their concern with social issues and social change strategies designed to improve the social service system.

The editors of this volume have been involved with various facets of social administration including practice the development of educational programs, teaching, and research. We have also been in constant contact with administrators in both the public and private sectors, those who served as field work mentors for our graduate students and those who participated in the numerous seminars, workshops, and conferences we have sponsored.

Through these varied experiences we found that a core of content, with some minor variation, was continuously being addressed. Consequently we designed this volume to reflect those content areas which we have found to be of general concern and interest to practicing administrators of the social services, areas representative of their interests and needs in the field. It has not been our intent to present either a comprehensive volume, such as Slavin's *Social Administration* (1978), or a unified text, such as Trecker's *Social Work Administration* (1971). Rather, we are presenting a volume of selected essays which address the various concerns and functions of the executive, and which, hopefully, will be of heuristic value.

The backgrounds of social administrators vary widely, and a useful book must meet their diverse needs. First, there are many practicing administrators who came up through the agency ranks on the basis of their clinical competence. Levinson and Klerman (1967) succinctly identify the needs of these clinician executives who must develop knowledge and skills unrelated to their original training. Second, a small but growing number of administrators, who may or may not have an MSW degree, who have been trained in various administration programs, including public administration and business administration. Finally, the number of students in academic social administration programs is rapidly increasing as schools of social work broaden their programs to include administration as a practice area (Kazmerski and Macarov, 1976).

Accordingly, the essays in this volume are intended for administrators and sub-executives of social service organizations that plan for or provide social services to clients, in both the public and the voluntary sectors. This volume will also be useful as a supplementary reader for students in social administration programs who have administration as their career goal.

The contributors to this volume have been selected on the basis of their roles as both educators and practitioners in a particular area of expertise. The essays are all original, designed for this volume.

After a dearth in the literature in social administration, we find that in this decade there is an awakening which reflects the increasing attention to the field. (A listing of pertinent works can be found in the references at the end of this preface.) In addition, the journal *Administration in Social Work* made its appearance in the spring of 1977. It is our hope that this volume, through its various administrative perspectives, will contribute to the field and enhance the practice of social administration.

The book is organized as follows: Part I includes two essays which are concerned with the theoretical foundations of social administration. Thus, Slavin provides a framework for social administration which serves as the backdrop for the chapters which follow. This broad perspective is followed by Gummer's essay, which focuses on organization theory and its relevance for administration.

Part II moves from the theoretical foundations to a concern with executive leadership. Perlmutter is concerned with the policy and political dimensions of administration as she identifies a series of constraints and contradictions which complicate the executive leadership role. Richan uses an important case study to illustrate how the administrator can function in the advocacy role, given these policy and political constraints. And since sanction and authority underpin the executive function, this section concludes with Rosenthal and Young's discussion of the governance of the social services. The authors examine the relationship of the executive to boards of directors and the nature, function, and process of working with boards.

Part III focuses on selected technical areas which are central to administrative practice. This section is organized on the premise that the administrator must understand the general aspects of these areas and must be able to link them to meet the mission and mandate of the organization; the essays are intended to help in the setting of guidelines and priorities, in decision-making, or in the hiring of personnel and/or external consultants in relation to these technical areas. Before we move into the individual discussions, Wilson's essay reinforces the orientation of the volume. This is followed by Lohmann's discussion of financial management, Weirich's chapter on information systems, Wilkerson's essay on project development, and Hirschhorn's discussion of evaluation. All of these discussions place the activity within a broader systems framework while simultaneously focusing on the specific technical processes involved.

The human resources of social administration is the concern of Part IV. Alexander and Kerson develop a structural argument vis-à-vis sexism, while Vargus' essay on the minority administrator has a psychological bent. The final essay is concerned with manpower training and preparation. Weiner focuses on the professional in the human service organization; he discusses staff development as an area concerned not only with building skills and knowledge but with developing group cohesion.

The contributors to this volume are all actively involved in social administration through teaching, direct practice, research, and/or supervision. It is our hope that these essays, which reflect this experience, will call attention to the critical areas and issues in the field and will thus contribute to the further development of effective administration of the social services.

Our colleagues and students at the School of Social Administration at Temple University have worked with us carefully as we have together shaped and fashioned our program in social administration. Ms. Barbara Brocklehurst, Ms. Charlotte Hill, and Ms. Lillian Gibson have provided invaluable secretarial assistance.

References

Atwater, Pierce. *Problems of Administration in Social Work*. Minneapolis: University of Minnesota Press, 1940.

Blumenthal, L. H. *Administration of Group Work*. New York: Association Press, 1948.

Dimock, H. S., ed. *Administration of the Modern Camp*. New York: Association Press, 1948.

Ehlers, W. H., M. J. Austin, and J.C. Prothero. *Administration for the Human Services*. New York: Harper and Row, 1976.

Johns, Ray. *Executive Responsibility*. New York: Association Press, 1954.

Kazmerski, K. J., and David Macarov. *Administration in the Social Work Curriculum*. New York: Council of Social Work Education, 1976.

Levinson, D. J., and G. L. Klerman. "The Clinician-Executive." *Psychiatry* 30 (1967): 3–15.

Levy, C. S. *Social Work Ethics*. New York: Human Sciences Press, 1976.

Reynolds, B. C. *Learning and Teaching in the Practice of Social Work*. New York: Rinehart 1942.

Sarri, R. C., and Yeheskel Hasenfeld, ed. *The Management of Human Services*. New York: Columbia University Press, 1978.

Schatz, H. A. *Social Work Administration*. New York: Council on Social Work Education, 1970.

Slavin, Simon. *Social Administration: The Management of the Social Services*. New York: Haworth Press and Council on Social Work Education, 1978.

Spencer, S. W., *The Administration Method in Social Work Education*. New York: Council on Social Work Education, 1959.

Street, E. A. *A Handbook for Social Agency Administration*. New York: Harper and Bros., 1947.

Steiner, R. *Managing the Human Service Organization*. Beverly Hills: Sage Publications, 1977.

Sutherland, J. W. *Managing Social Service Systems*. New York: PBI, 1977.

Trecker, H. B. *Group Process in Administration*. New York: Woman's Press, 1946.

————. *Social Work Administration*. New York: Association Press, 1971.

PART I:
CONCEPTUAL
FOUNDATIONS
OF SOCIAL
ADMINISTRATION

A THEORETICAL FRAMEWORK FOR SOCIAL ADMINISTRATION

Simon Slavin

1

Professor Slavin's essay provides the unifying theoretical statement for this volume. He addresses the critical need for theory building in social administration. Noting that management theory is an inadequately developed area in all disciplines, he tackles this challenge in relation to the social services.

The author identifies the three essential elements in the social services as the client/consumer, the practitioner or provider of the service, and the service agency. He views the administrator's task as that of "orchestrating" these diverse constituencies, with their different, and often conflicting, interests and needs. However, this role must be guided by a primacy of orientation towards the client/consumer. And it is this orientation which is his unique and distinctive contribution.

This orientation serves to set the stage for the inclusion of an advocacy role for administration. Included in this discussion are case advocacy, program advocacy, and policy advocacy. This theoretical framework provides a proactive view of the administrator's role and serves as a base for decision-making in the varied and diverse tasks to be performed. It is of direct relevance to all of the essays which follow.

Of the many aspects of social work practice, the least developed conceptually is administration. The literature is sparse, and the research embryonic. There is little that one can identify as useful theory, or even as thoughtful theoretical perspective.

In this respect, the situation in cognate disciplines is not much different. Other fields are, to one degree or another, similarly vague and indecisive (see Waldo, 1968, p. 6; Jaski, 1970, p. 303; Caiden, 1969, p. 338). Perspectives on organizational behavior are so diverse, and approaches to administration and management so disperate, that it is difficult to assume a theoretical foundation on which to build a view of administrative behavior in general, or social administration in particular. Indeed, one view suggests that a "unified theory of management is an impossibility" (Behling, 1970, p. 36). The intent of this chapter is to suggest some theoretical perspectives useful for viewing the administration of the social services as a distinctive aspect of professional practice with its own knowledge base, specialized skills, field of application, policy concerns, preoccupation with the delivery of social services to a delineated clientele, and history, culture, and value preferences. For present purposes administration and management are interchangeable terms.

The history of administration is, of course, as old as the social services themselves. Administrative careers, however, have tended to be built upon clinical practice. Competent practitioners have tended to move sequentially into supervisory, sub-executive, and executive roles, and the essential criterion for advancement has been the ability to perform clinical tasks with some distinction. Sarri has put the issue well:

> Reliance on the promotion of practitioners trained into direct service methods as the primary means for obtaining administrators and policy personnel is not appropriate. . . . There is some evidence that knowledge and skill in clinical practice may be antithetical to or dysfunctional for sound administration and policy development (1973, p. 43).

There is a growing conviction that administrative competence requires its own special preparation. The increasing number of programs in schools of social work that include both specialized courses and related field work (Kazmersky and Macarov, 1975, p. 43) and the emphasis given in recent years by several agencies of the Department of Health, Education, and Welfare, notably the Social and Rehabilitation Agency and the National Institute of Mental Health, to research and training grants in this field provide testimony to this trend.

Mapping The Territory

Delineating the social service field is a difficult task, made so by a complicated history and a diffuse tradition. Boundaries in human affairs tend to be arbitrary because the inevitable overlaps defy definition. Disciplines compete with one another in establishing their respective domains when some essential skills are shared, such as rehabilitation programs, or when new ones made an appearance, such as human services or resources. National patterns and tradition also vary. In England, for example, education, health, and housing are generally included in the social services. A study of British social service administration (Brown, 1975) includes in its purview health, social security ("payments to those in need"), and the personal social services (the provision of "help, social care and support in the community for individuals and groups who appear to be in need of it").

Some more or less arbitrary judgments must be made in mapping the territory for the essays in this volume, concerned as it is with the administration of the social services in America. In its most general sense social services refers to "communal provision to enhance individual and group development and well-being and to aid, rehabilitate, or treat those in difficulty or need" (Kahn, 1972, p. 17). These provisions are made through non-market mechanisms and include goods, services, and policies under public, voluntary, and mixed auspices.

In their comprehensive study of the social services in the United States, Kamerman and Kahn (1976) identify the main service systems as follows: child welfare programs; child care and related programs; social services for the aged; social services for families; homemakers, home help, home health aides; veterans programs; correctional and penal services; community centers, settlements, group programs; access services (e.g., information, referral, advice, case advocacy, liaison); special programs for refugees, native Americans, migrant workers; components of community mental health, retardation programs, community development. In addition, one might add school social work, medical social work and health planning, industrial and labor social work programs, and social planning and fund-raising.

Traditionally, social welfare has been concerned with specialized aspects of several other fields—for example, health, education, housing, employment and income maintenance—as well as with the personal social services. The core professions in most of these have been distinctive—for example, medicine in health and teaching in education. For our purposes, social work is the central professional discipline in the social services, and so our territory includes those special programs located in these service systems where social workers ply their distinctive skill. Because income maintenance programs have been so large a preoccupation of social workers, particularly with respect to social policy development and implementation, we should add this system to our list. With the exception of the general health service, our categories should, then, closely resemble those discussed by Brown.

The parallel attempt to define the essential domain of social administration as a discipline and as a professional practice encounters several significant difficulties, some relating to cognate disciplines and others internal to the social work profession itself. As an administrative discipline it shares certain technical processes with all other administrative enterprises, reflecting essentially their *organizational* requirements. To a greater or lesser degree, it also shares some structural and political dynamics. To illustrate, in the public sector, the social services constitute a sub-set of public administration, so administrators deal with political processes and action in undifferentiated ways. Again, the organizational structure of the public schools bears significant similarities to that of social agencies, so that board-executive-staff relationships and behaviors evolve in quite similar ways. The same can be said of many aspects of health administration in hospitals and in voluntary health associations.

In each of these instances, however, the range of substantive policy issues diverge materially, reflecting the socio-technical foundations of each as well as the fundamental purposes and objectives that gave rise historically to each set of endeavors. A continuing task for both theory and research is to differentiate the common, generic core, or G, factors that inhere in the administration of all cooperative organizational systems from those specific characteristic, or S, factors that tend to preoccupy each professional practice to a substantially greater extent than any other.

This question of boundaries and overlap between different systems has its internal counterpart in the social services. Administering these services in social agencies has always involved the development and implementation of social policies that defined the nature of the services to be provided. For some this suggests the essential unity of these two aspects of social service delivery systems (Gummer, 1975). Some graduate training programs in schools of social work organize their curricula on this basis; others develop separate tracks for each, differentiating both classroom instruction and field experience (Kazmersky and Macarov, 1976).

Here, too, we face the issue of common areas of knowledge and skill (G factors) and professional behaviors that have their own distinctive specifications (S factors). These differences are most readily seen in the contrast between some of the large public bureaucracies in the social services and the direct service, voluntary social agency in the community. Much of the professional activity of the former is devoted to developing social policies and procedures and monitoring their implementation, establishing standards, reviewing grant proposals and requests, and evaluating the progress of programs under their jurisdiction. In the latter, administrators preside over the actual delivery of services, organize, allocate, and monitor staff service roles, deal directly with served constituencies, and provide leadership to and develop relationships with boards of directors that generally reflect local community interests. One set of tasks is largely indirect in essence, some steps removed from the actual and specific provision of client services; the other set is preoccupied with immediate service delivery and the intimacy of practioner-client interaction.

The concern here is with the service-giving agency and some aspects of its administrative dynamics. We will explore the essential organizational elements of the social agency and the nature of its constituencies; some of the internal and external relationships that bind these constituencies; the diverse interests and needs of organizational participants; the essential process of organizational integration, administrative orientation, compliance, and advocacy; and finally some aspects of organizational change that flow from this analysis.

The Social Service Agency

All service-giving organizations combine three essential universal elements: the provider of the service (practitioner), the user of the service (client, consumer), and the organization (the service agency) that brings these two together. In its simplest form, the structure of the social agency can be pictured as follows:

PRACTITIONER ↔ ORGANIZATION ↔ CLIENT

These elements inevitably develop a network of relationships through which the essential objectives of the service-giving agency are achieved. Clients interact with practitioners, and both have a distinctive relationship with the organization; for example, clients meet eligibility requirements, and practitioners respond to conditions of hire.

The reality of the organizational system, however, is considerably more complicated when these organizational elements are viewed in their interaction. (Much of the following is drawn from Slavin, 1977.) This can perhaps best be seen in the matrix shown in Figure 1-1. Each cell in the ninefold table represents a central relationship in the agency system. Figure 1-1 presents three paired or reciprocal relationships between the organizational elements and three relationships internal to each element.

Cell 1 constitutes patterns of client interactions within the agency. There are at least two classes of interaction:

1. Those in which clients prepare one another for ways of working the system to their advantage. Thus, welfare neighbors tell prospective recipients how to approach welfare workers, how to make the case for benefit entitlements most telling, how to dress for interviews, how to deal with hidden resources, and the like. Tenants tell new tenants how to approach

Figure 1-1. Interrelationships between the elements
in the Agency Systems

	CLIENT	ORGANIZATION	PRACTITIONER
CLIENT	1	2	3
ORGANIZATION	4	5	6
PRACTITIONER	7	8	9

rent control officials and how to extract benefits from landlords. Prospective adoptive parents learn from other clients how to appear acceptable to agency norms.

2. Those in which clients compete with one another, either individually or in classes, for agency largess. In family service agencies, selected classes of clients, for example, the poor aged, compete for the organization's resources with fee-paying family clients or with other groups, such as immigrants. Housing programs deal with competing demands of low-income clients and the economically advantaged.

Cell 9 represents relationships within the practitioner group. This class of constituents is hardly homogeneous. Line workers' needs and interests are often substantially different from those of supervisors, department heads, or practitioners from different disciplines. Conflicts between group workers and recreationists in children's institutions, between social workers, counselors, and psychologists in multifunction agencies, between income maintenance workers and service-providing personnel in the public welfare agency, often come to the surface. Much of the administrator's time and attention is devoted to managing these conflicts.

The organization as a legal entity (cell 5), represented by the board of directors or trustees, similarly tends to incorporate a variety of interests and propensities. Indeed, if a board is properly constituted, it is necessarily composed of members who are representative of different constituencies. The administrator is continually engaged in maintaining consensus on essential organizational objectives on the part of the policy-determining body, and in dealing with internal board differences as they emerge from competing or conflicting motivations for board membership, from differing reference group interests, or from ideological differences.

The actual service transaction in the agency is reflected in cells 3 and 7. Practitioners engage clients, and clients engage practitioners, each from distinctive orientations. From the professional's viewpoint, a repertoire of intervention modes and skills furthers the objective of providing a service. A readiness to participate, either voluntarily or under compulsion, on the part of the client makes the service experience possible. The process is reciprocal, and the administrator needs to possess an awareness not only of the professional skills involved but of the ethical and moral basis that lies behind the service delivery. To the extent to which a distinctive methodology and technology is required to provide the agency's service to its clientele, to that extent the administrator requires substantive professional know-how in order to fulfil the professional leadership role so necessary for organizational vitality.

Cells 6 and 8 describe the reciprocal relationship between staff and agency. The agency's policies, purposes, and orientation either attract or repel prospective staff members. Similarly, the physical arrangements, the reward system, the standards of work, the basis of evaluation, and the fringe benefit system all suggest the ways in which organizations are forthcoming in respect to the service providers they engage. Practitioners view the organization as the locus of livelihood and the legitimizer of their professional skill. They approach their self-interest in respect to rewards, working conditions, and security either singly or collectively. Organizational and professional interests frequently diverge, providing an agenda for administrative action that recurs with substantial regularity.

Finally, cells 2 and 4 depict the ways in which clients view agencies and agencies view clients. There are several classes of issues here, involving such matters as: client participation in policy setting; availability, accessibility, and sufficiency of services; eligibility criteria and fee arrangements; and comprehensiveness and continuity of services. Public welfare agencies are frequently preoccupied with limiting service and establishing eligibility barriers. Troublesome clients may be eschewed, and institutional provision may become oppressive. Social agencies need clients to survive, and clients need agency programs that are responsive to their needs. Keeping this symbiotic relationship in constructive interaction is a significant dimension of administrative competence.

To this point, the social agency system has been viewed as bounded. While dynamic elements of analysis have been introduced, the organizational environment has been ignored. The social agency inevitably exists in a socio-political field of related and competing organizations and influences. Resources must be garnered from outside the organization, and increasingly from the public agency. Clients are referred to other services and accepted from them.

So far the discussion has been concerned with the internal, primary constituencies of the administrator. But neither client nor practitioner nor board of directors exists in isolation. Each is embedded in a network of relationships external to the organization. What appears at first sight as a simple structure of relationships is complicated by the fact that each of these elements themselves involve a complex set of relationships in the form of a multiplicity of constituencies that have a greater or lesser interest in what happens in the process of providing services. The administrator is confronted by several tiers of constituencies that differ in their closeness to the actual service provision. It may be convenient to think of primary, secondary, and tertiary constituencies. For example, the primary and most intimate concerns of the administrators are the staff group whose roles they allocate and monitor, the clients who are the immediate objects of the service, and the board of directors, which represents the legal entity of the agency. Much of the administrator's energy and time is devoted to managing these activities in the light of the philosophy, objectives, and policies that guide them.

None of these relationships, however, develops in an institutional vacuum, for each of the primary constituencies has its own constituencies which are ready to intercede in the ongoing activities of the agency, sometimes indirectly, at other times openly and forcefully. The primary staff group reflects the norms and standards of the profession to which it belongs and to which it refers when questions of professional practice are raised. Similarly, trade union organizations representing the staff constituency actively participate in establishing conditions of work.

In like manner, clients frequently belong to consumer organizations, parent associations, or tenant groups that reflect client interests and often become part of the process of establishing conditions affecting client service. In some instances, such associations become part of decision-making bodies, a formal representation of their essential interest in the organization's activities and purposes.

The service-giving agency is also directly related to other bodies in the institutional environment. Of primary interest here are service networks of which they are a part—such as sectarian and non-sectarian local service systems and city-wide, state-wide, or national networks. Funding sources, either voluntary or public, similarly represent immediate organizational relationships that affect the ability of social agencies to provide service.

Each of these primary and secondary constituencies is part of the organizational lifespace of the social administrator. There is, finally, a third tier that is part of this organizational reality, one that affects each of the elements in similar ways. Located here are the general public, whose sanction is the ultimate source of organizational legitimacy, the press and television, legislative bodies, regulatory agencies, and the like. Each of these has its occasion to influence the service-giving function, sometimes to the detriment of the service, sometimes to its flowering. This hierarchy of constituencies is shown in Figure 1-2.

This delineation suggests the vast complexity of the administrative enterprise and points to the many forces in the institutional environment with which the administrator must perforce be concerned. Ignoring any one of

Figure 1-2. Organizational Life Space of Social Administration:
The Constituencies of the Social Administrators

	PRACTITIONER (provider) ←→	ORGANIZATION (social agency) ←→	CLIENT (consumer)
	↓	↓	↓
PRIMARY (internal) constituencies	Staff system ↓	Trustee system ↓	Client system ↓
SECONDARY (external) constituencies*	Professional associations labor unions, alumni ↓	Institutional network, federations, funding agencies, coordinating bodies ↓	Parent associations, consumer groups, special interest groups ↓
TERTIARY (external) constituencies*	General community system Legislatures, federal, state, regional, local Regulatory bodies Media		

*These are illustrative and not intended to be comprehensive.

these elements and its constituencies can only be at the administrators peril. At different times their attention must be focused at specific points on the several networks of relationships. Anticipating when and where to focus is part of the administrative skill and art. Ultimately, the needs and/or interests of these multiple constituencies must be met.

In a non-market system of services, client satisfaction leads to organizational stability and continued utilization of the services. Staff satisfaction plays an important part in agency morale and low rates of turnover. Trustee identification with the organization flows from personal satisfaction in the work. In the secondary and tertiary systems, parent and consumer groups tend to mobilize against shabby or incompetent dealing with clients; professional bodies monitor and often police adequate standards of care; sources of funds attempt to judge the ways in which their resources are expended and provide sanctions where they feel results do not justify continued support. Finally, in a service system network where public funds play an increasingly significant role in supporting service agencies, public policy development and legislative enactments affect most social services in direct and critical ways.

While the conventional wisdom concerning social agencies suggests the mutuality of interests of organizational participants in achieving organizational objectives (Trecker, 1971), a closer examination of the realities of organizational life reveals a built-in set of contradictions and potential antagonisms. The conflict between professional and bureaucratic orientations has been frequently noted in the literature (Billingsley, 1964; Hanlan, 1972, p. 40; Smalley, 1969, p. 33; Freidson, 1970, pp. 138-139; Toren, 1969, p. 157; Reiff, 1971, p. 62; Merton, 1957; Rapoport, 1960, p. 71). But this is only one aspect of organizational conflict. Others reflect some of the distinctive needs and interests of each of the major organizational elements. Clients come to social agencies because they need service; professionals seek income and security, job satisfaction and career development; organizations pursue stability and growth, prestige and status. These needs and the interests they engender are not necessarily compatible (Epstein, 1973, p. 6; Schein, 1972, p. 18).

Illustrations of these differences and contradictions abound in actual practice. The divergence of practitioner-client interests is frequently the result of the "abrasive effects of sociocultural differences" (Bolman, 1972, p. 97). Clients often want and need extended hours for service; practitioners prefer to be available during conventional working hours. Even the definition of a client's problem can pose difficulty. Thus, the sociologist Goode states that "it is the practitioner who decides upon the client's needs, and the occupation will be classified as less professional if the client imposes his own judgment" (Goode, 1969, p. 278; see also Friedson, 1970, p. 169).

Practitioners often find themselves at odds with their agencies. This is particularly true in public welfare departments, where according to Scott (1969, p. 85) "many of the lay-determined laws and policies . . . constitute a source of strain and tension for the professionals who man the agencies." Organizations tend to eschew programs that are perceived as controversial and unpopular, even though clients and staff might believe they are important. School busing issues, inhospitality to speakers and consultants who express socially deviant viewpoints, for example, tend to be avoided because they might alienate important providers of resources, or affect legislators negatively. Challenges to conventional authority tend to precipitate conflict and hostility among trustees, professionals, and clients (Helfgot, 1974).

Conflicts internal to each of the elements also have their sources. Clinicians and researchers on professional staffs frequently differ when the latter wish to deny services to clients in order to ensure tidy experimental conditions. Clinicians of differing theoretical orientations often differ about the best approach to meeting a client's need. Class and social status differences among trustees often lead to conflict in the development of organizational policies. This has been especially prominent in community action—oriented agencies during the sixties. Finally, client differences get expressed in views about priorities of service, reflecting differences in categories of client need and in client reference groups. Well established client organizations have more "clout" than those that are new, weak or dissident, and hence are able to command greater attention from service giving agencies.

In summary, the administrator of a social agency always functions in a dynamic field of forces in which conflicting constituency interests contest for attention and response. The varying pressures and demands that result place powerful constraints on administrative authority. Power and influence tend to be unequally distributed among constituencies and make purely rational behavior by administrators problematical. Organizational-maintenance needs contend with the perceived requirements of clients and practitioners.

The administrator must bring these differing needs and interests into some form of balance or equilibrium—to orchestrate these diverse constituencies. Pusic (1974, p. 197) refers to the "interest-adjudicating and conflict-handling function of administration in which increasingly interested parties themselves are becoming involved through processes such as representation, bargaining participation, and self-management." This interest-balancing function of administration has frequently been noted (Bach, 1964, p. 191; Vickers, 1965, p. 195; Walton, 1959, p. 32).

Since each of the triad of organizational elements—client, practitioner, organization—inevitably attempts to enhance or maximize its position within the service system, we must consider the function of administrators in managing these frequently opposing pressures. Are they to maintain a rationally induced neutrality and objectivity, or are there normative or ethical standards to guide his behavior? If one assumes that there is a preferred orientation that guides administrative decision-making, the consequences of such a choice must be clearly understood. When the administrators sees their essential reference point as the organization, for example, they face the issues posed by compliance requirements of both clients and practitioners. Similarly, if the primacy of orientation is to the client, both organization and practitioner are perforce compelled to subordinate other interests to client service requirements.

The question of differential practitioner orientation has been studied and should cast some light on this issue of administrative orientation and organizational compliance. Billingsley (1964) examined social work practice in a family counseling agency and a child protective agency. When asked to choose between conflicting demands of agency policies, professional standards, the needs of clients or community demands, the great majority indicated that they would follow agency guidelines even if they conflicted with professional standards or the needs of clients. Mass (1964) presented case vignettes to seventy social workers in ten different agencies and asked them to choose from among five alternative intervention procedures. Roughly half the staff worked in psychiatric or family agencies, the others in public agencies. Staff choices reflected these agency orientations to a marked degree. Briar (1964) found that social workers' judgments concerning placement of children in need of substitute care tended to follow closely their own staff positions in either foster care programs or in institutional care.

In reviewing these studies, Kadushin (1965, pp. 44–45) concluded that "a worker in a particular agency . . . tends to reinterpret the client's problem situation in terms of the agency's service. . . . The agency's mandate (or the mandate of a particular department of an agency) determines what we choose to attend and makes for selective perception."

In a related field, Friedson (1970, p. 88) similarly concluded that organizational requirements often take precedence over professional norms in the practice of medicine.

> In a few systematic studies of medical practice that have been made, it was found that the association between medical education and subsequent performance was at best very weak. While the available evidence is scanty and poor, it points to variations in the organization of practice—that is, in the organized setting in which the professional works—as a more important influence than medical education on variation in performance.

What is true for practitioners tends also to be true for administrators. They are hired by boards of directors and are legally accountable to them. In a real sense, they are also directly accountable to funding sources. The power that comes from making resources available provides a powerful lever to constrain administrative action, especially through the threat to discontinue support. The pressures for establishing and maintaining the centrality of the organization's needs pose decisional problems for administrators as they seek to reconcile these needs with those of clients and practitioners. This is clearly one of the essential dilemmas all executives face, particularly when the interests of their several constituencies clash. When they do, the issue of primacy of orientation necessarily comes to the fore.

A brief look at some of the possible consequences of administrative choice may be instructive. For example, a preoccupation or overemphasis on organization needs often leads to goal displacement, where means become ends. Organizational neatness requirements can lead to an excessive emphasis on procedures, eligibility requirements, forms, and rigidities, where client needs tend to become subordinate. Red tape and ritualism become the ruling norms (Stein, 1961, 1962; Blau and Meyer, 1971; Bennis, 1970).

A widely accepted view places the social agency's defined function and purpose as the organizing principle of administrative action. Trecker (1971, p. 28), for example, states that "the purposes of an agency mirror the underlying value and philosophy of service which the agency represents. . . . Purpose, therefore, becomes the primary point of reference for the administrator and it should guide all his actions." The issue implicit here was sharply joined some years ago by the emminent psychologist Allport (1960, p. 283):

> Increasing emphasis on defining "agency function" can lead to a ratrace of referrals, sometimes demoralizing to the client and hence unethical. Even if referrals themselves do not damage the client, he may find at the end of his track that there is no rubric for his distress and therefore no agency to help him. An unmarried girl in a certain town could find no help: she was seven months pregnant, and the only appropriate agency had a rule that no applicant more than six months pregnant could be accepted. Good casework, the agency said, could not be done at this late stage of pregnancy. But is good casework an end in itself? Are we wrong in assuming that social service exists to aid mortals in distress, not to sharpen skills or gratify the professional self-image of the worker?

The point here is that while organizational needs and interests, and their related purposes, procedures, and the like, are indeed a necessary aspect of the delivery of social services, where these become the focal point of emphasis and orientation, both client needs and professional interests become secondary, often to their disadvantage. Clients who do not fit exact agency requirements for either the substance of the service or its accessibility and availability often do not receive the benefits they need. Individual responsiveness and adaptability is often inhibited by general organization prescriptions.

Organizational convenience, eschewing controversial issues, and subservience to funding sources can, and often do, supersede the client service objectives of service agencies; voluntary foundations tend to overwhelm the social agency's independence in responding to objective social need assessment. Organizational maintenance needs tend to encroach on service considerations.

There are consequences, similarly, to an overemphasis on the professional practitioner's needs and requirements. Staff interest in research and training feeds professional status needs more than regular service provision. Interest in unusual, exotic, or specialized client problems can lead to neglect or oversight of other, more numerous, and more characteristic client demands. The movement of practitioners from social agency to private practice, from the public agency to the fee-paying private agency, from institutional settings for the aged and mentally retarded to the more

highly regarded clinical counseling services, are all ways in which professional self-preoccupation may go counter to the broad range of general
client needs. Within the agency, professional overidentification may lead
to rigid professional boundaries and make responsive inter-disciplinary
work more difficult. Since client problems do not necessarily develop in
accordance with the ways professionals package their skills, the question
arises, Which should be responsive to the other? Where the orientation is
essentially professional, clients either adapt to worker's requirements or
leave the service.

When a client perspective becomes the focal point of orientation, both
organization and practitioner are constrained to pursue their interests in
the light of their impact on the integrity of client services. There are, of
course, many problems associated with such a client orientation, not the
least of which is the very identification of the client. This is not as obvious as
would appear to be the case. Thus, Bledsoe and his associates (1972, p.
800), writing out of their experience in California during Governor
Reagan's incumbency, give their definition:

> Who is the client for social services who must be satisfied? The critical client
> is the taxpayer. He pays the tab for the programs and derives the benefits, if
> any, of the services. Thus he, more than the individual recipient of specific
> services, represents the prime target for client-satisfaction efforts. (Another
> important client group . . . consists of elected officials.) A key question is how
> to determine that the taxpayer is satisfied with the services.

Defining the client and client interests is both a value problem and a
problem of professional assessment. The client as the recipient and user of
service provides the essential generative principle for the establishment of
any social service. Social agencies provide an organized response to human
need. Without some perceived default in social development on the part of
individuals or collectivities of individuals there is no basis for creating a
social service. When people cannot reach some desired goal unaided, a
service encounter becomes possible. Parsons (1934, p. 672) defines service
as "any act of an individual so far as it contributes to the realization of the
ends of other individuals." The social agency makes this possible. Service
needs set the conditions for creating an organization to meet them and
should, as a normative principle, define the essential value orientation of
those responsible for administering the service response.

The professional issue goes to the heart of the question of identifying the
client's problem as the basis for practitioner intervention. In the view of
some, only the professional has the ability, by virture of training and
insight, to pose the "real" problem after appropriately analyzing the "presenting" problem and its underlying dynamics. A proper client perspective
suggests a more definitive role for the client in assessing the need that is the

subject of the service transaction. Many problems *are* what they appear. Professional redefinition is often made in light of the agency's philosophical and ideological biases, as we noted above.

One implication of the primacy of orientation to the client and to the integrity of the client service is an administrative advocacy role prescription. In the words of Caiden (1969, p. 14), "the administrator is a social entrepreneur, an advocate for his clientele and a humanizer of institutions." In this posture, the administrator guards against the necessary imposition of agency maintenance needs and practitioner self-interest when they pose negative consequences for agency clients. In this vein, Friedson (1970, p. 168) argues that "professional dominance creates sufficient problems to require the development of a stronger countervailing administrative management and of a better organized clientele."

Advocacy in social work (see Chapter 4, below) is normally seen as adversarial to administration, as a corrective action against arbitrary or destructive agency behavior. The target of advocacy action is most generally authority, the "powers," or organizational policy, the very aspects of the social agency with which the administrator is most centrally identified. On the one hand this makes it extremely difficult for the administrator to project a client advocacy posture. On the other hand, when deftly managed, the authority position of the administrator can facilitate advocacy behavior by staff members, clients, client organizations, and community consumer bodies. Easy access to board members both individually and collectively places the administrator in a strategic position of influence internally. Relationships with key persons of influence in the community, with organizations positively associated with advocacy goals, and with the media can be used to further client objectives.

The focus thus far has been on case advocacy, enhancing individual client service. Administrative advocacy moves in two additional directions, program advocacy and policy advocacy. These are closely related to the concept of administrative leadership that defines the central role of the executive. There is little question that the executives are the central management officers. To the extent that they are also viewed as the chief service officer, providing professional direction to the agency and ensuring service integrity, advocacy is a natural part of the executive role repertoire. In this sense the administrator is not value free, but carries an essential client bias, guided by a service ethic that is rooted in the articulated value system of the profession. Much of the discussion of the clinician-executive centers on these considerations, particularly in the mental health field (Levinson and Klerman, 1972).

Program advocacy gives the administrator responsibility for developing initiatives for organizational growth and responsiveness to changing needs and developing technology. It demands professional alertness, keeping abreast of new patterns of work, and intimate acquaintance with the results of research, particularly on practice. Policy advocacy demands familiarity with social trends, problem analysis, and policy initiatives in legislative and planning bodies and a willingness to risk involvement in the political process.

The client perspective advocated here suggests another point of vantage for the administrator—it provides an essential link to purposive organizational change. If we define organizational change as those modifications and shifts in organizational programs, processes, objectives, or structure that align them with client service needs and interests, then the administrator's assessment of any such disjunction establishes an agenda for change. Thus, there is a direct causal chain from the primacy of orientation to the client, through administrative client advocacy, to a change process that has as its sole end improved service delivery. But this is a sequence that can entail great difficulty for the administrators, bringing them into conflict with trustees, staff members, funding and monitoring agencies, and the like. Long ago, Machiavelli described the essential resistance to novelty in social affairs:

> There is nothing more difficult to carry out, nor more doubtful of success, nor more dangerous to handle than to initiate a new order of things. For the reformer has enemies in all who profit by the old order, and only lukewarm defenders in all those who would profit by the new order. This lukewarmness arises partly from fear of their adversaries, who have the law in their favor; and partly from the incredibility of mankind, who do not truly believe in anything new until they have had actual experience of it (quoted in Caiden, 1969, p. 18).

Yet the executive who is guided by a service ethic is compelled to develop the skills that inform and guide organizational change. The literature on engineering social agency change is now fairly extensive (Brager, and Halloway, 1978; Patti, 1974; Rothman, 1974). From the perspective of this volume, the administrative role includes the management of the change process, focused and oriented to client need and to the integrity of the client service. Such a view places managerial technology—budgeting, information systems, cost-benefit analysis, decision theory—in a context that is essentially and primarily sanctioned by service considerations and by quality standards, and where ultimate accountability is located in the served clientele.

A Theoretical Perspective

What has been sketched above is the outlines of a theory of social service administration or, better, a partial theory or theoretical perspectives. It approaches, essentially, a structural-humanistic theory that identifies normative principles for administrative practice and the major elements that inhere in the locus of the work. It is structural in the sense that it develops from a depiction of the organizational lifespace and its interacting formal and informal relationships. It is humanistic in its central and primary concern for the essential human needs that occasioned the establishment of the social service in the first instance.

A more complete theory would have to incorporate certain other perspectives in the general paradigm. Interest-group theory is useful for defining the position of the several constituencies located in the organizational space. The political context of the community's establishment and continued support of service institutions, its social meaning, similarly provides a theoretical vantage point. Again, contingency considerations found so frequently in the general management literature set some boundaries for the cogency of managerial propositions, their conditional nature, and their reliance on context, social constraints, and ethical imperatives.

The current national emphasis on efficiency, cost containment, and quantifiable objectives often mythologizes management and its power, and tends to lead to a narrow technicism which will "set matters right." The reliance on technically trained managers, drawn from disciplines often removed from the experience of the social services in many of the public bureaucracies dealing with human need, has created as many problems for client service integrity as it has solved.

This chapter provides a rationale and framework for a value-based, ethically directed administrative orientation that has as its ultimate purpose a humane, adequate, and competent social service delivery system.

References

Allport, Gordon W. *Personality and Social Encounter*. Boston: Beacon, 1960.

Bach, G. L. "Universities, Business Schools and Business." In Harold Koontz, ed., *Toward a Unified Theory of Management*, pp. 189-203. New York: McGraw-Hill, 1964.

Behling, Orlando. "Unification of Management Theory: A Pessimistic View." In Max S. Wortman and Fred Luthans, eds., *Emerging Concepts in Management*, pp. 34-43. London: Macmillan, 1969.

Bennis, Warren, G., ed. *American Bureaucracy*. New York: Aldine, 1970.

Billingsley, Andrew. "Bureaucratic and Professional Orientation Patterns in Social Case Work." *Social Service Review* 38. no. 4 (Dec. 1964): 400–407.

Blau, Peter, and Marshall W. Meyer. *Bureaucracy in Modern Society*, Rev. ed. New York: Random House, 1971.

Bledsoe, Ralph C., Dennis R. Denny, Charles D. Hobbs, and Raymond S. Long. "Productivity Management in the California Services Program." *Public Administration Review* 32, no. 6 (Nov.–Dec. 1972): 799–803.

Bolman, William M. "Community Control of the Mental Health Center." *American Journal of Psychiatry* 129, no. 2 (Aug. 1972): 95–100.

Brager, George, and Stephen Holloway, *Changing Human Service Organizations: Politics and Practice*, New York: Free Press, 1978.

Briar, Scott, "Clinical Judgment in Foster Care Placement," *Child Welfare* 42, no. 4 (April 1963): 161–172.

Brown, R. G. S. *The Management of Welfare: A Study of British Social Service Administration*. London: Martin Robertson, 1975.

Caiden, Gerald E. *Administrative Reform*. Chicago: Aldine, 1969.

Charlesworth, James C. *Theory and Practice of Public Administration: Scope, Objectives and Methods*. Philadelphia: American Academy of Political and Social Science, Oct. 1968.

Epstein, Laura. "Is Autonomous Practice Possible." *Social Work* 18, no. 2 (March 1973): 5–12.

Etzioni, Amitai, ed. *The Semi-Professions and Their Organization*. New York: Free Press, 1969.

Goode, William J. "The Theoretical Limits of Professionalization." In Amitai Etzioni, ed., *The Semi-Professions and Their Organization*, pp. 266–313. New York: Free Press, 1969.

Gummer, Burton. "Social Planning and Social Administration: Implications for Curriculum Development." *Journal of Education for Social Work* 11, no. 1 (Winter 1975): 66–73.

Hanlan, Archie. "Changing Functions and Structures." In Florence W. Kaslow and associates, *Issues in Human Services*, pp. 39–50. San Francisco: Jossey-Bass, 1972.

Helfgot, Joseph. "Professional Reform Organizations and the Symbolic Representation of the Poor." *American Sociological Review* 39, no. 4 (Aug. 1974): 475–491.

Jaski, Ernest B. Review of F. A. Snyder and R. D. Peterson. *Dynamics of Elementary School Administration* (1970). *Administrative Science Quarterly* 17, no. 1 (June 1972: 303–304.

Kadushin, Alfred. Discussion of Dr. Andrew Billingsley's paper, "Education for Strategic Uncertainty in Social Welfare." *In Institure Proceedings: Education for Social Work with "Unmotivated Clients."* Florence Heller Graduate School for Advanced Studies in Social Welfare, 1965.

Kahn, Alfred J. "Public Social Services: The Next Phase." *Public Welfare* 30 no. 1 (Winter 1972): 15–24.

Kammerman, Sheila B., and Alfred J. Kahn. *Social Services in the United States*. Philadelphia: Temple University Press, 1976.

Kaslow, Florence W., and associates. *Issues in Human Services*. San Francisco: Jossey-Bass, 1972.

Kazmerski, K. J., and David Macarov. *Administration in the Social Work Curriculum: Report of a Survey*. New York: Council on Social Work Education, 1976.

Koontz, Harold. *Toward a Unified Theory of Management*. New York: McGraw-Hill, 1964.

Levinson, Daniel J., and Gerald L. Klerman. "The Clinician-Executive," *Administration in Mental Health*, vol. 1 (Winter 1972): 53–67.

Maas, Henry. "Group Influences on Worker Client Interactions." *Social Work* 9, no. 2 (April 1964): 70–79.

Merton, Robert K. *Social Theory and Social Structure*. Glencoe, Ill: Free Press, 1957.

Parsons, Talcott. "Service." *Encyclopaedia of the Social Services*, Reissue, vol. 13. New York: Macmillan, 1937.

Patti, Rino J. "Organizational Resistance to Change: The View from Below." *Social Service Review* 48, no. 3 (Sept. 1974): 367–383.

Perlmutter, Felice D., ed. *A Design for Social Work Practice*. New York: Columbia University Press, 1974.

Pusić, Eugen. "The Administration of Welfare." In Felice D. Perlmutter, ed., *A Design for Social Work Practice*. New York: Columbia University Press, 1974.

Rapoport, Lydia. "In Defense of Social Work: An Examination of Stress in the Profession." *Social Service Review* 36, no. 1 (March 1960): 62–74.

Reiff, Robert. "The Danger of the Techni-Pro: Democratizing the Human Service Professions." *Social Policy* 2, no. 1 (May-June 1971): 62–64.

Rothman, Jack. *Planning and Organizing for Social Change*. New York: Columbia University Press, 1974.

Sarri, Rosemary C. "Effective Social Work Intervention in Administration and Planning Roles: Implications for Education." *Facing the Challenge*, New York: Council on Social Work Education, 1973.

Schein, Edgar H. *Professional Education*. New York: McGraw-Hill, 1972.

Scott, W. Richards. "Professional Employees in a Bureaucratic Structure in Social Work." In Amitai Etzioni, ed., *The Semi-Professions and their Organization*. New York: Free Press, 1969.

Smalley, Ruth E. "Values and Directions in Social Work Education." *Journal of Social Work Process* 17, no. 33 (1969): 11–36.

Stein, Herman. "Administrative Implications of Bureaucratic Theory." *Social Work* 6, no. 3 (July 1961): 14–21.

————. "The Study of Organizational Effectiveness." In National Association of Social Workers, *Research in Social Welfare Administration*. New York, National Association of Social Workers, 1962. 22–32.

Toren, Nina. "Semi-Professionalism and Social Work: A Theoretical Perspective." In Amitai Etzioni, ed., *The Semi-Professions and Their Organizations*. New York: Free Press, 1969.

Trecker, Harleigh B. *Social Work Administration: Principles and Practices*. New York: Association Press, 1971.

Vickers, Geoffrey. *The Art of Judgment*. New York: Basic Books, 1965.

Waldo, Dwight. "Scope of the Theory of Public Administration." in James C. Charlesworth, ed., *Theory and Practice of Public Administration*. Philadelphia: American Academy of Political and Social Science, 1968.

Walton, John. *Administration and Policy-Making in Education*. Baltimore: The Johns Hopkins University Press, 1959.

Wortman, Max S., and Fred Luthans. *Emerging Concepts in Management*. London: Macmillan, 1969.

ORGANIZATION THEORY FOR SOCIAL ADMINISTRATION

Burton Gummer

2

Organization theory provides administrators with a conceptual scheme for understanding the structure and dynamics of their social service systems. Without some coherent perspective from which to view things, the day-to-day activities of a complex organization such as the social service agency would appear unrelated, random, and seemingly purposeless.

Professor Gummer succinctly presents three models of organizational behavior: the rational model, the natural-system model, and the power-politics model. He suggests that these models deal with different aspects or circumstances related to the organization and need not be viewed as competing, or all-explanatory. Rather, familiarity with the elements of each model provides administrators with a system of analysis wherein they can better understand their organizations and therefore are better able to provide effective leadership. The author's discussion of the power-politics model is directly applicable to the advocacy and social change issues addressed later in this volume by Perlmutter, Richan, Alexander and Kerson, and Vargus. The discussion is enriched throughout by a series of illustrations from the social services.

This chapter presents an overview of the major theoretical approaches used to explain the behavior of formal organizations. The rationale for the inclusion of this material in the present volume proceeds from the assumption that an understanding of relevant theories is as important for the practitioner of administration as it is for practitioners of other social work methods. In much the same way that personality theory offers the caseworker a framework for understanding and analyzing individual behaviors, organization theory provides the administrator with a conceptual device for comprehending organizational behaviors. Without some coherent perspective from which to view things, the day-to-day activities of a complex organization would appear unrelated, random, and beyond comprehension. In the same way that personality theory enables the counselor to look beyond the endless array of behaviors presented by the client and get at the underlying personality structures upon which these behaviors are predicated, organization theory offers the administrator a way of understanding the events and activities of organizational life as a function of the underlying structures and environmental conditions which, in Selznick's (1960, p. xi) words, "constrain and summon" behavior.

The framework used for examining these perspectives is an extension of a scheme first developed by Gouldner (1959). Gouldner sees theories of organizations falling into two broad categories. In the first, the organization is seen as a "rational instrument" for accomplishing some specific purpose, while in the second it is seen as a "natural system" that has the same system maintaining and enhancing requirements of any other social system. A third perspective, the organization as an arena for the exercise of "power-politics," will be added to draw attention to the importance for organizational structure and behavior of the way in which resources are obtained and the internal mechanisms for their allocation (Gummer, 1978; Wamsley and Zald, 1976). The three models will be analyzed by first looking at the major variables that make up the model, and then examining the dynamic processes that connect these variables with each other (see Figure 2–1).

Figure 2–1. Major Variables and Dynamics in the
Rational, Natural-System, and
Power-Politics Models of Organizations

	RATIONAL	NATURAL-SYSTEM	POWER-POLITICS
VARIABLES	Production goals	Subsystem goals	Resource characteristics
	Technologies	Informal structure	Control structure
DYNAMICS	Maximization of rationality	Management of internal conflict	Adaptation to changes in resource availability
	Reduction of uncertainty	Maintenance of the character of the system	

The Rational Model

The oldest, and consequently most venerable, approach to the study of organizations is the rational model in which, as Gouldner (*1959*, p. *404*) observes, the organization "is conceived as an "instrument"—that is, as a rationally conceived means to the realization of expressly advanced group goals. Its structures are understood as tools deliberately established for the efficient realization of these group purposes." This approach is predicated on the assumption that the *raison d'être* of an organization is that it is the best (i.e., the most efficient) means for achieving a goal. This model has its roots in the writings of Max Weber (1964), who developed the classic conception of the rational organization in his work on bureaucracy.

ORGANIZATIONAL GOALS

Two organizational variables central to the rational model are the goals of the organization and the technologies employed to pursue those goals. Within this model goals are usually defined in product terms. That is, the primary concern of an organization is the production of a product or service, and the organization exists exclusively for that purpose. Since the efficient attainment of goals is the central purpose of an organization, the identification and specification of goals becomes critical since all other organizational activities are dependent upon them. Selznick (1957, pp. 61–64), for instance, considers the setting of goals ("the identification of institutional mission and role") as one of the major functions of leadership in an organization.

One aspect of organization goals of particular concern here is the degree to which they can be specified. That is, organizational goal statements can vary along a dimension that goes from concrete, specific goals to abstract, general goals. An example of the former would be Day Care Agency X, which states that its goal is to serve 100 children (from specified socio-economic backgrounds, and with certain family characteristics) per week, with a program that is an equal mixture of socialization and educational components, with the intention of developing specific educational and interpersonal skills within the child during a set period of time. Day Care Agency Y, on the other hand, has as its goal a statement that the purpose of the agency is to "enhance the growth and development of children through the provision of quality day care services." The latter statement offers little in the way of guidance as to how one should structure activities to achieve that goal. Within the rational model the goal of the organization is the keystone to the entire structure. It is the source of the major criterion by which organizational performance is evaluated; namely, is a particular piece of structure or unit of activity more efficient in the attainment of goals than some other structure or activity? If an organization does not cast its goals in specific, operational language, then goal statements will not direct internal decision-making. This, in turn, seriously limits the extent to which the organization can be viewed as a rational instrument for the pursuit of goals.

A second, related aspect of organizational goals is the amount of consensus that exists among organizational members around the stated goal (assuming that the goal is stated in specific terms). Barnard (1968, p. 65) has drawn attention to the importance of cooperation in organizations in his definition of an organization as a "cooperative system." One factor that affects an individual's willingness to cooperate is the extent to which he or she can identify with the goals of the organization. The degree to which one is able to accept the goals will, in turn, determine the extent to which one will voluntarily submit to the directives of organizational leaders. The voluntary nature of an individual's conformance to organizational directives, moreover, constitutes the heart of Weber's (1964) theory of authority (or "imperative coordination"), which he defines as:

> the probability that certain specific commands . . . from a given source will be obeyed by a given group of persons. . . . A criterion of every true relation of imperative control . . . is a certain minimum of voluntary submission; thus an interest (based on ulterior motives or genuine acceptance) is obedience. . . . It is an induction from experience that no system of authority voluntarily limits itself to the appeal to material or affectual or ideal motives as a basis for guaranteeing its continuance. In addition every such system attempts to establish and to cultivate the belief in its "legitimacy" (pp 324–325).

However, the degree of consensus about goals in a social agency will, in all likelihood, be fairly low due to the highly normative nature of social welfare activities. That is, social agencies ultimately concern themselves with how people *ought* to behave, and thus must address themselves to some notion of what Donnison (1955, pp. 349–350) has termed the "social health" of its clientele. Moreover, as Donnison goes on to say, "there is no generally understood state of 'social health' toward which all people strive; our disagreements on this question form the subject matter of politics the world over."

From this perspective the goal formation process in a social agency can be seen as essentially a political one in which various interest groups—both within and outside of the organization—attempt to influence or dominate the setting of the agency's major purposes. An example of this is the debates that have taken place over the purposes of day-care programs. One can identify at least three major interests that have opposing conceptions of what functions a day-care center should perform. Feminists see this as a major tool for effecting equality between the sexes since it offers relief from child-care responsibilities and an opportunity for women to pursue other interests. From this perspective the purposes of day care should be just that, to offer care of children during the day to whomever wishes to use it. Another interest group is child-development specialists, who see this as an opportunity to introduce "good" (i.e., middle-class) child-rearing practices to the general population. This group frequently advocates confining day-care services to those people experiencing difficulties in raising their children, and have as their goal the changing of parental attitudes and behavior as well as providing care for children. Finally, the advocates of traditional income maintenance policies see day care as essentially a device for ensuring that income maintenance programs do not undermine work incentives. For them, the major purpose of a day-care program is to reduce the possibility that those receiving public funds will use their parental responsibilities as an "excuse" for not seeking work.

Not only are the goals of social agencies highly controversial, but the people who work in these agencies, that is, social workers and especially professionally trained social workers, are generally sensitive to these controversies and quite likely to have well-developed normative and ideological systems of their own (Scott, 1969; Zald and McCarthy, 1975). To the extent that a consensus about organizational objectives is not present, administrators must pursue a variety of strategies for inducing member participation and cooperation. Cyert and MacCrimmon (1968, pp. 570–72) identify the major strategies used for this purpose as "bargaining" and "side payments," both of which require expenditures of resources beyond what would be required if the member was in agreement with organizational goals. This results in a net loss of efficiency for the organization.

Not only does a lack of consensus affect the nature of member participation, it has an impact on the entire decision-making process within an organization. The rational model assumes that organizational decisions will be made according to the criterion of what is the most effective and efficient way of attaining a given goal. However, when there is no consensus about the purposes of the organization or the means for achieving them (i.e., under conditions of uncertainty), then non-efficiency criteria are used. Pfeffer and his colleagues (1976) found, for instance, that under conditions of uncertainty social influences dominate organizational decision-making, with social relationships and social attraction becoming the bases for decisions. A foster-care agency that is not clear as to what constitutes an "adequate" foster-care family, and has varying points of view about this represented on its staff, is an example of an organization that can be expected to operate on subjective criteria. Families may be selected because they are personally liked by the workers, come from the same ethnic, racial, or religious background, or have similar political and social views. Any decision will be just as good as any other since there is no authoritative statement about what constitutes a "good" family. This procedure is in direct contradiction to Weber's (1958) concept of a bureaucracy (i.e., a rational organization) as an impersonal mechanism:

Bureaucratization offers above all the optimum possibility for carrying through the principle of specializing administrative functions according to purely objective considerations. . . . The "objective" discharge of business primarily means discharge of business according to *calculable rules* and "without regard for persons" (p. 215, emphasis in original).

TECHNOLOGY IN ORGANIZATIONS

A second critical variable in the rational model is the nature of the technologies employed by an organization. Technology in organizations is defined by Perrow (1967) as:

the actions that an individual performs upon an object, with or without the aid of tools or mechanical devices, in order to make some change in that object. The object, or "raw material," may be a living being, human or otherwise, a symbol, or an inanimate object (p. 202).

Thompson (1967) identifies three major types of technologies: long-linked, mediating, and intensive. The first involves serial interdependence, in that act Z can be performed only after the successful completion of act Y, such as the work on an assembly line. Mediating technologies are employed by organizations whose function is to link clients or customers who are or wish to be interdependent, such as commercial banks who link depositors to borrowers. The term intensive is used to refer to technologies in which

a variety of techniques [are] drawn upon to achieve a change in some specific object; but the selection, combination, and order of application are determined by feedback from the object itself. When the object is human this intensive technology is regarded as "therapeutic," but the same technical logic is found also in the construction industry . . . and in research where the objects of concern are non-human (pp. 15–18).

Perrow (1967) develops a typology based on two aspects of technology: the number of exceptional cases encountered in the work, and the nature of the search process undertaken when exceptions occur. The first variable is measured on a scale going from low to high. The second involves two types of search processes:

The first . . . involves a search which can be conducted on a logical, analytical basis. . . . This is exemplified by the mechanical engineering unit of a firm building large machinery. . . . The second . . . occurs when the problem is so vague and poorly conceptualized as to make it virtually unanalyzable. In this case, no "formal" search is undertaken, but instead one draws upon the residue of unanalyzed experience or intuition, or relies upon chance and guesswork. Examples would be work with exotic metals or nuclear fuels, psychiatric casework, and some kinds of advertising (pp. 195–197).

These and other approaches to classifying organizational technologies (Litwak, 1961; Woodward, 1965) all employ a general analytical framework which looks at the nature of the work done and the nature of the object upon which the work is done. The first factor moves along a continuum that goes from kinds of work in which there is a great deal of knowledge about each component activity that goes into the work, to those kinds of work in which the component activities cannot be separated out and the work is seen as an undifferentiated whole. An example of the former would be a public assistance agency where the major technologies are the determination of eligibility according to predetermined rules; the disbursing of public monies according to established schedules for payment; and accounting for these expenditures. An example of the latter would be a child-guidance clinic in which the diagnosis and treatment of psychological problems in children is the major technology. These activities are usually seen as part of a highly interdependent and interactive process that must be treated as one unitary activity. The degree to which the work of an agency can be dis-aggregated into finite steps has important implications for the nature of the division of labor in that organization. In the first instance the work can be broken up into its constituent parts and activities assigned to different people. This, in turn, necessitates a large administrative component in the organization so that the various activities can be coordinated. One conse-quence of this is that the individuals performing the work do not have to be highly trained because they only have to deal with one aspect of the job. In the second case, the child-guidance clinic where the work cannot be disaggregated, the division of labor will be more limited and the individual performing the work will have to do most of the activities entailed in the job. This, in turn, will require more training for the worker and will lessen the need for an elaborate administrative structure, since coordination takes place at the level of the worker. These two ways of organizing work are usually referred to as *bureaucratic* and *professional* organizations, respec-tively (Litwak, 1961; Scott, 1966).

A salient characteristic of the nature of the object upon which the work is performed is the extent to which the object *reacts* to the worker. This can be measured on a scale that goes from non-reactive objects (e.g., stable metals) to highly reactive objects (e.g., human beings). The amount of reactivity on the part of the object has important implications for the amount of discretion that must be granted to the worker. In the first case the worker will need little discretion because the non-reactive nature of the object means that its characteristics can be predicted over time and the work applied to it routinized. Procedures can be specified in advance and the worker's job will consist, in great part, of applying these predetermined procedures to specific situations. In the case of reactive objects whose characteristics cannot be predicted over time, procedures cannot be specified in advance and the worker will have to have a considerable amount of discretion to take actions based upon the needs of the situation as they arise.

For the most part social agencies deal with situations best characterized as reactive. Within this category, however, the degree of reactivity of the client to the worker will vary, and consequently so will the amount of discretion that has to be given the worker. Two factors affecting the amount of reactivity in a situation are the degree of stress the client is experiencing, and the amount of pathology—physical, psychological, or social—present in the client. Clients experiencing extreme stress, and whose behavior or condition is considered pathological, will tend to be volatile and erratic, and the worker will need considerable leeway in determining the most appropriate course of action. Examples of such situations are the onset of acute illness (physical or mental), sudden death, unexpected loss of a job or living arrangement, and abandonment of a spouse and/or children. These situations tend to be idiosyncratic and unpredictable and agencies find there are few specific guidelines that can be offered to the worker. On the other hand, situations in which clients are not experiencing undue stress, and whose behavior and condition is within normal limits, will be more predictable and thus more amenable to routine, predetermined procedures set by the agency. Examples of this are recreational and leisure-time activities, chronic-care facilities, and long-term counseling.

The reactivity of the client has implications for organizational structure quite similar to those coming out of the nature of the work itself. Organizations dealing with relatively non-reactive situations will lend themselves to a bureaucratic structure more readily, while those dealing with highly reactive situations will be constrained to organize themselves along professional lines because of the need for highly trained workers who will be able to make sound discretionary judgments.

RATIONALITY AND UNCERTAINTY

The major dynamic processes within the rational model are the *maximization of rationality* and the *reduction of uncertainty*. Proponents of the rational model argue that the primary force that powers and shapes organizational development is the increase in rational arrangements within the organization. The criterion of efficiency permeates all aspects of organizational behavior with the result that, to paraphrase Gresham's Law, efficiency criteria drive out all other criteria. A major obstacle to the pursuit of rational action is the existence of uncertainty, whether this pertains to confusion or unclarity about organizational goals, the nature of the technologies employed, or unpredictable elements in the environment. In order to increase an organization's capacity for rational action organization-al leaders will seek to reduce uncertainty by the extension of administrative controls over both internal and external factors. Uncertainties within the organization will be dealt with by efforts to regularize and routinize as many aspects of organizational behavior as possible. These efforts will persist even when the nature of the activities do not lend themselves to such control. Goffman's (1961) analysis of the nature of "total institutions" can be seen as one example of an attempt to impose bureaucratic control mechanisms over highly reactive situations (i.e., hospitalized mental patients) as a way of increasing the predictability and tractability of the behavior of the inmates. In that case, concerns of administrative control completely supplanted concerns of therapeutic effectiveness.

When facing uncertainty in the environment, organizations attempt to extend control over critical elements in the environment as a way of reducing this. In economic organizations this is referred to as "vertical integration" whereby a firm extends its control over organizations which supply resources needed for production as well as those organizations responsible for the product's distribution (e.g., oil companies and automobile manufacturers). The social service agency must also deal with an unpredictable environment, although the strategy of directly incorporating other organizations is generally not available to it. One strategy that is often used is that of laying claim to what Levine and White (1961, p. 597) have termed an organization's "domain," which is defined as the "specific goals it wishes to pursue and the functions it undertakes to implement its goals." Warren (1972) extended this concept to include the function domain plays in ensuring to an organization an undisputed claim to necessary resources:

> Organizational domain is the organization's locus in the interorganizational network, including its legitimated "right" to operate in specific geographic and functional areas and its channels of access to . . . resources. The two important components here are the organization's right to do something, and its access to the resources it needs in order to do it. . . . In its interaction with other organizations, an organization acts to preserve or expand its domain (p. 22).

Establishing a claim to a particular domain, however, is a difficult strategy to employ because claims to legitimacy as a service provider are difficult to advance and sustain in a field where there is so little consensus both about who should offer a particular service and the best way for delivering that service. An example of competition for domain is found in the community mental health field between agencies offering direct services and those offering preventive services (i.e., the "consultation and education" components of community mental health centers). In the area of services to the elderly there has traditionally been competition between social workers and nurses for control of these programs, as there has been in public schools between school social workers and guidance counselors. Lack of "domain consensus" in most service areas means that, in general, the social agency will be less able to control its environment and its efforts at promoting rational internal operations will be hampered to the degree that it must continually deal with uncertainties in terms of funding sources, access to clients, and claims to functional specialization (Kirk and Greenley, 1974).

The Natural-System Model

In the natural-system approach the organization is seen as a type of social system, and the processes that characterize the functioning of social systems in general are used to explain the operations of complex organizations. A major way in which this approach differs from the rational model is in the number and kinds of goals that an organization is seen as pursuing. In the rational model the organization has only one goal, the efficient production of a service or product. In the natural-system model the generation of products or services is but one of several goals that the organization must attend to. Any social unit that can be viewed as a social system is assumed to have two types of goals. The first is the production of an output, the need for which motivated the founding of the organization (Parsons, 1956). Once the organization has been brought into existence, however, a new set of goals is generated which have to do with the maintenance of the system as a distinct social entity. Moreover, system maintenance goals become as important as the original production goals. Thus, a major concern within the natural-system model is the *relationship between production and maintenance goals* within an organization.

These models also differ in the way an organization member is viewed. In the rational model the individual is seen primarily as a role incumbent. That is, the only part of the individual's total life situation deemed relevant is that part directly pertaining to role performance within the organization. Other factors such as one's emotional or social life are not considered necessary for an understanding of how one behaves in the organization. It is assumed that the organization member will act in a rational manner and thereby complete tasks in the most efficient way possible. The natural-system model, on the other hand, argues that this is an unrealistic and artificial view of human behavior and that the total person must be considered. Attention is therefore directed to the *informal structure* of an organization, which can be defined as the patterned relationships that evolve between and among organization members based on their total social and emotional needs. This is in contrast to the rational model's emphasis on the *formal structure* of an organization, which is the pattern of interactions between and among members based on the requirements of their official organizational roles.

SUBSYSTEM GOALS

A social system can be defined as a group of elements (individuals, groups, offices) that exist within some boundary and are related to each other in a patterned way in order to accomplish some goal. The system functions by taking resources (inputs) from its environment, transforming them by means of a production process (throughput), and delivering back into the environment a product made up of the transformed resources (output). Systems are composed of subsystems, each of which performs a function necessary to the system's ongoing operation.

In their analysis of the complex organization as a social system, Katz and Kahn (1966, pp. 39–47) identify the following subsystems within an organization: production or technical, supportive, maintenance, adaptive, and managerial. The production subsystem is concerned with the throughput function of the actual work of the organization. Its goal is the production of a service or product and is thus analogous to the goal of the organization as a whole in the rational model. That is, what the rational model posits as the goal of the entire organization, the natural-system model sees as the goal of the production subsystem only. The function of the supportive subsystem is to ensure a steady supply of resources and to see that the finished product is distributed, that is, to make sure that there is a consumer for the organization's product. The maintenance subsystem is concerned with what Selznick (1948, p. 29) refers to as the "integrity and continuity of the system itself." Since a social system consists of the patterned interactions of individuals within the system, the goal of the maintenance subsystem is to ensure that organization members function in conformance with organizationally sanctioned procedures. That is, it is concerned with seeing to it that members accept the goals, rules, and general format of operations that have developed in the organization.

The adaptive subsystem is concerned with the capacity of the organization to adjust to changes within its environment. These changes may take the form of shifting values, alterations in the political or economic systems, introduction of new, competitive organizations, and the like. Its goal is to identify changes in the environment pertinent to the operation of the organization and develop ways in which the organization can react to these changes. The managerial subsystem's function is to see that the other subsystems operate in a coordinated fashion. It must ensure the integrated functioning of all parts of the system so that the goals of the system as a whole may be realized.

In a child-welfare agency, for example, the workers dealing directly with clients constitute the production subsystem and their function is to offer the services of the organization (counseling, placement, and adoption). The executive director and the members of the board operate as the supportive subsystem and are concerned with ensuring adequate financing, clients, and facilities. The maintenance subsystem's function of ensuring comformance with agency-prescribed ways of behaving has its formal expression in the written rules and regulations of the organization and in the supervisory structure and procedures. Its equally important but informal expression is found in the ways in which organizational leaders create a "climate" within the organization by espousing and supporting certain ways of acting and thinking and by stigmatizing and opposing ways of behaving that are not considered "appropriate" to the agency (Argyris, 1976). The adaptive function of monitoring and responding to new developments in the organization's environment is performed by those with responsibility for program planning and development. (Interestingly enough, this function is frequently given the least priority in many social agencies because it is seen as diverting resources away from delivering services, yet it probably has the greatest potential for increasing services through the identification of new sources of support.) Finally, the various supervisors and department heads act as the managerial subsystem and function to coordinate the organization's overall activities.

This conceptualization of the organization as composed of subsystems, each performing a different function and pursuing different goals, draws attention to the potential for *goal conflicts within the organization*. The natural-system model assumes that an organization member will be more influenced by the goals of his or her unit than by the overall purposes of the organization. For example, a person involved in the production subsystem will be primarily interested in perfecting the technical capacities of that unit so that it can go about its work in the most efficient and effective way. In the case of the social service agency, the production subsystem will be primarily concerned with improving the technical competence of the members of the unit. Emphasis will be placed on recruiting and hiring individuals with the most and best training possible, reducing staff turnover so that people have sustained experiences in an area of work, and, in general, creating a stable situation in which people will be able to develop their technical skills. In that same agency, however, the program development section (i.e., the adaptive subsystem) will be concerned with increasing the agency's capacity to adapt to a changing and shifting environment. The interests of this unit will probably conflict with those of the service unit since program planners and developers will be concerned with increasing the agency's capacity to respond flexibly to external changes while the service workers will be arguing for stable and routinized operations. As another example, those responsible for fund-raising (the supportive subsystem) may want the service unit to develop new programs in order to attract new monies, an initiative the service people may resist because of their lack of expertise in the proposed program areas. Because of the existence of these potential conflicts between and among subsystems, a major goal for the managerial subsystem is the maintenance of a balance between the units. (This will be discussed at further length below since it constitutes the major dynamic factor within the natural-system model.)

INFORMAL STRUCTURE

In addition to the variable of subsystem functions and goals, the natural-system model stresses the importance of the informal (i.e., not organizationally sanctioned) structures in an organization. Gouldner (1959) defines informal structures in the following way:

> Some informal patterns are organizationally unprescribed culture structures—that is, patterns of belief and sentiment; for example, the belief that one should not be a "rate buster." Other informal patterns are organizationally unprescribed social structures, i.e., the cliques that develop among those working near one another (p. 410).

The importance of informal structures in organizations was first noted in the now famous research on worker performance in the Hawthorne Works of the Western Electric Company during the 1920's (Mayo, 1960; Roethlisberger and Dickson, 1939). In that study it was found that the informal relationships that evolve among people who work together are just as important in determining worker behavior as official organizational policies and regulations.

Moreover, the logic of informal structures is based in the social and psychological needs of individuals (i.e., those aspects of one's life not directly connected with performance on the job) and is thus quite different from the logic of the formal structure, which is based in the need to design a structure that will enhance the efficient and effective achievement of organizational goals. One example of the ways in which these two structures conflict has to do with the issue of job security for organization members. Etzioni (1964, p. 3) lists as one of the defining characteristics of an organization "the substitution of personnel, i.e., unsatisfactory persons can be removed and others assigned their tasks." The importance of this is best understood from the rational model perspective, in which the personnel of an organization are viewed, in a sense, as interchangeable parts that can be eliminated, added, or altered depending upon the needs of the organization. From this point of view, job security will be dysfunctional because it may lead to inefficiency if the person is either incompetent or in some other way inappropriate for the position. From an individual perspective, however, job security is of paramount concern; economically, socially, and psychologically, people need steady and rewarding work and adequate income. The need for security serves as the basis for a type of informal structure found in all organizations, namely, some system of mutual protection among people working together. Workers can be expected to "look out" for each other's interests in ways that will run counter to the attempts of organization leaders to develop monitoring and evaluative devices aimed at identifying and weeding out incompetents. These informal arrangements can take the form of a group of workers covering for each other's poor performances, or group resistance to and sabotage of managerial efforts to impose objective and standardized performance-rating devices.

While the informal arrangements within an organization may have negative consequences in terms of undermining efforts to maximize rational procedures, they can have a positive impact on overall organizational functioning because of the role they can play in maintaining a high degree of morale among the workers. Individuals who are able to exert some influence and control over the conditions of their work can be expected to identify more readily with the organization than those who feel powerless in the face of formal organizational requirements (Ouchi and Johnson, 1978). This identification, moreover, serves as the basis of a stronger commitment on the part of the worker to the organization. As an individual's investment in an organization grows because it is a "nice place to work," that is, organization leaders accept and encourage the existence of informal arrangements, then the organization's potential control over the worker is increased since a "nice place to work" is also a hard place to leave, and the worker has a greater stake in remaining with the organization (Tannenbaum, 1968, pp. 3–29). This factor is particularly important in the social welfare agency where, due to the value-laden nature of the work, acceptance of organizational goals and strategies by workers directly increases organizational efficiency since workers will not act in opposition to an organization towards which there are strong commitments.

SYSTEM MAINTENANCE

The natural-system model posits as a central dynamic process the maintenance of the *character of the system* over time. The word "character" is used advisedly because its reference point in individual personality development provides a useful analogy for looking at organizational development. As an individual grows and matures, a process of character or identity formation occurs. The young person experiments with a variety of ways of doing and being in terms of occupation, interpersonal relationships, and overall conceptions of what kind of person he or she will become. Over time individuals select one or another of these ways, or develop new ones, which then become the dominant ways in which the person conducts his or her life. It is at this point that we say that a person's character or identity has been formed.

In much the same way new organizations experiment with different ways of being. There are many ways to structure an organization. Decision-making, for instance, can be centralized so that a few elite members make all major decisions, or it can be decentralized to promote broad participation by many organization members. The strategy for delivering services may emphasize quantity and attach great importance to the number of clients reached; or it may concentrate on quality and direct attention to the technical competence of the staff. Internal relationships may be structured along collegial lines and stress peer interactions, or they may develop along hierarchical lines that emphasize superordinate and subordinate interactions.

As the organization "matures," it selects particular ways of doing things and structuring itself and, like the individual, will be said to have developed a character or, to use Boulding's (1956) term, an "image." The reasons why an organization develops one form and not another are complex and go beyond the scope of the present discussion. Some salient factors in the process, however, are the historical period in which the organization was formed, the nature of the technologies available, dominant values in the larger society, and the values and styles of the founders of the organization (Stinchcombe, 1965).

Once the organization has settled on a purpose, and its internal patterns of relationships have been established, a constant force operates within the organization to maintain this pattern. As the organization becomes an ongoing concern, its members develop commitment to its continued existence; the basis of this commitment is the benefits that organization members derive from the continued existence of the organization in *its present form*. These commitments will vary, therefore, according to benefit received; organizational leaders and those in dominant roles will obviously have a greater investment than others. However, for any organization to continue to function as a system the majority of the members must perceive their situations to be better as a result of their involvement in the organization than would be the case if they were to leave. That is, the organization member must feel that the benefits received are sufficient to warrant her or his continued participation (Barnard, 1968; Simon, 1964).

Commitment to the maintenance of the system, then, is a function of the system's ability to produce benefits for its members. If such benefits are lessened by major changes in the organization's environment, it can be expected that internal commitments to organizational maintenance will also lessen. Changes in the environment usually lead to organizational change, both in overall purposes and internal arrangments; for if the goals pursued by the organization are no longer relevant to its "output set" (Evan, 1966), then it will not be able to recruit the resources necessary for its ongoing operation. In order to survive, the organization will have to alter its goals to conform to new expectations from the environment; this, in turn, will alter the internal structure of the organization as new goals require new patterns of interactions among the organization's subsystems and change the pattern for the distribution of benefits. Once this new pattern is consolidated, however, staff will develop the same strong commitment to its maintenance; this commitment can be expected to continue until the system's function is once again challenged by changes in the environment.

MANAGEMENT OF INTERNAL CONFLICT

Another dynamic process in the organizational system is the need to manage the conflicts that arise from the fact that the system is made up of subsystems which pursue their own goals. Internal conflict is seen as a natural occurence arising out of the normal operations of the system. That is, the model emphasizes the organization as a cause of intraorganizational conflict rather than the malicious, perverse, or pathological actions of organization members (although they, too, may cause some forms of conflict).

The problem of internal conflict becomes particularly serious when any one of the organizational subsystems emerges as a "leading" subsystem and threatens to dominate or eclipse the other subsystems. While the natural-system model stresses the equal importance of all subsystems for the overall functioning of the organization, one of the subsystems can assume greater importance than others under certain conditions. For example, in the earlier discussion of organizational development is was pointed out that agencies will usually select one or another service strategy as their preferred one, emphasizing either quantity or quality of services. In the former case, where volume is the key, one can expect the supportive and adaptive subsystems to assume key roles because of the constant need for new monies, more clients, and expanded facilities. In a quality strategy, the service or technical subsystem will be predominant, and concerns will be focussed on staff development, inservice training, and similar issues.

A critical function for the manager is the maintenance of equilibrium within the organization. When the functions of one subsystem are stressed by the organization, it would be detrimental to the organization's overall effectiveness to allow that subsystem to dominate others. Such dominance would result in a distortion of the purposes of the organization and a subsequent weakening of the organization's capacities to perform all necessary functions. In the example given above, a social agency in which the technical or service subsystem dominates would have a lessened capacity to recruit new funds and identify critical changes in the environment. If the managerial subsystem is functioning properly (which may not be the case if the agency administrators come from a service background and are biased in that direction), it will develop strategies for reducing the hegemony of the service subsystem and ensure that all functions within the organization are attended to.

The Power-Politics Model

A third theme in the study of organizations is one that views the organization as primarily a political arena in which interest groups compete for the control of organizational resources. While this approach does not have the coherence of the other models, there is a sufficient convergence of the conceptual and analytical emphases of a number of writers that warrant their being grouped as a "power-politics model." Two themes characterize this approach. The first theme is the importance assigned to resources, particularly their source, the amount available, and the means for deciding their distribution within the organization, as determinants of organizational structure and behavior (White, 1974; Zald, 1970). The second is an emphasis on political processes within the organization as the chief mechanism for determining the distribution of resources (Benson, 1977; Burns, 1961; Pettigrew, 1973; Zald, 1970).

All students of organizations recognize the importance of resources since organizations would cease to function if they were unable to secure a regular and sufficient supply of resources. The students of the power-politics approach, however, draw attention to the fact that resources, aside from their importance in the organization's productive work, are also the basis for power, be it on an interpersonal, group, or organizational level. Power has been defined as the ability of person A to control and direct the behavior of person B by means of A's *control over resources* needed by B (Buckley, 1967, pp. 176–185; Dahl, 1957; Emerson, 1962; French and Raven, 1968). By extension, organizational power is generated when a person, or unit, within the organization is able to establish control over resources, thus enabling that person or unit to direct the behavior of other persons or units dependent upon those resources (Tannenbaum, 1968). The power-politics approach, moreover, stresses political processes as the primary way in which individuals or units are able to establish control over resources. Politics is defined by Banfield (1955, p. 304) as "the activity (negotiation, argument, discussion, application of force, persuasion, etc.) by which an issue is agitated or settled." The issue to be settled is how and by whom decisions about resource allocations are to be made, or, in Lasswell's (1958) classic phrase, "who gets what, when, how."

The rational model assumes that resources will be allocated according to rational criteria, that is, they will go where they are most needed for efficient goal attainment. The natural-system model assumes that resources will be allocated along lines that promote system maintenance and enhancement. These assumptions have been criticized as overly simplistic in the first case and overly abstract and unspecified in the second (Benson, 1977; Georgiou, 1973). A political approach to resource allocation proceeds from the assumption that organization members seek to promote their self interests, and their behavior within the organization will be guided by that consideration (Downs, 1967; Tullock, 1965). An individual's organizational interests, moreover, are determined by his or her place within the organization, place being a function of hierarchical position and functional specialty. Political behavior in this context can be viewed as behavior aimed at securing and enhancing one's place in the organization. Pettigrew's (1973) description of organizational politics illuminates this process:

> The division of work in an organization creates sub-units. These sub-units develop interests based on specialized functions and responsibilities. Although such sub-units have specialized tasks, they may also be interdependent. This interdependence may be played out within a joint decision-making process. Within such decision-making processes, interest-based demands are made. Given heterogeneity in the demand-generating process and the absence of a clearly set system of priorities between those demands, conflict is likely to ensue. Sub-units with differential interests make claims on scarce organizational resources. . . . The success any claimant has in furthering his interests will be a consequence of his ability to generate support for his demand.
>
> It is the involvement of sub-units in such demand- and support-generating processes within the decision-making processes of the organization that constitute the political dimension. Political behaviour is defined as behaviour by individuals, or, in collective terms, by sub-units, within an organization that makes a claim against the resource-shaping system of the organization (pp. 17–18).

The major variables in this model are (1) the character of the organization's resources and (2) the nature of its control structure. The central operating dynamic is the impact that shifting patterns of resource availability have on the internal structure of an organization.

RESOURCES

Organizational resources are defined by Yuchtman and Seashore (1967) as more or less "generalized means, or facilities, that are potentially controllable by social organizations and that are potentially usable—however indirectly—in relationships between the organization and its environment," (p. 900). Resources, then, are means for accomplishing organizational purposes that are "imported" by the organization from its environment. In the social welfare organization, for example, the principle resources are money, personnel, clients, and sanctions from the community. Since the present concern is with resources as the bases for power in organizations, the two aspects of this definition that are most critical are the degree to which resources are generalizable and controllable.

The generalizability of a resource has two dimensions: the degree to which one resource can be exchanged for another, or what Yuchtman and Seashore (1967, p. 900) call a resource's "liquidity," and the extent to which one resource can be used for a variety of purposes, which will be referred to here as its "transferability." Money and credit are high in liquidity, while availability of time or ideological commitment to a particular program are low. A psychiatric social worker specializing in the problems of autistic children is an example of a highly non-transferrable resource, while a social worker with a general background is a highly transferrable resource. Organizations with resources high in liquidity and/or transferability can be expected to have a high level of internal political activity due to the efforts of sub-units to gain control of these resources. These kinds of resources, because of their generalizability, can be used by a variety of organizational units, regardless of the unit's functional specialty.

The controllability of a resource refers to the ease with which individuals within the organization are able to establish control over the use of a resource. This, in turn, is a function of the extent to which the resource comes into the organization unencumbered by external constraints on its use. The kinds of external constraints on resources that can be placed on social welfare organizations range from the statutory prescriptions for the use of public monies to the demands of client-advocacy groups that clients be dealt with in ways specified by them (White, 1974, pp. 367–368). The number of external constraints placed on the use of an organizational resource, regardless of the generalizability of the resource itself, will affect the degree of political bargaining that can take place within the organization over the disposition of the resource. That is, resources designated for a particular use by an outside body cannot be bargained for within the organization. An example of a liquid resource that, while highly generalizable, has become less amenable to control by recipient organizations is the federal funds granted to the states in support of social services. In 1963 the federal government spent a little under 200 million dollars in social services grants to the states; by 1972 this figure had risen to over 1.5 billion dollars (Derthick, 1975, table 1 at p. 8). Moreover, as Derthick (1975, pp. 1–14) points out in her thorough and astute analysis of this situation, the funds were "uncontrolled" because the federal government attached few or no conditions to their use. The lack of external constraints on these funds made them highly controllable by the recipient organization, which was free to use them for its own purposes. Since 1972, however, the pendulum has swung in the opposite direction, with the federal government imposing stricter guidelines and accountability procedures on the use of these monies, thus reducing their controllability by recipient organizations (Mogulof, 1973; Newman and Turem, 1974; Smith, 1971). The resource retained its liquidity—it's still money—but lost its controllability (by recipient organizations). Taken together, generalizability and controllability of resources can be viewed as the necessary and sufficient conditions for determining the absolute level of political activity within an organization.

CONTROL STRUCTURE

Tannenbaum (1968) defines control in organizations as:

> any process in which a person or group of persons or organization of persons determines, that is, intentionally affects, the behavior of another person, group, or organization. . . . The exercise of control may be viewed as an exchange of some valued resource dispensed by one person in return for compliance on the part of another (pp. 5, 15).

Control, then, is synonymous with power, and the control structure of an organization is another way of talking about the distribution of power within the organization. The aspect of the control or power structure most relevant to the present discussion is the extent to which power is concentrated in the hands of a few individuals, or whether it is dispersed among many individuals throughout the organization. The first situation is usually referred to as a *centralized* control structure, while the second is a *decentralized* structure (Meyer, 1968; Scott and Mitchell, 1972, p. 150).

Since power is based on control of resources, the amount of power an individual or unit can exercise is directly related to the amount of resources at their disposal. In organizations where many units have access to resources, and no one unit is in a position to exercise control over the bulk of the resources coming into the organization, we can speak of a highly diffuse power situation in which political activity between units will be high as they compete and negotiate with each other to secure and expand their share of resources. In organizations in which one unit is able to exercise total, or near-total, control over the bulk of the resources, we have a concentrated power situation and can expect internal political activity to decrease. The latter situation will best be analyzed in terms of the rational model since the dominant power group will be able to establish its goals as the overall goals of the organization and will be able to make rational decisions in pursuit of those goals since it has the power to implement decisions.

Politics and rationality can be seen as competing methods for deciding on the distribution of resources within an organization. In a scientifically oriented society such as the American one, rationality is stressed. That is, *ceteris paribus,* rational decisions will be preferred over non-rational ones. However, rationality assumes a clear statement of objectives and the ability to rank preferentially the alternatives for reaching those objectives, with efficiency being the criterion for establishing the rank order. In the absence of either of these conditions another way must be found for deciding how resources are to be distributed. The power-politics approach suggests that the ability to organize and agitate issues (i.e., to engage in political behavior) comes into play when the conditions for rational decision-making about resource distribution are not present.

The proponents of the rational model argue that rationality determines the shape of the control structure, that is, those who have the most power in an organization *should* have that power because they are the people or units most suited to direct the operations of the organization, given its goals. The power-politics approach reverses this argument. The goals of an organization are not completely pre-determined, but evolve out of the struggle for control over resources. The goals of an organization at any given time are the goals of the group within the organization that has attained ascendancy in the competition for resources. Those people who are able to gain control over resources are then able to impose their goals on the organization as a whole. Whatever rationality there is in the structure and operations of the organization is a function of the ability of one group, or unit, to "seize the day," to establish its dominance over other groups through their control of resources.

SHIFTING PATTERNS OF RESOURCE AVAILABILITY

One of the leading proponents of a political approach to studying organizations argues that a central strength of this orientation is the insights it offers to an understanding of the nature of organizational change: "The political-economy framework is not a substitute for decision-theory, the human-relations approach, or the concept of organizational rationality. For analysis of organizational change, however, it does claim to subsume these others" (Zald, 1970, p. 241). The power-politics approach is explicitly concerned with the processes of organizational change. Flowing from its concern with resources as determinants of organizational behavior, change in organizations is viewed as primarily a function of the shifting patterns of resource availability. That is, as the kinds and amounts of resources available changes, the internal arrangements for their control and distribution (i.e., the structure of the organization) will change in a process of organizational adaptation to its environment.

As a productive system an organization is constantly using up resources in its work. These come from the organization's environment, which allocates resources for those things it "wants done or can be persuaded to support" (Thompson and McEwen, 1958, p. 23). The organization is dependent upon its environment since it must adapt its internal structure and operations to respond to changing environmental requirements. The power-politics model suggests that this process of adaptation can best be understood in terms of the capacities of different units in the organization to establish hegemony over other units by means of their access to and control over new resources.

It has been argued here that the structure of an organization at any given time is best seen as the product of the most recent struggle for power among organizational subunits, with the "winner" (i.e., the unit able to establish control over resources) establishing the agenda for organizational action. The dominant unit is able to elevate its goals and priorities to the level of the goals and priorities for the total organization. The reason why a particular unit is able to establish this control is a function of two factors: the degree to which the unit is organized to take action on its own behalf in negotiating for resources, and the relevance of the unit's functional specialty to the demands placed on the organization by its significant "publics." In a sense, the unit must be able to "sell" itself and have something to "sell." Moreover, of the two factors the second will be the deciding one in a struggle for control. A unit may have great potential for engaging in internal political struggles because of its cohesiveness, high morale, and effective and ambitious leadership, but be lacking in the functional specialization needed by the organization. It is possible that this unit may be able to establish control over resources because of its strength as a cohesive and purposeful social unit. This victory, however, will be short-lived unless the unit is able to acquire or develop the technical capabilities needed by the organization to satisfy the expectations set in its environment.

Developments in the operation of public assistance programs over the past fifteen years offer an illustration of how this process works. Public assistance agencies generally involve three functional specializations: management, eligibility determination, and social services. The period from 1945 to 1962 saw the steady rise in the influence of one of these functional groups, the social services (Gilbert, 1966; Kahn, 1965). Starting with the publication in 1945 of Charlotte Towle's *Common Human Needs* and culminating with the passage of the 1962 Amendments to the Social Security Act (sometimes referred to as the "services amendment"), the influence of the social service (i.e., casework) perspective came to dominate the entire public assistance operation. The functional specialty offered by caseworkers includes a method for individual rehabilitation and change through counseling. The reason why this unit was able to attain the dominance it did within public assistance was the congruence between its specialized skills and the prevailing mood of the time as regards the nature of financial dependency. Namely, the causes of poverty were to be found in the short-comings and defects (usually of a psychological nature) of the poor, with the solution being some form of psychological rehabilitation (Mencher, 1963; Lukoff and Mencher, 1962). The goals of social workers became the goals of public assistance, and the 1962 amendments provided for the allocation of monies exlusively for the purposes of expanding the casework capacities of public welfare agencies.

Contrary to all expectations, the 1960's saw the most dramatic rise in the number of people receiving assistance since the inception of the program (Lynch, 1967). As a result, the public agenda shifted from a concern with rehabilitating the poor (assuming that that was once a real concern of the general public and not just of social workers) to ways of dealing with the mounting costs of the public assistance program ("Crisis in Welfare," 1969). Federal and state legislatures began to redeploy public assistance funds from service activities and placed the highest priority on the development of effective management. The influence of the caseworkers waned and the "age of the manager" arrived with consequent changes in the internal structure of the public assistance agency (Gruber, 1974; Turem, 1974).

A Note on the Use of the Framework

In order to apply this framework there must be guidelines for its use. The purpose of any conceptual framework is to further understanding through the application of relevant theoretical schemes. Three theoretical models have been presented here and the question now is when and for what purposes are they to be used.

The rational model is most appropriate when there is a clear and concrete specification of objectives and widespread support for these objectives among the members of the organization, and when the means for pursuing these objectives are developed to the point where one alternative can be clearly distinguished from another. (Casework, family therapy, and group therapy, for instance, cannot be neatly separated into three distinct methods because of the considerable overlapping of techniques employed by all three.) The situation conducive to rational analysis must be the *opposite* of what Cohen and his colleagues (1972) refer to as "organized anarchies:"

These are organizations—or decision situations—characterized by three properties. The first is problematic preferences. . . . The organization operates on the basis of a variety of inconsistent and ill-defined preferences. . . . The second property is unclear technology. Although the organization manages to survive and even produce, its own processes are not understood by its members. . . . The third property is fluid participation. Participants vary in the amount of time and effort they devote to different domains; involvement varies from one time to another (p. 1).

Many social welfare organizations do not meet the requirements of the rational model because of dissensus over goals and the diffuse nature of the technologies employed. While this is true for the organization as a whole, it will be less true as one looks at subunits within the organization. As one moves from macro- to micro-levels of analysis, from the total operation to specific aspects of that operation, the probabilities for rational action increase. This is mainly due to the greater clarity and agreement about goals and means found in small, cohesive groups, compared to large, heterogenous conglomerates. The rational model, then, will most likely be an appropriate framework for looking at the actions of subunits within organizations. As one goes beyond the operations of a specific unit and looks at overall organizational behavior, the rational approach becomes less useable, except in instances when the total organization is pursuing agreed-upon, specific objectives and has clearly identifiable technological means to choose from.

The natural-system model stresses the importance of coordinating the various subunits of an organization so that the system as a whole can function effectively. This approach assumes a high degree of interdependence among the units of a system in that one unit will not be able to function unless its activities are articulated with all other units. The degree of system interdependence, however, is an empirical question and cannot be assumed. Gouldner (1959) sheds considerable light on the ways in which interdependence can vary in social systems through his concept of the "functional autonomy" of the parts of a system. Functional autonomy is defined as:

> the degree to which any one part is dependent on others for the satisfaction of its needs. Systems in which parts have "high" functional autonomy may be regarded as having a "low" degree of system interdependence; conversely, systems in which parts have "low" functional autonomy have a "high" degree of system interdependence. The concept of functional autonomy directs attention to the fact that some parts may survive separation from others, that parts vary in their dependence upon one another, and that their interdependence is not necessarily symmetrical (p. 419).

An organization can be viewed in systemic terms, and analyzed as such, to the extent that the various units comprising it can be shown to *have to rely on each other* in order to get their work done. That is, must I wait until you complete your job before I can start mine? In a child-guidance agency, for example, can the family therapist begin work with a family before the intake worker has completed the initial interviews? Can the intake worker elect to continue seeing a family, thus circumventing the need to involve the family therapist? If either of these situations exist, then these units are operating in a *parallel* rather than interdependent fashion, and it would be inappropriate to view them as part of an integrated system of activities. These are the kinds of empirical questions that must be asked, and answered, about an organization in order to determine the extent of system interdependence and, consequently, the appropriateness of the natural-system model for analysis.

The power-politics approach proceeds from the assumption of the ubiquity of self-interest as a motivating force in all human behavior, including behavior in organizations. Individuals in organizations will act to secure and promote their interests, these being determined by one's location in the structure. Action directed toward the interests of the organization as a whole (whether these interests are defined in terms of maximizing efficient production or securing system integration) will occur only if there is some force operating to constrain self-interest behavior (Olsen, 1971, pp. 5–52). That is, unless the conditions noted above as necessary for an organization to operate either in the rational pursuit of a goal or to sustain and enhance itself as an integrated social system are clearly present, then it is safe to assume that behavior in the organization will best be explained along the lines suggested in the power-politics model.

References

Argyris, Chris. "Single-loop and Double-loop Models in Research in Decision-making." *Administrative Science Quarterly* 21 (1976): 363–375.

Banfield, Edward C. "Note on Conceptual Scheme." In Martin Meyerson and Edward C. Banfield, *Politics, Planning and the Public Interest*. Glencoe, Ill.: Free Press, 1955.

Barnard, Chester I. *The Functions of the Executive*. 30th ed. Cambridge, Mass.: Harvard University Press, 1968.

Benson, J. Kenneth. "Organizations: A Dialectical View." *Administrative Science Quarterly* 22, no. 1 (1977): 1–21.

Boulding, Kenneth. *The Image*. Ann Arbor, Mich.: University of Michigan Press, 1956.

Buckley, Walter. *Sociology and Modern Systems Theory*. Englewood Cliffs, N.J.: Prentice-Hall, 1967.

Burns, Tom. "Micro-politics: Mechanisms of Institutional Change." *Administrative Science Quarterly* 6, no. 2 (1961): 257–281.

Cohen, Michael D., James G. March, and Johan P. Olsen. "A Garbage Can Model of Organizational Choice." *Administrative Science Quarterly* 17, no. 1 (1972): 1–25.

"Crisis in Welfare," *The Public Interest,* Number 16 (Summer 1969), entire issue.

Cyert, Richard M., and Kenneth R. MacCrimmon. "Organizations." In Gardner Lindzey and Eelliot Aronson, eds., *The Handbook of Social Psychology,* 1: 568–611. Reading, Mass.: Addison-Wesley, 1968.

Dahl, Robert A. "The concept of power." *Behavioral Science* 2(1957): 201–215.

Derthick, Martha. *Uncontrollable Spending for Social Services Grants.* Washington, D.C.: Brookings Institution, 1975.

Donnison, David D. "Observations on University Training for Social Workers in Great Britain and North America." *Social Service Review* 29 (1955): 341–350.

Downs, Anthony. *Inside Bureaucracy.* Boston: Little, Brown, 1967.

Emerson, Richard M. "Power-Dependence Relations." *American Sociological Review* 27 (1962): 31–41.

Etzioni, Amitai. *Modern Organizations.* Englewood Cliffs, J.J.: Prentice-Hall, 1964.

Evan, William M. "The Organization-set: Toward a Theory of Inter-organizational Relations." In James D. Thompson, ed., *Approaches to Organizational Design.* Pittsburgh: University of Pittsburgh Press, 1966.

French, John R. P., Jr., and Bertram Raven. "The Bases of Social Power." In Dorwin Cartwright and Alvin Zander, eds., *Group Dynamics: Research and Theory.* 3rd ed. New York: Harper & Row, 1968.

Georgiou, Petro. "The Goal Paradigm and Notes towards a Counter Paradigm." *Administrative Science Quarterly* 18 (1973): 291–310.

Gilbert, Charles E. "Policy-making in Public Welfare: The 1962 Amendments." *Political Science Quarterly* 81 (1966): 196–224.

Goffman, Erving. *Asylums: Essays on the Social Situation of Mental Patients and Other Inmates.* Garden City, N.Y.: Anchor, 1961.

Gouldner, Alvin W. "Organizational analysis." In Robert K. Merton, Leonard Bloom, and L. Edward S. Cottrell, eds., *Sociology Today.* New York: Basic Books, 1959.

Gruber, Murray. "Total Administration." *Social Work* 19 (1974): 625–636.

Gummer, Burton. "A Power-politics Approach to Social Welfare Organizations." *Social Service Review* 52, no. 3 (1978): 349–361.

Kahn, Alfred J. "Social Services in Relation to Income Security." *Social Service Review* 39 (1965): 381–389.

Katz, Daniel and Robert L. Kahn. *The Social Psychology of Organizations.* New York: John Wiley, 1966.

Kirk, Stuart A., and James R. Greenley. "Denying or Deliverying Services?" *Social Work* 19 (1974): 439–447.

Lasswell, Harold. *Politics: Who Gets What, When, How.* New York: Meridian Books, World, 1958.

Levine, Sol, and Paul E. White. "Exchange as a Conceptual Framework for the Study of Interorganizational Relationships." *Administrative Science Quarterly* 5 (1961): 583–601.

Litwak, Eugene. "Models of Bureaucracy Which Permit Conflict." *American Journal of Sociology* 67 (1961): 177–184.

Lukoff, Irving F., and Samuel Mencher. "A Critique of the Conceptual Foundation of Community Research Associates. *Social Service Review* 36 (1962): 433–443.

Lynch, John M. "Trends in Number of AFDC Recipients, 1961–1965." *Welfare in Review* 5 (1967): 7–13.

Mayo, Elton. *The Human Problems of an Industrial Civilization* New York: Compass Books, Viking, 1960.

Mencher, Samuel. "Perspectives on Recent Welfare Legislation, Fore and Aft." *Social Work* 8 (1963): 59–64.

Meyer, Marshall W. "The Two Authority Structures of Bureaucratic Organization." *Administrative Science Quarterly* 13 (1968): 211–228.

Mogulof, Melvin. "Elements of a Special-revenue-sharing Proposal for the Social Services: Goal Setting, Decategorization, Planning, and Evaluation." *Social Service Review* 47 (1973): 593–604.

Newman, Edward and Jerry Turem. "The Crisis of Accountability." *Social Work* 19 (1974): 5–16.

Olsen, Mancus. *The Logic of Collective Action: Public Goods and the Theory of Groups.* Cambridge, Mass.: Harvard University Press, 1971.

Ouchi, William G., and Jerry B. Johnson. "Types of Organizational Control and their Relationship to Emotional Well-being." *Administrative Science Quarterly* 23, no. 2 (1978): 293–317.

Parsons, Talcott. "Suggestions for a Sociological Approach to the Study of Organizations—I." *Administrative Science Quarterly* 1, no. 1 (1956): 63–75.

Perrow, Charles. "A Framework for the Comparative Analysis of Organizations." *American Sociological Review* 32, no. 3 (1967): 194–208.

Pettigrew, Andrew M. *The Politics of Organizational Decision-making.* London: Tavistock, 1973.

Pfeffer, Jeffrey, Gerald R. Salancik, and Husespin Leblebici. "The Effect of Uncertainty on the Use of Social Influence in Organizational Decision Making." *Administrative Science Quarterly* 21, no. 2 (1976): 227–245.

Roethlisberger, Fritz J., and William J. Dickson. *Management and the Worker.* Cambridge, Mass.: Harvard University Press, 1939.

Scott, W. Richard. "Professionals in Bureaucracies—Areas of Conflict." In H. M. Vollmer and D. L. Mills, eds., *Professionalization.* Englewood Cliffs, N.J.: Prentice-Hall, 1966.

Scott, W. Richard. "Professional Employees in a Bureaucratic Structure: Social Work." In A. Etzioni, ed., *The Semi-Professions and Their Organization.* New York: Free Press, 1969.

Scott, William G. and T. C. Mitchell. *Organization Theory: A Structural and Behavioral Approach.* Rev. ed. Homewood, Ill.: Irwin-Dorsey, 1972.

Selznick, Philip. "Foundations of the Theory of Organization." *American Sociological Review* 13 (1948): 25–35.

Selznick, Philip. *Leadership in Administration: A Sociological Interpretation*. New York: Harper & Row, 1957.

Selznick, Philip. *The Organizational Weapon: A Study of Bolshevik Strategy and Tactics*. 2nd ed. New York: Free Press, 1960.

Simon, Herbert A. "On the Concept of Organizational Goal." *Administrative Science Quarterly* 8 (1964) : 1–22.

Stinchcombe, Arthur L. "Social Structure and Organization." In James G. March, ed., *The Handbook of Organizations*. Chicago: Rand-McNally, 1965.

Tannenbaum, Arnold S. *Control in Organizations*. New York: McGraw-Hill, 1968.

Thompson, James D. *Organizations in Action*. New York: McGraw-Hill, 1967.

Thompson, James D. and William J. McEwen. "Organizational Goals and Environment: Goal-setting as an Interaction Process." *American Sociological Review*, 23, no. 1 (1958): 23–31.

Towle, Charlotte. *Common Human Needs*. New York: National Association of Social Workers, 1945.

Tullock, Gordon. *The Politics of Bureaucracy*. Washington, D.C.: Public Affairs Press, 1965.

Turem, Jerry. "The Call for a Management Stance." *Social Work* 19 (1974): 625–636.

Wamsley, Gary L., and Mayer N. Zald. *The Political Economy of Public Organizations: A Critique and Approach to the Study of Public Administration*. Bloomington, Ind.: Indiana University Press, 1976.

Warren, Roland L. "The Concerting of Decisions as a Variable in Organizational Interaction." In Matthew Tuite, Roger Chisholm, and Michael Radnoes, eds., *Interorganizational Decision Making*. Chicago: Aldine, 1972.

Weber, Max. "Bureaucracy." In Hans H. Gerth and C, Wright Mills, eds. and trans., *From Max Weber: Essays in Sociology*. New York: Oxford University Press, 1958.

Weber, Max. *The Theory of Social and Economic Organizations*, trans. A. M. Henderson and Talcott Parsons. New York: Free Press Paperbacks, 1964.

White, Paul E. "Resources as Determinants of Organizational Behavior." *Administrative Science Quarterly* 19 (1974): 366–379.

Woodward, John. *Industrial Organization*. London: Oxford University Press, 1965.

Yuchtman, Ephraim and Stanley E. Seashore. "A System Resource Approach to Organizational Effectiveness." *American Sociological Review* 32 (1967): 891–903.

Zald, Mayer N. *Organizational Change: The Political Economy of the YMCA*. Chicago: University of Chicago Press, 1970.

———— and John D. McCarthy. "Organizational Intellectuals and the Criticism of Society." *Social Service Review* 49 (1975): 344–362.

PART II: LEADERSHIP IN SOCIAL ADMINISTRATION

THE EXECUTIVE BIND: CONSTRAINTS UPON LEADERSHIP

Felice Davidson Perlmutter

3

Given the turbulent environment in which we live, and especially in which the social services are embedded, executives of the social services are increasingly faced with complex conditions and circumstances within which they must function. In this chapter, Professor Perlmutter identifies a series of these administrative constraints upon leadership.

From her research in various welfare programs, Professor Perlmutter identifies three broad categories of constraints: (1) policy constraints, (2) political constraints, and (3) professional constraints. While she recognizes that they overlap, and each affects and is affected by the others, she presents them as distinct groupings in order to clarify and highlight the various constraints within each category.

The theoretical perspectives suggested by Professor Slavin in Chapter 1 should provide an orientation which the administrator can use as a basis for dealing with these various constraints upon leadership. And the clarification of these constraints provides the administrator with a sounder basis for the advocacy role discussed by Richan.

The Executive Bind: Constraints
Upon Leadership

Traditionally, administration has been viewed optimistically and positively (Selznick, 1957), for it was assumed that creative leadership, through the use of various analytic, technical, and interactional skills (Neugeboren, 1971), embodied the art of the possible. Recently, however, attention has increasingly been paid to the complexities of management, especially in the human services (Slavin, 1977), both in the public (Bower, 1977) and

53

nonprofit (Mittenthal and Mahoney, 1977) sectors. Given an increasingly turbulent organizational environment (Emery and Trist, 1965), it appears that there is a need for flexible leadership to meet the ever-changing demands of different administrative situations (Skinner and Sasser, 1977). And the capacity for this leadership will depend on a realistic understanding of the actual roles performed by the executive, since an important element in the learning of the executive is insight into the specific "pressures and dilemmas" of his or her job (Mintzberg, 1975, p. 60).

A central aspect of the reality of social administration is that it both reflects and is involved with the major social problems and social dilemmas of the twentieth century. Thus Drucker discusses management as a "generic function" common to all societies (1973, p. 17). It is therefore essential that the constraints upon leadership, its pressures and dilemmas, be identified, since it is our assumption that knowledge should be the basis for action and that understanding will enable the executive to develop more effective administrative strategies to create "conditions that will make possible in the future what is excluded in the present" (Selznick, 1957).

Leadership is a proactive function, and the executive must bear final responsibility for the decisions made in his or her organization. This is especially the case in human service systems, since all other decision-makers in the organization can abdicate their responsibility and defer decisions to the administrator, and the board of directors, despite its responsibility for setting policy, tends to yield this function to the executive, as its membership is often short-term and reflects changing interest groups and constituencies.

The purpose of this chapter is to describe several types of administrative constraints which affect social administration on the assumption that the executive, in the process of maximizing his/her options, will be more effective if the constraints in the system are understood. While the case material used in the discussion is drawn from the American context,* the concepts discussed are probably applicable to other societies.

Three types of constraints have been identified through research in human services administration: (1) policy constraints; (2) political constraints; and (3) professional constraints. While the major part of the discussion concerns the constraints associated with policy, the executive must be equally sensitive to the constraints which stem from political and professional factors. Each of these constraints will be clarified through the use of case illustrations and implications for executive behavior will be detailed.

*The author was principal investigator of the following projects from which the case material is drawn: *Prevention Programs in CMH Centers*, supported by NIMH Grant MH-25351, 1973–1977; *The United Services Agency Evaluation Project*, HEW, SRS Project 11-p-578 2013, Title X, Sec. 1115 of the Social Security Act, 1974–1977.

Case Studies

As a result of two very different empirical studies it has become increasingly clear that executive leadership would be facilitated, and executive burn-out inhibited, if the constraints intrinsic to and inherent in a given situation were made clear. The two studies will be briefly described in order that the case material which will be used in this chapter can be better understood. They are quite different, not only in terms of the content addressed, but also in terms of the methodology employed.

PREVENTION PROGRAMS IN COMMUNITY MENTAL HEALTH CENTERS

The first study was an exploratory one, and examined the Community Mental Health Centers (CMHCs), a radically new structure for mental health care in the United States. The regulations that accompanied the Mental Retardation and Community Mental Health Construction Act of 1963 had specified that five essential services be provided if a program were to be designated a community mental health center: (1) in-patient services; (2) out-patient services; (3) partial hospitalization services, including at least day care; (4) emergency 24-hour service; and (5) consultation and education.

The redefinition of the model for mental health care in the United States entailed several fundamental changes including: first, the development of the program under federal initiative through Public Law 88–164, a major transformation vis-à-vis federal involvement; second, the shift from state hospitals as the chief locale of treatment for mental illness "to the community as a potential arena for the engagement of mental health problems" (Cowen et al., 1967, p. 9); third, a change in the traditional one-to-one relationship between the psychiatrist and the patient, with its emphasis on the individual's adjustment, to a community-oriented, broad-spectrum approach (Musto, 1975); and finally, and relevant to our study, the addition of the public health focus on the prevention of illness and the promotion of health to a medically based, treatment-oriented system.

The service that was identified with the prevention mandate was consultation and education (C and E):

> Consultation and Education is a promising new mental health tool. . . . Four of the five essential elements of service required for a comprehensive community mental health center focus on new methods of treatment and care. The fifth, consultation and education to community agencies and professionals, is concerned with the prevention of mental illness and the promotion of mental health (NIMH, 1966, foreword).

In the early years of the CMHC program there were many strains and struggles in the centers, frequently located in C and E (Perlmutter and

Silverman, 1972). Consequently the study was designed with two objectives: (1) to obtain an understanding of the new service which was specially designed for and developed by the CMHC—consultation and education—through a survey of all C and E programs in all community mental health centers in Region III (Pennsylvania, Delaware, Maryland, Washington, D.C., Virginia, and West Virginia), federally funded prior to January 1973; (2) to contribute to the understanding of prevention in the field of mental health as it affects program development in consultation and education. This exploratory study served to highlight a number of constraints relevant to administration.

THE UNITED SERVICES AGENCY
EVALUATION PROJECT

The second study was a program evaluation of a demonstration project in services integration at the local level in Luzerne and Wyoming Counties of Pennsylvania, in a newly created agency called the United Services Agency (USA). A local catastrophe (i.e., a flood) provided the opportunity to experiment with new administrative arrangements as five public agencies were merged, including the County Board of Assistance, Aging, Child Welfare, Juvenile Probation, and Mental Health–Mental Retardation (MH–MR).

The USA had seven major objectives: (1) All the services of the five programs would be *integrated* at the local level; not only would there be entry into the system through a single point of access (i.e., a case manager), but the provision of the services would also be integrated, performed by a generic worker. (2) Services would be highly *decentralized*, available at seven local multiservice centers located throughout the two-county area to assure easy access. (3) Eligibility for services would be *universal* and all income-related requirements were to be waived. This would, it was hoped, broaden the consumer base of the multiservice centers and help to lessen the stigma of the "welfare image" which might otherwise be associated with the Centers.* (4) A *partnership* between USA and other public and voluntary agencies would encourage the more efficient and effective utilization of present resources and the planning for and development of additional human services in the two-county area being served. (5) *Advocacy* was a vital objective for the USA. The original conception for the advocacy function was the development of an independent spokesman, in the style of an ombudsman. (6). An *advisory* function for the USA was viewed as essential in order to involve community leaders in the development of the USA system. (7) And, finally, a strong *central administrative* role was conceived which would actively be concerned with an array of functions,

---

*Unfortunately, shortly after the inception of USA, new federal legislation attached income limits to all services funded under the Social Security Act.

including the design of a unified information system and fiscal responsibility, as well as research, evaluation, and planning.

The original concept for the USA was the result of a long, evolutionary process of concern and discussion about human services by state welfare leaders, started in the 1950's and culminating with the appointment of a secretary of welfare in 1971 who was committed to services integration in order to replace the "non-system" in human services. Thus, this demonstration project provided the opportunity to operationalize what had until now been theoretically conceived of as an ideal structure (Perlmutter, Richan, and Weirich, 1977). And this demonstration project provided an excellent opportunity to examine the constraints inherent in a situation when an ideal organizational concept is implemented in an ongoing service delivery system.

SIMILARITIES AND CONTRASTS
BETWEEN THE USA AND THE CMHCS

The similarities and differences between the two projects will now be highlighted.

Six similarities are noted: First, both projects were involved with complex human service systems which included policy, administration as well as program. Second, at least two governmental levels were involved: in the CMHC study the focus was on the federal and the local level; in the USA study, the state was also vitally involved. Third, both systems included highly trained professionals with preferences, experience, and skill. Fourth, both programs were involved with fundamental innovations and program change throughout the period of the study. Fifth, both studies took place in the first half of the 1970's, within a similar social, political, and professional climate. And, finally, both studies were conducted by an outside researcher who was not part of the system under study.

The differences between the two projects are equally salient. First, whereas the United Services Agency was a demonstration project, delimited in time, the CMHC is an ongoing program. Second, the CMH centers are entities clearly created as a result of specific federal legislation in contrast to the United Services Agency, which was a product of demonstration waivers obtained for that situation only. Third, the CMHC findings are of national interest, as they seek to clarify concepts and develop new professional approaches for all CMHCs; by contrast, the USA was created by one State Department of Public Welfare's initiative, in a unique circumstance and within a particular local setting (although on the assumption that it would be transferrable to other settings).

These two programs, the Community Mental Health Centers in Region III and the United Services Agency in Luzerne and Wyoming Counties, Pennsylvania, provide the case material for our discussion.

Constraints upon Leadership

The three types of constraints upon leadership—policy, political, and professional—will now be discussed. For the purpose of this discussion, we distinguish between policy and politics as follows. Policy is defined as program intent which reflects decisions made on the basis of principle with a supporting rationale. By contrast, politics is viewed as the action of interest groups affecting and affected by the policy who are motivated by self-interest. Although professionals can function as an interest group, we handle the constraints posed by professionalism as a distinctive category.

POLICY CONSTRAINTS

Ideally the program of a human service system should reflect and reinforce the policy frame from which it receives its sanction. In reality, this is often an area of great tension as policy and program often appear to be independent of each other. While there has been discussion in the literature of goal displacement as a cause of this incompatability and tension (Sills, 1966), the recent expansion of human service activity in and through the public sector highlights some additional problems in the policy arena.

Two broad sets of problems related to policy are here identified as a result of our research in the field; they are conceived as *internal* binds and *external* binds. Within the former category (i.e., internal binds) are the constraints intrinsic to the mandates themselves, which include (1) *competing* mandates, (2) *conflicting* mandates, and (3) *ambiguous* mandates. Within the latter category (i.e., external binds) are those constraints associated with (1) *incompatible sources of mandates* and (2) *long-term and short-term requirements*.

The Internal Bind.   In regard to *competing mandates*, the situation frequently obtains where there are several policies underpinning a program which are appropriate both on their own terms and compatible with each other. A problem arises when there are no clear priorities set, choices must be made between them, and the resources are inadequate to support all.

Thus, for example, the Community Mental Health Centers were given the mandate to provide for both the *treatment* and the *prevention* of mental illness, two important areas of activity essential for the mental health of the nation (Joint Commission, 1961). While compatible on a theoretical level, an understanding of the historical development of mental health services yields a different perspective on the juxtaposition of these two mandates.

Historically the CMHC program developed within the context of the mental health establishment which was focused totally on the treatment of the mentally ill. Many of the past practices in this field were now being questioned such as the extensive hospitalization of the mentally ill away from their community base, as well as the reliance on the traditional therapeutic hour as the basic treatment modality, both costly to the patient and manpower intensive. New forms of mental health treatment were being tried abroad, such as crisis-intervention teams in Amsterdam (Bellak, 1964) and therapeutic community in England (Jones, 1953), which helped to stimulate the interest in a new form of mental health service in the United States. However, it should be noted that the historical thread was clearly within the treatment arena; the prevention of mental illness and the promotion of mental health were not orientations of the field.

At the same time, the Poverty Program was enacted in the United States in a decade of social and political unrest and upheaval vis-à-vis the Viet Nam war, the widespread resistance to racial equality, and the intractability of poverty. Increasingly, personality and also symptoms of mental illness were seen "as having been molded by social institutions" (Alexander and Selesnick, 1966, p. 445). Thus Caplan (1974) talked about combatting harmful influences which operate in the community and strengthening the capacity of people to withstand stress, while Wagenfield and Robin (1976 suggested "a lowering of the incidence rate of disorder through an alteration of certain institutions . . . of the society viewed by community mental health practitioners as pathogenic . . . (e.g., poverty, racism, inequality of opportunity)."

We now saw a social problem orientation introduced into a field where until now a medical, illness model held sway. This historical collision of two different public programs (i.e., Poverty Program and CMHC) served to create a fusion of goals in the new mental health program: *prevention*, the concern of the Poverty Program, was thus added to, and linked with, *treatment* at the *policy level*.

And yet, a decade later, the tension created by the juxtaposition of these two important goals has not been reduced. Prevention has remained a second-class citizen in a treatment-oriented system with little understanding of the problem or the process for change (Perlmutter, 1973a).

The task for the executive, when faced with competing mandates, is complex. The mere recognition and clarification of the elements involved is an important and essential first step, for this enables the executive to examine a variety of possible options, given that the problem is not one of conflict or incompatibility. In fact the appropriate strategy to consider may be one of garnering increasing resources in order to fulfill the several competing mandates simultaneously. Or, if increasing the resources is not possible, the ordering of priorities and the development of a long-term plan may be another effective strategy (Perlmutter and Vayda, 1978).

In this first illustration the *competing* mandates have been defined by the policy base and the practical problem is one of operationalizing two mandates on a program level even though they are often compatible. The second problem in the policy area occurs when there are *conflicting* mandates built into one human service system. This second type of policy constraint created many difficulties for the United Services Agency.

As described earlier, the USA was designed to integrate a variety of services at the front line of actual delivery; thus the generic worker was to serve all clients and their needs whether they were children, adults, or elderly, whether they had mental health or corrections problems. However, the underlying policy did not support service integration, as all funding and accountability remained in the separate program areas of mental health, child welfare, aging, and corrections. Although functioning with a generic concept when delivering services, each worker continued not only to be paid by, but also to be supervised within, his or her specialized program. And although the administrative heads of the separate programs were not given direct line responsibility within the new integrated structure, their presence in a staff capacity in central administration was a constant source of tension. Thus the policy frame designed sui generis for USA was in conflict with other ongoing mandates.

In the case of conflicting mandates the executive has few viable options; a choice must be made to support one *or* the other mandate. The executive must examine the options and choose the best direction open to him or her. In some cases the executive can use his or her analytic skill to redefine the problem and find different alternatives based on a new perspective.

The third policy constraint of *ambiguous* mandates, wherein an existing policy is unclear, is illustrated by the CMHC experience. In the late 1960's social action and institutional change were incorporated as strategies within the social-political model of primary prevention (Kaplan and Roman, 1973; Gottesfield, 1972; Mechanic, 1969). Centers, usually in large urban areas, became the sites of activities directed towards broad-based social change, with a focus on correcting social inequities. This model was not uniformly accepted across the nation and to this very day debate continues about the limits of primary prevention activity (Vayda and Perlmutter, 1977). But significant to our discussion is the fact that the ambiguity of the prevention mandate made it possible for very different patterns to emerge within the Consultation and Education Services of individual CMHCs, differences that reflected either the needs of the catchment area or the particular interests of the professional staff.

The constraints created by ambiguous mandates can be viewed as an opportunity since they leave the executive room for decision-making and action: since the signals are unclear, there is greater latitude for individual interpretation. This is a state to be desired by a risk-taker who can use this lack of clarity to press for unorthodox options and alternatives. A more conservative administrator might prefer to press for the formulation of mandates in these unchartered areas in order to be protected, and thereby lose an opportunity for innovative action. Furthermore, in the press for greater clarity, the executive could precipitate a less satisfactory solution (i.e., the formulation of new competing or conflicting mandates).

The External Bind.   Incompatible sources of mandates become a constraint when public policy which affects the same organization is initiated at different levels of government. When human service agencies were primarily organized in the private sector, their unique mission, goals, and objectives were defined by a lay board of directors which was close to the local community whose needs stimulated the formation of the local agency. Consequently the local boards had a stake in the formulation and protection of these organizational goals and objectives (Perlmutter, 1973b). However, in the case of the Community Mental Health Centers, the mission for this system was not defined by the individual CMHC at the local level but by the federal legislation, far removed from the individual catchment areas. Consequently the local boards were not close to or involved with the policy-making process and tended to focus on the treatment function of the CMH center, since this is what they understood.

As a result, the federal legislative intent was not operationalized at the local level. The implications of these findings were profound: it was clear that executive leadership was critical in addressing this inconsistency since there was clearly a misfit between federal and local interests (Perlmutter and Vayda, 1978).

The USA also provides us with several illustrations of the problem created by incompatible sources of mandates. Although the agency had "consumer advocacy" as one of its goals when it applied for funds to implement activity in this area, the Pennsylvania Department of Public Welfare turned down the request on the grounds that the state could not legally fund an advocacy program (Perlmutter, Richan, and Weirich, VI, 1977). Thus the USA could not meet one of its own goals because its parent agency at the next governmental level did not support the local unit's activity. And yet the local agency was dependent upon the state agency for resources to implement this goal, which not only had been approved at the federal level but had been defined at the state level.

As another example, the thrust for services integration in the USA reflected the interest of some of the critical actors in the Department of Public Welfare at the state level (State and Local Commission, 1963) and at the federal level (Richardson, 1971). Yet there was little commitment or concern for this policy at the local level, either with the county commissioners or with the local service system (Perlmutter, Richan, and Weirich, II, 1977). The project was able to develop only because of the special local circumstance (i.e., the flood and the attendant funding); it certainly did not reflect the interests and orientations of the local community.

There is usually little stake in new policies at the local level when a program is designed at the federal level; therefore, extensive support and clarification are essential from the level of origin (Rein, 1961). Unfortunately, federal leadership both in regard to services integration (Gage, 1976) and community mental health (Goldston, 1976) have been sorely lacking. The cost of attempting to implement the federal and state policy in both the CMHC and the USA systems was profound in many respects, especially so because it created enormous administrative and professional tensions.

And yet the reality is that the incompatibility of the sources of policy will continue to affect the human services. How can the executive cope with this fact of life? Slavin's concept of executive leadership that orchestrates a variety of interests (see Chapter 1) suggests several strategies. First, the executive can articulate the differences and press for resolution between the different levels, thus inducing a change in the system's functioning. Second, the executive may prefer not to articulate the differences, but rather use those differences to enlist commitment on different levels. Third, the executive may choose to redefine the situation either by introducing a new mandate or by focusing on the overarching concerns of the present ones. And, finally, the executive can seek new constituencies or interest groups which can bring a new perspective to the situation.

The final policy constraint associated with long-term versus short-term factors can be discussed from two aspects: first, the accelerated pace of activity in the social services and, second, the problems related to time-limited demonstration projects.

The first problem is addressed by a Family Service Agency executive:

> As you may know, I came into administration like most executives of my vintage—through the skill of being a pretty good practitioner and then a good supervisor. . . . Fortunately I did come into the job as executive . . . when there was still the usual rhythm of going on year to year, and changes, if they occurred, took about two to four years and you had a lot of time to get used to them. I don't believe that there is any place in the country that such a rhythm is possible, today, at least if one is going to survive.*

This accelerated pace places enormous demand upon administration and puts it into a crisis-management framework. The challenge for the executive is to manage this year-to-year rhythm while *simultaneously* being concerned with the long range planning essential to the growth and de-

---

*Letter to The Reverend Arnold Purdie, Deceased, former Executive Director, Episcopal Community Services of Pennsylvania, which was shared with the author.

velopment of the organization. For if the executive can only address the year-by-year requirements, Selznick's concept of executive leadership as future oriented would be a futile dream.

In addition to the tension created by the accelerated time frame are those tensions intrinsic to a demonstration project. When an agency becomes involved in a demonstration project, it must clearly identify those elements which are compatible with its operations and which can be incorporated into the ongoing agency program. It must avoid those which are not organically related to the program and will usually be sloughed off at the project's end.

The United Services Agency is an example of a demonstration project constructed within a fundamentally incompatible policy framework. Although formal sovereignty over the local programs in Luzerne and Wyoming Counties was assigned to the central administration of USA, this did not guarantee the integration of local services nor the continuity of this service delivery approach. In fact, the USA experience illustrates the difficulties of changing the practices of established programs and the behavior of seasoned professionals. Although the funding agreement for USA between the Pennsylvania Department of Public Welfare and the county commissioners envisioned complete control by USA, even during the demonstration period the separate programs constituents (i.e., Child Welfare, Aging, MH-MR) retained much of their prior power and even maintained services independent of the USA model. For the reality was that the demonstration funds could only support the planning and administrative work of the USA leadership; the actual funding of services remained under the individual programs. Furthermore, the professionals strongly identified with their former programs and roles and resisted identifying with USA and their new generic roles. Thus, not only did the agency experience continuous conflict as a result of this incompatability but, since it was a five-year demonstration project, it was difficult to develop commitment to the new system when all the actors believed the integrated program would be dismantled when the project terminated.

A demonstration project can provide an enormous opportunity to introduce innovation into a human service system. However, the executive, both in the private and the public sectors, is continuously faced by both long-term and short-term requirements in the agency's programs. It is essential that the executive first identify these different processes in order to be able to plan a better means of handling them. Thus, the response to continuous crisis which is cyclical, but expected, will be different from the activity necessary to deal with a short-term, one-shot demonstration project where the executive must consciously and carefully include in his or her calculations the cost of this strategy and the investments which must be made to protect and stabilize the innovations.

POLITICAL CONSTRAINTS

Although political constraints are inextricably linked to policy constraints, we prefer to treat them separately in order to highlight them. The above discussion of the misfit between federal-level policy applied to local-level programs illustrates the political constraints which exist between governmental structures. However, in addition to vertical federal, state, and local relationships, there are also horizontal relationships at the local level (Warren, 1963). The United Services Agency provides excellent case material vis-à-vis the problems in the political arena.

In regard to vertical political processes, the USA was a demonstration project under the aegis of the Pennsylvania Department of Public Welfare; in the beginning of the project, the special support of the Welfare Secretary served to give it a special status as a semi-autonomous unit or "mini-region" (Perlmutter, Richan, and Weirich, II, 1977). This was a critical political asset and served to get the organization started in spite of the numerous and inherent policy contradictions. In fact, without this special relationship with the state the agency might never have successfully come into existence.

While federal interest was also important, it eventually waned. For its part, the state bureaucracy never understood the special needs of this demonstration project and through normal routine placed enormous impediments in USA's path. For example, since funding was categorical in nature, while the USA services were integrated, a central challenge for USA fiscal management was to integrate funding streams as well as to control them. (i.e., allocation and accountability). Proper management of resources required an understanding of a unique and complex programmatic design. Although USA was given the local control of its resources, it remained under direct supervision of the Pennsylvania Department of Public Welfare comptroller. Thus the USA Fiscal Division was headed by a position not under USA's authority. Little understanding of the program's unique needs existed at the state level, and eventually USA was accused of stepping beyond the bounds of local authority and bypassing state perogatives (Perlmutter, Richan, and Weirich, IX, 1977). The ability of USA's executive to work creatively with this fiscal reality must be noted, since the new and innovative programs required heroic efforts.

In the Community Mental Health Center program, the federal government assumed major staffing responsibility for an eight-year period, with a gradual decrease based upon the expectation that funds would be generated from other sources, including state and local government. In reality this financial intent has never been achieved, and "often centers were forced either to cut services, especially nonreimbursable services (consultation and education programs) or to increase income from direct clinical services" (Landsberg and Hammer, 1977, p. 64). Furthermore, under third-party payments, prevention services were not funded. Thus, the federal design was never accepted at the state or local level.

On the horizontal level, other problems existed from the start in the United Services Agency, not only between the public agencies but also between the USA and the voluntary sector. Both public and private agencies alike were concerned that USA would usurp enormous power which would undermine the integrity, if not the existence, of their programs. Since welfare agencies are extremely dependent upon one another for the exchange of resources such as clients, referrals, and programs (Morris and Lescohier, 1978), it was essential that the USA administration concern itself with relationships at the horizontal level. This could not be done with verbal assurances alone, but required a *quid pro quo*. The extensive use of contracting with the private sector provided a major source of leverage for USA; however, it should be noted that the contracts were in new areas of service and did not threaten the domain of the voluntary sector.

An excellent illustration of a successful resolution in the political arena is provided by the USA in its experience with the Family Service Association of Wyoming Valley (FSA). The FSA had established a claim to information and referral services in 1972, at the same time that the USA was started. In response to the chaos occasioned by the flood, FSA extended its target population to include all of the residents of Wilkes-Barre; the original intent to respond only to flood-related problems was soon broadened to become a permanent program with wide-ranging services.

USA, meanwhile, also had plans to provide information and referral services, since its constituent programs (Child Welfare, MH-MR, and Aging) were operating information and referral programs for their respective clients. The USA leadership wanted both to expand services to cover the two-county area, with an around-the-clock provision, as well as to have the services reflect the "generic" approach. However, not only was the USA constrained by inadequate staffing levels and restrictions on after-hours work, but was also aware that, with FSA operating such a service, unnecessary duplication would occur. Furthermore, it was clear that FSA was not going to give up the program it had worked so hard to establish.

Consequently the USA approached FSA with the request to expand their services to cover the whole two-county area and to ensure continuous phone coverage. The negotiations were long and hard, and there were many technical problems involved in setting up such an extensive contract. But in January 1975, a contract between the USA and Family Service was achieved, *with FSA acting as the sponsoring and administrating agency*. FSA's original fears of a USA takeover were soothed, and USA was satisfied that its regional mandate for I and R services would be implemented. A few months after this initial agreement, another arrangement was made which added crisis intervention and emergency services to the joint program, and a help-line was also formed, using a team approach for emergency after-hours provision of services.

This program illustrates a significant cooperative effort between the various participants, while at the same time allowing each service domain to protect its interests. For example, MH-MR's contention that special expertise was needed to deliver crisis services was respected and the MH-MR centers largely determined and controlled these services. What is significant, however, is that in addition to expanded services, the arrangement also served to increase the collaboration among the various public and private agencies as staffs, services, clientele, and funding were mixed together. This overlapping, and interdependency, resulted in significant changes in the political relationships among the agencies.

However, it is not sufficient to identify the organizational processes involved. Equally important in these horizontal and vertical relationships was the leadership available in the USA system. While the first executive played an important function in initiating the new USA agency, his focus was on the internal technical, formal installation of the agency system rather than on the intersystem relationships in the social service network. The external resistance was enormous, however, and might in fact have impeded the USA operation had not the second executive recognized the priority of establishing these external working relationships and focused her energy in this area. The power inherent in the USA was not enough to carry off this innovation; the careful use of charismatic leadership was a critical element in this highly political process.

This experience highlights the importance of the executive attending to the problems in the vertical and horizontal networks of his or her program to assure the agency's capacity not only to survive but also to progress. Furthermore, it is necessary that the executive assess the interpersonal skills required for the particular negotiations in order to ensure success.

PROFESSIONAL CONSTRAINTS

The behavior of professionals in human service organizations has been discussed in the literature (Goode, 1969; Rose, 1974); we wish to focus on three aspects of professionalism, including (1) ideological orientations, (2) technical expertise, and (3) structural factors.

The CMHC study highlighted the critical role *ideology* plays in the behavior of professionals in a human service system. As the CMHC program began to develop, the claimed monopoly of the medical profession over the treatment of mental illness was no longer, a priori, accepted.

> In the absence of more specfic and definitive scientific evidence of the causes of mental illness, psychiatry and the allied mental health professions should adapt and practice a broad, liberal philosophy of what constitutes and who can do treatment within the framework of their hospitals, clinics, or other professional service agencies (Joint Commission, IX, 1961).

The shifting ideological orientations occurred primarily in the Consultation and Education Service (Perlmutter and Silverman, 1973), with social and institutional change accepted as organizational goals (Hersch, 1972). This shift in orientations introduced a broad and diverse set of values and objectives into the mental health field, most concisely presented in Baker and Schulberg's *Community Mental Health Ideology Scale* (1967).

It has been assumed that, whereas the medically trained professionals in the CMHCs (e.g., psychiatrists) would resist the new orientations, social workers, because of their community orientations, would be "in a unique position to contribute to the support of those functions and objectives which are least well implemented and staffed, namely work with other social and community systems" (National Conference on Social Welfare Task Force, 1975).

And yet our CMHC study found that the professional orientations of the social workers vis-à-vis prevention in C and E did not reflect the unique and distinctive activist orientation of their profession; rather it was the position of the professional in the CMHC which was the more decisive factor. The C and E directors were the most activistically and community-oriented cohort (Perlmutter and Vayda, 1978); their orientations were *not* compatible with those of their center directors, who were more traditional in their views. Since the C and E director is directly accountable to the center director, it became apparent that the top executive must examine, explore, and expand his or her orientations in order to fulfill the mission of the program, especially when it is a new and innovative one. The lack of understanding, and therefore support, of the dual mandate of prevention *and* treatment is an example of a default of leadership.

A second professional constraint is the problem related to *technical expertise*. This was very evident in USA, when the workers from the categorical programs (i.e., Aging, Child Welfare, Mental Health–Mental Retardation) were expected to become "generic" workers in the newly organized structure. Consequently, despite the new job descriptions and work roles, USA workers retained their self-identification with their base, specialized programs. This problem was exacerbated by the fact that not only was there a lack of clarity in the plan for manpower utilization, but the agency was in a continuous state of organizational crisis and uncertainty (Perlmutter, Richan, and Weirich, V, 1977).

A carefully designed staff development program could have served to teach new skills needed for the new roles. A major problem in both the CMHC and USA programs was due to the fact that the professional had not been trained to perform either a "preventive" or a "generic" function. Since workers at the front line can either promote or undermine the organization's objectives (Smith, 1965), it is imperative that the executive give priority to designing a staff training program which will help the professionals to understand not only the design and intent of the new system but also their new roles.

In both the CMHC program and in the USA the critical function of staff training was not appreciated by the executives. Thus, in the USA, the training program was never organized around the major programmatic goals of service integration, but rather responded to and utilized the expertise available within its member programs. For example, the USA contracted with MH-MR to conduct its initial training sessions with a focus on mental health principles instead of using these early sessions to interpret and explain the new program in order to influence the orientations of the professional staff. Similarly, the leadership in the CMHCs never recognized its critical role in using staff training as a vehicle for incorporating the new concepts and strategies implicit in the CMHC program.

Both of these case studies highlight the fact that the executive can neither assume that professional staff will adjust to or accept organizational change nor that the sub-executives and supervisory staff will clearly understand what is required to help the rest of the staff function effectively in the new context. While the executive must delegate staff development and supervision to other administrators, it is essential that leadership be clearly asserted to help professionals work effectively and appropriately to implement new programs.

Finally, problems with professional staff were further exacerbated by some of the *structural* characteristics of the organization. In addition to the problem identified in the above discussion of professional constraints (where workers had to shift their work to new methods for which they were neither trained nor oriented), another major obstacle was due to the fact that the professionals were on different payrolls (e.g., county funds for Child Welfare and Aging, and state funds of the Board of Assistance). Consequently, salaries for workers performing the same tasks were often very disparate. In addition the State Civil Service classifications created inequities when the regulations reduced the flexibility of USA in personnel assignments; as a result, while workers with similar education and experience were assigned to new and diverse positions, they were locked into old job titles with a salary differential of as much as 20 percent (Perlmutter, Richan, and Weirich, V, 1977).

There is no question that these structural problems are the most difficult to handle. This is where the advocacy role of the executive, discussed in Richan's chapter, becomes critical as the executive serves to bridge practice reality with policy intent.

Conclusion

This discussion has identified various constraints upon leadership in the human services on the assumption that knowledge and insights into the pressures and dilemmas of administration leads to more effective action. Although this chapter has used case material from two particular programs, the executive bind created by the various constraints discussed here appears to be relevant to social administration regardless of context.

References

Alexander, F. G., and S. T. Selesnick. *The History of Psychiatry*. New York: Mentor, 1966.

Baker, Frank, and H. C. Schulberg. "The Development of a Community Mental Health Ideology Scale." *Community Mental Health Journal* 3 (1967): 216–225.

Bellak, Leopold. *Handbook of Community Psychiatry and Community Mental Health*. New York: Grune and Stratton, 1964.

Bower, J. L. "Effective Public Management." *Harvard Business Review* 55 (March–April 1977): 131–140.

Caplan, Gerald. *Support Systems and Community Mental Health*. New York: Behavioral Publications, 1974.

Cowen, E. I., E. A. Gardner, and M. Zax. *Emergent Approaches to Mental Health Problems*. New York: Appleton-Century-Crofts, 1967.

Drucker, P. F. *Management: Tasks, Responsibilities, Practices*. New York: Harper and Row, 1973.

Emery, F. E., and E. D. Trist. "The Causal Texture of Organizational Environment." *Human Relations* 18 (1965): 21–32.

Gage, R. W. "Integration of Human Service Delivery Systems." *Public Welfare* 34 (1976): 27–33.

Goldston, S. E. "Primary Prevention: A View from the Federal Scene." In G. W. Albee and M. J. Joffee, eds., *Primary Prevention in Psychopathology*. Hanover, N.H.: University Press of New England, 1977.

Goode, W. J. "The Theoretical Limits of Professionalization." A. Etzioni, ed., In *The Semi-Professions and Their Organization*. New York: Free Press, 1969.

Gottesfeld, Harry, ed. *The Critical Issues of Community Mental Health*. New York: Behavioral Publications, 1972.

Hersch, C. "Social History, Mental Health and Community Control." *American Psychology* 27 (1972): 749–754.

Joint Commission on Mental Illness. *Action for Mental Health*. New York: Basic Books, 1961.

Jones, Maxwell, et al. *The Therapeutic Community: A New Treatment Method in Psychiatry*. New York: Basic Books, 1953.

Kaplan, S. R., and Melvin Roman. *The Organization and Delivery of Mental Health Services in the Ghetto. New York: Praeger*, 1973.

Landsberg, Gerald, and Roni Hammer. "Possible Programmatic Consequences of Community Mental Health Center Funding Arrangements." *Community Mental Health Journal* 13 (Spring 1977): 63–67.

Mechanic, David. *Mental Health and Social Policy*. Englewood Cliffs, N.J.: Prentice-Hall, 1969.

Mintzberg, H. "The Manager's Job: Folklore and Fact." *Harvard Business Review* 53 (July-August 1975): 49–61.

Mittenthal, B. A., and B. W. Mahoney. "Getting Management Help in the Nonprofit Sector." *Harvard Business Review* 55 (Sept.-Oct. 1977): 95–102.

Morris, Robert, and I. H. Lescohier. "Service Integration: Real versus Illusory Solutions to Welfare Dilemmas." In R. C. Sarri and Y. Hasenfeld, eds., *The Management of Human Services*. New York: Columbia University Press, 1978.

Musto, R. F. "Whatever Happened to Community Mental Health?" *The Public Interest* 39 (1975): 53–79.

National Conference in Social Welfare Task Force. *Roles for Social Work in Community Mental Health Programs*. Task Force Report. 1975.

National Institute of Mental Health. *Consultation and Education: A Service of the Community Mental Health Center*. Washington, D.C.: National Institute of Mental Health, 1966.

Neugeboren, Bernard. "Developing Specialized Programs in Social Work Administration in the Master's Degree Program: Field Practice Component." *Education for Social Work* 7 (1971): 35–47.

Perlmutter, F. D. [a]. "Prevention and Treatment: A Strategy for Survival." *Community Mental Health Journal* 10 (1973): 276–281.

————. "Citizen Participation and Professionalism: A Developmental Relationship," *Public Welfare* 31 (1973b): 25–28.

————, W. Richan, and T. Weirich. *Final Report of the United Services Agency Evaluation Project* (Philadelphia: Temple University, School of Social Administration, 1977). Monograph I: *The United Services Agency as a Services Integration Project*. Monograph II: *The Political and Policy Contexts of the United Services Agency*. Monograph III: *Planning in the United Services Agency*. Monograph IV: *The Service Delivery System of the United Services Agency*. Monograph V: *Personnel Utilization in the United Services Agency*. Monograph VI: *Consumer Advocacy in the United Services Agency*. Monograph VII: *Management Information Systems and the United Services Agency*. Monograph VIII: *Public Administration in the United Services Agency*. Monograph IX: *Transferability and the United Services Agency*. Monograph X: *Technical Appendix for United Services Agency Evaluation Project*.

_____ and H. A. Silverman. "Conflict in Consultation-Education." *Community Mental Health Journal* 9 (1973): 116-122.

_____. "The Community Mental Health Center: A Structural Anachronism." *Social Work* 17 (1972): 72–84.

_____ and A. M. Vayda. "Barriers to Prevention Programs in Community Mental Health Centers." *Administration in Mental Health* 5 (1978): 140–153.

Rein, Martin. *An Organizational Analysis of a National Agency's Local Affiliates in Their Community Contexts*. New York: Planned Parenthood, 1961.

Richardson, Eliot. "A Proposed Strategy of HEW Services Reform." A Memorandum for the President, Washington, D.C.: Dec. 23, 1971.

Rose, Gordon, "Issues in Professionalism: British Social Work Triumphant," In F. D. Perlmutter. ed., *A Design for Social Work Practice*. New York: Columbia University Press, 1974.

Selznick, Philip. *Leadership in Administration*. New York: Harper and Row, 1957.

Sills, D. L. "Goal Succession in Four Voluntary Associations." In W. A. Glaser. and D. L. Sills, eds., *The Government of Associations. Totowa, N.J.: Bedminister,* 1966.

Skinner, W., and W. E. Sasser. "Managers with Impact: Versatile and Inconsistent." *Harvard Business Review* 55 (Nov.-Dec. 1977): 140–148.

Slavin, Simon, ed. *Social Administration: The Management of the Social Services*. New York: Haworth Press and Council on Social Work Education, 1978.

Smith, D. E. "Front-line Organization of the State Mental Hospital." *Administrative Science Quarterly* 10 (1965): 381–399.

State and Local Welfare Commission. *A Reallocation of Public Welfare Responsibilities*. (Harrisburg, Pa.: Department of Public Welfare, 1963).

Vayda, A. M., and F. D. Perlmutter. "Primary Prevention Programs in Community Mental Health Centers: A Survey of Current Activity." *Community Mental Health Journal* 13 (1977): 343–351.

Wagenfield, M. O., and S. S. Robin. "Boundary Busting in the Role of the Community Mental Health Worker." *Journal of Health and Social Behavior* 17 (1976): 111–121.

Warren, R. L. *The Community in America*. Chicago: Rand McNally, 1963.

THE ADMINISTRATOR AS ADVOCATE

Willard C. Richan

4

Advocacy is easier to advocate than to activate. In this essay Professor Richan discusses the complexity of administrative advocacy, and supports the views of the editors that it is an essential component in the role of the social administrator. The chapter illustrates the theoretical issues identified by Slavin, Gummer, and Perlmutter.

Professor Richan chooses to address this topic through a unique case illustration from the social services. We are presented with an historical process, which began in 1969, when a top administrator was hired to head a juvenile correctional system, and ended in 1977, when this administrator left the formal bureaucracy to become an advocate from outside the system. Political, professional, organizational, and personal elements are presented which provide us with an opportunity to use this case heuristically as a basis for defining our own responsibility for and relationship to the advocacy role.

It may seem like a contradiction in terms to speak of administration and advocacy* in the same breath. Advocacy in behalf of consumers of social services is usually thought of as directed *at* administrators instead of *by* them. Yet there are several reasons why the administrator of social services as advocate is a highly appropriate role.

Advocacy is entirely consistent with the leadership role which both Katz and Kahn (1966, pp. 300–355) and Selznick (1957) see as central to the administrative function. The administrator needs to have a "systemic perspective" (Katz and Kahn, 1966, pp. 315–318) which transcends the special

---

*Defined here as action in behalf of an aggrieved person, through direct intervention, or an entire class of aggrieved persons, through attempted change in policy. See Ad Hoc Committee on Advocacy, 1969.

interests of any one group within or around the organization. While this orientation would presumably give organizational interests primacy over client interests, the model espoused by these writers clearly suggests the kind of vision which can see the vital connection between the organization's long-term self-interest and the welfare of one of its key resources, its clientele.

Weinberger's skepticism (in Richan, 1969, pp. 294–302) about the freedom of the executive to assert such leadership led him to propose that responsibility for monitoring and reforming social service organizations be vested in professional associations. This view ignores the fact that professional associations, insofar as they have leverage of any kind, are far more likely to be able to exert it with their members who are administrators than directly with service systems, over which they have no direct authority. The National Association of Social Workers (NASW) specifically noted this distinction in one policy statement on standards for social service organizations (see *Standards*, 1975).

When NASW formulated a policy on advocacy, it defined this role as obligatory for all social workers and spoke directly to the responsibility of the administrator, "who then is bound to act as an advocate on behalf of clients under his jurisdiction. A collateral obligation would be the responsibility of the supervisor or administrator to create the climate in which direct-service workers can discharge their advocacy obligations" (Ad Hoc Committee on Advocacy, 1968). It is not generally realized that this obligation is an official part of the NASW professional standards and as such is technically enforceable under the formal adjudication procedures of the Association. Admittedly the willingness and ability of NASW to sanction violations of these obligations have not been tested. However, on the positive side, the Association has stepped in to provide legal and other assistance to at least one welfare agency executive who was dismissed for fighting in behalf of clients. ("Berkan Appealing Dismissal," 1972).

Clearly the willingness of social work administrators to act as advocates in behalf of a relatively powerless constituency will depend largely on their belief that they have the freedom and power to do so. While it must be acknowledged that the position of the social agency executive is exposed and vulnerable as perhaps no other professional role is, administrators are not without resources. And they know it. In his research, Weinberger (in Richan, 1969) found that

administrators express a high degree of satisfaction with their ability to implement program changes whether or not their board initially concurred with new plans. Selected comments indicated board acceptance of program changes and innovations in those situations where the executive informed and explained to the board the rationale for policy change (p. 295).

This view is corroborated by Senor (1963) and Hoshino (1967) in the private and public sectors of social welfare, respectively. This chapter proposes to examine the resources available to administrators and ways in which these can be exploited. For illustrative material I shall take a field which has a well-earned reputation for resisting change, juvenile corrections.* Its ability to fend off attempted reforms led one witness at a 1971 congressional subcommittee hearing to declare:

> I think the history of correctional reform is that it never occurs. The most one can hope for is a great deal of brouhaha every 5, 10 or 15 years following a series of scandals or upsets. In the more liberal States maybe the old programs will be redone in new buildings, but in terms of basic reform, I think the system is so self-protective, so self-insulated, that it is able to absorb any substantive reform and devour it over a period of time (*Hearings*, 1971).

The speaker was Dr. Jerome Miller, whose leadership in correctional reform defied his own dismal assessment. The reforms which he set in motion as an administrator, first in Massachusetts and later in Pennsylvania, made significant inroads on the warehousing of youth in correctional facilities, and, contrary to widespread belief, the reforms have not all been devoured. The Miller experience is not completely a success story nor without mistakes, which makes it all the more valuable as an illustration of the potential of the administrator as advocate in the real world.

The Miller Crusade

The juvenile justice field is capable of virtually all of the mortifications of flesh and spirit that are associated with the adult criminal justice system. But it carries an extra burden, a strong professional commitment to rehabilitate the offender. While this mission has helped to focus public attention on the worst sins of the juvenile justice system and acted as a goad to reform, more frequently it has lent itself to abuse of the civil rights of offenders in the name of treatment and to a kind of self-righteousness which has tended to deflect attempts at reform. Said the director of one juvenile correctional facility:

> You can't force an institution to take the kind of kids that require the facility, not provide the necessary resources, and then criticize them because they tried to do their best. . . . You can't take a kid who has experienced 15 years of the kinds of experiences that our kids experienced in the past and expect

---

*This discussion is concerned with the administrative tactics related to advocacy; it does not address problems of deinstitutionalization per se.

them overnight to respond to program. So the kind of kids that require more than the usual control, . . . it takes time for them to respond to the relationships or program or what have you. *(Child Abuse at Taxpayers' Expense,* 1974, p. 44).

This speaker, a professional social worker, presided over an institution in which a boy had been fatally burned in a detention cell, an orientation program was likened to classical brainwashing techniques, and children were kept locked in total isolation for weeks at a time. This director was later dismissed, the standard solution to outside criticism of juvenile correctional programs. The professional literature is littered with pessimistic reports on the possibility of truly reforming the juvenile justice system (see Cheatwood, 1974; James, 1970; Lerman, 1968; Polsky, 1967).

Jerome Miller took over the Massachusetts juvenile correctional system in 1969 with all of the anger and brashness associated with the late sixties. But Miller was no revolutionary. A psychiatric social worker who had been teaching in a school of social work, he set out to develop a more humanistic and therapeutic climate in the massive training schools for juvenile offenders. He launched ambitious staff training programs and sought to open better lines of communication to the youthful charges in the system. It was a tactic which had been tried many times before—moderate reform of the existing system. It was when this course of action failed that he turned to stronger medicine—deinstitutionalization (Rutherford, 1974; Ohlin, Coates, and Miller, 1974).

Miller conducted a campaign which was bold and imaginative if one liked it and aggressive and reckless if one did not. In the process he effectively closed down a number of huge training schools where youthful offenders had been subjected to treatment so abusive that it had caused a major scandal. Without Miller's leadership the system could have rapidly recovered from the scandals and gone back to business as usual. Under his direction the system took a major leap into a diversified program with an emphasis on community-based programs. After Miller left Massachusetts in 1973, his hand-picked successor carried on the work of consolidating the gains, and as of this writing the Massachusetts juvenile correctional system has not reverted to its former status.

Likewise, in Pennsylvania, Miller was able to eliminate the use of an adult penitentiary for juvenile offenders and set in motion the development of community alternatives for juvenile correctional institutions. While in time Miller's own position in the Pennsylvania hierarchy was seriously weakened, the reforms which he initiated went forward under the leadership of others.

For the purposes of this analysis, the details of the reform program are less important than the factors which appear to have allowed it to happen.

We shall consider three major elements: formal authority, control over resources, and control over information. All three factors need to be present in substantial degree for the administrator-as-advocate to be able to function effectively. While this case concerns state-level administration, the underlying principles should apply equally to the executive of a direct service delivery system and to advocacy on a case as well as a policy level. The complementary nature of the three factors—formal authority, resource control, and information control—becomes clear as one considers Dr. Miller's attempts at juvenile justice reform in Massachusetts and later in Pennsylvania.

Formal Authority to Act

Formal authority, or legitimate influence, is inherent in the administrator's role. The legitimacy is an important element for two reasons. In the first place, it lessens the need of the person wielding authority to engage in exchange relationships (Levine and White, 1961) in order to maintain influence over others. Secondly, it establishes a status quo which has general acceptability and which other interested parties are hesitant to challenge. Both of these aspects of formal authority were important to Jerome Miller's advocacy of change.

In 1948 the Massachusetts legislature made a major innovation in the state's juvenile justice system: it removed the power to make placements from juvenile judges and gave it to a new Youth Service Board (YSB), nominally within the Department of Education but functionally autonomous (Ohlin, Coates, and Miller, 1974). On the surface, the change seemed to have little effect on the fortunes of juvenile offenders. The old outlook prevailed in the correctional system, and the practices of the Division of Youth Services, the administrative counterpart of the YSB, continued to draw the fire of liberal critics. But the shift of control of commitments from individual judges to a unitary administrative arm had laid the foundation for later reform.

In contrast, Pennsylvania juvenile judges have the power to assign offenders to specific institutional facilities. This fact stood like a huge boulder in Jerome Miller's path throughout his attempts to reform the Pennsylvania juvenile correctional system. It did not prevent reforms from taking place, but it severely constrained their pace and extent and attenuated those changes which have occurred.

When Miller's attempt to remove juvenile offenders from an adult penitentiary, Camp Hill, was threatened by the power of the juvenile judges, he turned to the formal authority of the state attorney general for support. Miller reasoned that as long as judges could keep filling up Camp Hill with new bodies, it did little good to move out those already there. At his urging, the attorney general issued a letter to all juvenile judges, citing the violation of existing statutes and court decisions as the basis for his stand. The letter declared in part:

> This Department will seek the cooperation of all judges in the State in order to prevent further commitments of deprived or delinquent children to Camp Hill. In this regard, this Department must provide a major commitment to assist the judiciary in finding alternate placements for these children. You are advised that this Department will resist through all lawful channels the placement of any deprived or delinquent child in Camp Hill after August 15, 1975, and that appropriate action will be taken to review the status of juveniles now incarcerated (Letter, 1975).

While the tone of the letter was more conciliatory than Miller might have wished, and several judges threatened to test the authority of the attorney general to interfere with their prerogatives, the fact is that the commitment of juvenile offenders to Camp Hill from the juvenile courts of Pennsylvania effectively ceased as of that time. The legal situation was cloudy enough so that no one saw fit to make an overt contest of it. But a change in actors on the scene or a further hardening of the public mood against juvenile crime could easily resume the flow of youth into Camp Hill. And the formal authority to send youths to specific juvenile facilities in Pennsylvania still sits with the judges, successfully limiting the ability to make major inroads on that system.

Conceivably public sentiment against juvenile crime in Massachusetts could be stirred up to the point where commitment powers would be returned to the judges of that state, but this is relatively unlikely. Once the power to act has acquired legal sanction it is relatively hard to dislodge. This principle worked in Miller's favor in Massachusetts but was a major stumbling block to his efforts in Pennsylvania.

Formal authority was important to Miller in other ways in Massachusetts. As head of the reorganized Department of Youth Services (DYS) he had the power to make crucial decisions in all juvenile correctional operations, and he was not hesitant to use these powers on many occasions. He was in a position to order the closing of a facility and have it stick. He could also move personnal around and hire new people, although the ability to fire was sharply constrained by civil service requirements.

The key to much of Miller's freedom to act was the staunch support of Governor Francis Sargent, a moderate Republican. It allowed the DYS commissioner to survive more than one legislative investigation. In sharp contrast was his experience in Illinois, where he briefly headed up services for children and youth. He soon left that position, complaining about a lack of support from the administration (see Santiestevan, 1975).

Formal authority was a major issue for Dr. Miller in Pennsylvania. He was brought in as Governor Milton Shapp's special assistant for community programs, but did not have line authority over juvenile correctional programs. Later Miller became commissioner of children and youth. In this position he was responsible for youth programs but reported to the secretary of welfare, who made the major budgetary and other decisions. In time, as Miller's political power eroded, even this authority was taken from him, and was eventually reduced to virtually a token position, with those in charge of operations reporting to other officials.

Miller's formal authority was further limited by the large-scale use of private juvenile institutions in Pennsylvania. The State Department of Public Welfare was charged with monitoring private agencies, but it had exercised this power sparingly, generally only when a major crisis occured (see *Child Abuse at Taxpayers' Expense*, 1974).

An incident which occurred during a conference on community alternatives illustrates the erosion of Miller's authority. A heated exchange between the commissioner and a juvenile judge ended with Miller angrily stalking out of the room. Although he told his subordinates to leave with him, some stayed on and one left with him only to return shortly afterward (Interview, 1977).

Control over Resources

The power to obtain and allocate tangible resources such as money, materials, equipment, and personnel is a key factor in the administrator's capacity to act in behalf of aggrieved consumers or bring about system change. Conversely, the administrator's freedom of action is continually constrained by the threat of losing this power. White (1974), Levine and White (1961), and Yuchtman and Seashore (1967) all stress the importance of resources in inter- and intra-organizational relationships. Control over tangible resources may undercut formal hierarchical relationships, as Belknap (1956) found in the case of a state mental hospital.

The importance of access to resources in determining power relationships in prison communities has been noted by Clemmer (1958), McCleery (in Cressey, 1961, pp. 149–188), and others. Line staff in correctional facilities must reckon with the power of others over their livelihood, because they lack alternative careers and because they frequently get their jobs through political influence (Clemmer, 1958). Because of powerful informal influence patterns within the staff and inmate subsystems, correctional administrators need to control the allocation of rewards if they hope to influence the system (Cressey, 1959; Duffee, 1974; Polsky, 1967; Thatcher, in Bakal, 1973). Externally, the administrator needs to be assured of a flow of resources into the organization, and frequently reform efforts demand resources beyond those normally available.

Miller was blessed with generous federal support when he sought to reform the juvenile correctional system of Massachusetts. Yet a series of financial crises in 1973 threatened to undo his work (Rutherford, 1974). Miller was imaginative and free-wheeling in his use of available resources to advance his reforms. When he found civil service rules blocking his attempt to get rid of old line personnel, he simply left them there and added his own people to the staff. But in order to accomplish this he had to carry a double burden of personnel costs. The DYS budget more than doubled between 1969 and 1974. Clearly the extra external funds were Miller's ace-in-the-hole.

Miller's Pennsylvania strategy hinged in large part on two devices for gaining and allocating financial resources. One was new money from the federal government; the other was a shift in the state funding formula for institutional versus community programs. A federal grant of $1.9 million supported the first year's development of community alternatives to the incarceration of juveniles. This amount was halved in the second year, sharply curtailing the program (Interview, 1977). The revised funding formula, passed by the General Assembly in the summer of 1976, called for 75–90 percent funding of community programs and 50 percent funding for institutional care, essentially reversing the rates that had prevailed in the past (Combined History, 1974, p. A-113). But, significantly, the administration of funds was out of Miller's control by this time.

Control over Information

For his formal authority and control over tangible resources an administrator is largely dependent on others. The administrator who is alert to their importance may seek to expand both, but in each instance his or her control is limited. In contrast, the flow of information is much more within the control of the administrator. Wager (1972) points out that internally the administrator as a "linking pin" has access to more sources of information than anybody else in the organization and thus more control over what gets communicated to whom. Externally, the key administrative role is that of interpreter (Dubin, 1968; Drucker, 1974, pp. 481–493; Selznick, 1957). Effective communication is thus particularly important to the administrator as advocate, since through it he or she may magnify potential assets and neutralize potential threats.

Jerome Miller understood this principle and made effective use of it when he entered the Massachusetts juvenile correctional picture in 1969. From the outset he set about to seize the initiative. Capitalizing on strong legislative and administrative mandates and wide public support for reform, he launched a one-man campaign through the mass media and numerous public appearances. One of his first acts as DYS director was to issue a so-called "haircut edict." Henceforth inmates in state training schools were free to wear their hair as they wished. Underscoring the directive was the fact that Miller himself wore his hair longer than any other official, soon earning him the nickname of the "hippy commissioner" (Ohlin, Coates, and Miller, 1974).

The haircut edict was characteristic of what was soon to become a Miller trademark: the sudden symbolic act guaranteed to dramatize an issue and get maximum reaction from the target system. To the lay person, hair style among inmates may seem like a trivial issue—and so it is in objective terms. But its symbolic importance to inmates and correctional staff is great. A worker in one training school got this reply to his query as to why an inmate had been punished for wearing his hair in corn-rowed style:

> Hair style is not the issue. . . . An individual's self-pride and image of himself is enhanced only if he can, with consistency, present himself physically and socially as positively as possible. Toward this end, exposed underwear, walking on heels, corn-rowed hair, earrings—as a few examples—hardly identify "individual black pride." On the contrary, they identify hostility and conflict and—since we do have the rule—lack of self-discipline. (*Child Abuse at Taxpayers' Expense*, 1974).

In the ensuing months, Miller never gave away the initiative. Other directives followed, abolishing the standard practice of marching inmates from place to place in silent formation and allowing them to wear street clothes instead of prison garb. The predictable reaction of correctional personnel mounted and then subsided, demonstrating clearly that the new commissioner was formally in charge. In the general community, Miller's bold tactics captured the public imagination. Supporters were heartened and critics kept off balance. The success of the blitz approach is demonstrated by the fact that it was able to carry Miller through a series of legislative investigations and early reversals.

Even failure was turned into success: When initial efforts to turn the human warehouses into therapeutic communities were manifestly unsuccessful, Miller used this fact to show that, rather than being too drastic, the reforms were too timid. The interpretation was accepted by the public. National recognition further enhanced Miller's image as the campaign moved ahead (see Kovach, 1972). Aiding the commissioner throughout was a superb command of language and what seemed at the time to be an uncanny ability to read his audience. Crucial to his management of the communication process was access to strategic information. Miller knew his facts and could summon them up when challenged by reporters, hecklers, and antagonistic legislators.

Pennsylvania in 1975 was not Massachusetts in 1969. Although a large Eastern industrial state, Pennsylvania lacked the tradition of strong liberalism that has dominated Massachusetts politics in recent years. In the correctional field, the vested interests of private institutions and county judges have predominated. The law-and-order regime of Philadelphia's Mayor Frank Rizzo symbolized a powerful undercurrent of antagonism to offenders—especially young offenders—especially young black offenders. Miller entered the Pennsylvania scene with additional burdens—rumors (mostly untrue) of failure of the Massachusetts reform and reports that he had undermined professional standards during his brief tenure as head of child welfare services in Illinois (Santiestevan, 1975). This last criticism was especially damaging, since Miller needed the support of human service professionals to offset the opposition of correctional conservatives in Pennsylvania.

But his rhetoric tended to continue the same bold attack that had worked so well in Massachusetts. "A national scandal," said Jerome Miller of Camp Hill, the adult penitentiary to which Pennsylvania juvenile judges were continuing to send more than fifty youths a month. "This can't be allowed to continue," Miller said in one of his first public statements (Kotzbauer, 1975). There was no attempt to soften the impact of the verbal barrage. Aided by mounting citizen fury over two fatal burnings at private training schools and a suicide at Camp Hill, Miller began to focus public attention on the issue of juvenile institutions. With increasing frequency, headlines began to appear in the newspapers around the state, and Miller's face became a familiar sight on TV news shows. He made good copy, and the news media readily responded. Occasionally he had to issue a clarification or claim that he was misquoted when the enthusiasm of the press went too far. One news item quoted Miller to the effect that the state was planning totally to close down Camp Hill, the state's largest "youth development center" (training school), and the detention center serving Philadelphia, an agenda far beyond anything previously announced. (Lear, 1975). Miller issued a denial, saying he had been misquoted.

Initially, the opposition was relatively muted and fragmented. But, unlike the case of Massachusetts, it was not thrown off balance. Armed with the reports of failure in Massachusetts and disruption in Illinois, Miller's critics became increasingly vocal. The groundswell of organized citizen support which had been so vital to the earlier reform movement failed to gain the required momentum. Miller had his supporters, but many tended to be controversial themselves. The drive for reform eventually stalled, though not until after the assignment of juveniles to Camp Hill had been shut off and the bulk of those youths already in residence had been moved elsewhere. It was neither a total failure, nor a repeat of the dazzling performance in Massachusetts.

At best, public information campaigns have time-limited value. Eventually the novelty of the issue wears off, and the fragile reform coalition begins to fall apart as new causes attract the interest of the reformers. Meanwhile the hard core opposition, with a vital stake in the status quo, remains. This may suggest that reform efforts themselves are often effective only for a limited time. But it is important to add that public media campaigns are not the beginning and end of information control. Major attention to the flow of information, inside and outside the system, is always a major task of the administrator. The would-be advocate needs to be prepared to use data to mobilize support, neutralize opposition, and focus attention on relevant issues.

Conclusion

We have seen how one administrator was able to bring about significant and lasting changes in a sector of social services with a reputation for intractability. The experience of Jerome Miller in Massachusetts and later in Pennsylvania points up the crucial importance of three factors in institutional change: formal authority, control of resources, and control of information. These are assets which are part and parcel of the administrative role, thus supporting the importance of the administrator as an advocate.

The nature of the authority vested in the position of administrator varies with the particular situation. To the degree that it is formally recognized, officially sanctioned, relatively autonomous, and supported by the prevailing political climate, it is a potent weapon for bringing about changes. Like any asset, authority can become eroded, so the administrator needs to be constantly aware of his or her authority position.

While control of tangible resources is one dimension of formal authority, informal exchange relationships will often control the actual allocation of resources, and access to resources and the ability to allocate them selectively can offset limitations on formal authority. Conversely, an administrator's real influence may be undermined if financial and other tangible support shrinks.

Jerome Miller could not unilaterally alter the formal authority of the Pennsylvania juvenile judges to place youth in training schools, nor could he wish into existence more funds to facilitate community placement. But he did have control over his own use of the communication process, and here Miller was not entirely helpful to his cause in Pennsylvania. At the time he entered the state, he could not undo the reputation that had preceded him, but in time he might have altered it. Evaluations of the Massachusetts experience suggest that Miller may not have been entirely aware of the impact of some of his pronouncements on his audience (Ohlin, Coates, and Miller, 1974). His use of information was often intuitive rather than carefully thought out, and he therefore did not adjust his rhetoric to the more conservative environment in Pennsylvania.

But without Miller's audacious tactics, the gains that were made might not have occurred. The lesson to be drawn is not that provocation should necessarily be avoided but rather that one should seek to assess one's audience accurately and anticipate the impact of information upon it. In the last analysis, the art of advocacy, as of any other aspect of administration, is the art of succeeding. If events had aborted the crusade in Massachusetts in its early stages, no one would have heard about Jerome Miller. If conditions had been more conducive to change in Pennsylvania, undoubtedly analysts would be trying to comprehend Miller's genius.

There is one asset which Miller had in abundance, something that enabled him to rise above the generally uninspiring record of social service administrators as advocates. That was the willingness to risk himself in behalf of a cause he believed in. Upon reflection, it is probably the most important factor of all.

Epilogue

At the end of 1977, Jerome Miller left the Pennsylvania Department of Public Welfare and became the head of an action organization on institutionalization and alternatives, in Washington. But it was readily agreed by informed persons that he had long since ceased to be a significant actor in the Pennsylvania system. The role of outsider to the bureaucracy seemed to fit him best, even when he was placed in charge of it. There are lessons to be learned from the experience of Dr. Miller in reforming the youth correctional systems in two states, but it is doubtful that the conditions which fostered his rapid rise to a key decision-making position will often be found in public welfare systems. At best, the charismatic and bold sytle which he brought to juvenile corrections will be a transitory phenomenon in such systems. The awareness of this on the part of career bureaucrats is one of the factors that limits the long-term impact of administrators like Dr. Miller.

References

Ad Hoc Committee on Advocacy. "The Social Worker as Advocate: Champion of Social Victims." *Social Work* 14, no. 2 (1969): 16–22.

Bakal, Y, ed. *Closing Correctional Institutions*. Lexington, Mass.: Lexington, 1973.

Belknap, I. *Human Problems of a State Mental Hospital. New York: McGraw-Hill*, 1956.

"Berkan Appealing Dismissal as County Director, May Go to State Court." *NASW News* 17, no. 5 (1972): 4.

Camp Hill Fact Kit. Concordville, Pa.: Campaign for Alternatives to Training Schools, 1975. Mimeo.

Cheatwood, A. D. "The Staff in Correctional Settings: An Empirical Investigation of Frying Pans and Fires." *Journal of Research in Crime and Delinquency* 2 (1974): 173–179.

Child Abuse at Taxpayers' Expense. Concordville, Pa.: Friends Suburban Project, 1974.

Clemmer, D. *The Prison Community*. New York: Rinehart, 1958.

Combined History of Senate and House Bills, Sessions of 1975 and 1976 of General Assembly, Commonwealth of Pennsylvania. 1976.

Cressey, D. R., ed. *The Prison: Studies in Institutional Organization and Change*. New York: Holt, Rinehart and Winston, 1961.

Drucker, P. F. *Management: Tasks, Responsibilities and Practice*. 2nd ed. New York: Harper and Row, 1974.

Dubin, R. *Human Relations in Administration*. 3rd ed. Englewood Cliffs, N.J.: Prentice-Hall, 1968.

Duffee, D. "The Correctional Officer Subculture and Organizational Change." *Journal of Research in Crime and Delinquency* 2 (1974): 155–172.

Hearings before Subcommittee No. 3 of the Committee on the Judiciary, House of Representatives, Ninety-Second Congress. First Session on Corrections, Part V, Prisons, Prison Reform, and Prisoner's Rights: Massachusetts. Washington: U.S. Government Printing Office, 1972.

Hoshino, G. "Simplification of the Means Test and Its Consequences." *Social Service Review* 41, no. 3 (1967): 237–249.

Interview with Pennsylvania State Department of Public Welfare officials, Jan. 31, 1977.

James, Howard. *Children in Trouble*. New York: Pocketbooks, 1970.

Katz, D., and R. L. Kahn. *The Social Psychology of Organizations*. New York: Wiley, 1966.

Kotzbauer, R. W. "Criticisms of Youth Detention Centers Increases." *The Sunday Bulletin* (Philadelphia), March 2, 1975, p. 36.

Kovach, B. "Massachusetts Reforms to Doom Youth Prisons." *New York Times*, Jan. 31, 1972, p. 1.

Lear, L. "State to Close Youth Study Center, YDC and Camp Hill." *Philadelphia Tribune*, June 28, 1975, p. 1.

Lerman, P. "Evaluation Studies of Institutions for Delinquents: Implications for Research and Social Policy." *Social Work* 13, no. 3 (1968): 55–64.

Letter to Pennsylvania Juvenile Judges from Robert P. Kane, Attorney General, April 15, 1975.

Levine, S., and P. E. White. "Exchange as a Conceptual Framework for the Study of Interorganizational Relationships." *Administrative Science Quarterly* 5 (1961): 583–601.

Ohlin, L. E., R. B. Coates, and A. D. Miller. "Radical Correctional Reform: A Case Study of the Massachusetts Youth Correctional System." *Harvard Educational Review* 44 (1974): 74–111.

Polsky, H. W. *Cottage Six: The Social System of Delinquent Boys in Residential Treatment*. New York: Wiley, 1967.

Richan, W. C., ed. *Human Services and Social Work Responsibility*. New York: National Association of Social Workers, 1969.

Rutherford, A. *The Dissolution of the Training Schools in Massachusetts*. Columbus, Ohio: Academy for Contemporary Problems, 1974.

Santiestevan, H. *Deinstitutionalization: Out of Their Beds and into the Streets*. Washington: American Federation of State, County and Municipal Employees, 1975.

Selznick, P. *Leadership in Administration: A Sociological Interpretation*. New York: Harper and Row, 1957.

Senor, J. M. "Another Look at the Executive-Board Relationship." *Social Work* 8, no. 2 (1963): 19–25.

Standards for Social Services. Washington: National Association of Social Workers, 1975 (unpub. draft).

Wager, L. W. "Organizational 'Linking Pins': Hierarchical Status and Communicative Roles in Interlevel Conferences." *Human Relations* 25, no. 4 (1972): 307–326.

White, P. E. "Resources as Determinants of Organizational Behavior." *Administrative Science Quarterly* 19 (1974): 366–379.

Yuchtman, E., and S. E. Seashore. "A System Resource Approach to Organizational Effectiveness." *American Sociological Review* 32 (1967): 891–903.

THE GOVERNANCE
OF THE
SOCIAL SERVICES

Seymour J. Rosenthal
and James E. Young

5

The last decade has brought about a major shift in the governance of the social services. Whereas, prior to the 1960's, governance was the province of "noblesse oblige" boards in the voluntary sector, an altogether different reality exists today. Professors Rosenthal and Young present a broad overview of these changes, tracing the historical development and the policy context of governance.

The authors, calling upon their extensive experience in the field, first draw the important distinction between governing and advisory boards. In addition to discussing the functions of these boards, they carefully delineate the separate roles and responsibilities of board and staff. They also address the structure and development of the board as areas of executive concern. And finally they suggest a means for determining board accountability.

A major element in the executives' work is with their board of directors. This essay is sensitive not only to the political realities of this relationship but also to the practical demands involved in ensuring effective governance. It places in a practical context many of the theoretical elements identified by Slavin.

Introduction

Few functions are more demanding or vital for the administrator than the organization and maintenance of agency advisory and/or governance boards. Such groups represent the principal mechanism through which agency policy is formulated and the external environment is managed.

Their utilization is increasing, and the composition of such groups is undergoing major alterations, within both public and pri ate social services delivery agencies.

The purpose of this chapter is to examine the effects of recent developments on the mandate, composition, structure, and functions of advisory and governance boards. These developments reflect major shifts in the expectations of citizens in relation to the institutions which serve them. The spirit and tone for these shifts was captured in 1968 by former Secretary of Health, Education and Welfare Wilbur Cohen. He stated:

> Throughout our land today there is a great new spirit of involvement and participation. It is part of this social ferment that is transforming our society and its institutions. More people are becoming aware of their rights and responsibilities as citizens. People from all walks of life want a greater voice in solving their own problems and guiding their own destinies. Young people want to belong, to contribute, to have a hand in decision making processes in their schools and jobs. Poor people want a greater role in the systems and institutions that govern their lives. All public agencies need to reexamine their policies and reshape their structures where necessary to make room for genuine widespread public participation.

This chapter will trace the shift within the United States from the private voluntary social welfare board of privilege to the consumer-oriented "representative" boards toward which most social service delivery agencies are moving. It will distinguish the mandates of the governing or policy board from that of the advisory boards, discuss the structures of differing types of boards, and identify their policy planning functions. Board-staff relationships will be explored through an analysis of management styles and board-staff roles. The effectiveness of the board will be viewed in relation to composition, structure, and training support. Finally, we will speculate as to the future directions such boards may take in the administration of social welfare programs.

Historical Context

The development and expansion and utilization of public and private governing and advisory boards has paralleled increasing industrialization, governmental intervention, and the attendant and complex institutionalization of relationships within society. Since the end of the middle ages boards were used to some extent by most European governments, and the American colonies in the eighteenth century formed councils to the government, but little other use of boards and committees was employed (Fairlee, 1958).

Until recently, however, the substantial preponderance of board activity has not taken place within the public sector, but rather within the private voluntarily social service network. The Voluntary Social Agency Board has been described as follows:

> With the exception of some agencies under sectarian auspices, private agencies in the United States typically have a lay board and control. Such boards have evolved from the early years when a group of wealthy persons would constitute themselves the patrons of a charity. Their major function then (since welfare work was mainly confined to relief giving) was often little more than supplying funds out of their own pockets and those of their friends. With the growth of federated financing direct involvement of social delivery boards in fund raising has declined. But, indirectly, through the influence on the allocation of jointly raised funds their importance in this area remains. It represents the agency in community and intra-agency relationships and most important, from the viewpoint of everyday welfare practice, it has the power to set policy in all phases of agency operation, from rules governing client eligibility to pay scales for professional staff (Wilensky and Lebeaux, 1958).

The shifts within the private voluntary sector from the "noblesse oblige" board to more broadly based representation was stimulated and paralleled by a marked change in the nature of relationships surrounding the planning and delivery of social services which took place during the decade of the 1960's. Beginning during the Kennedy administration and accelerating through the Johnson administration, the balance of activity within social services shifted from the control of resources by the private sector to the allocation of resources by the public sector.

The President's Committee on Juvenile Delinquency was a forerunner of the programs which began to search out viable roles for recipients in policy formation. Clearly the Economic Opportunity Act of 1964 with its "maximum feasible participation" requirement set in motion the policies which broke the monopoly on the governance of social services previously held by the power elite. The "maximum feasible participation" manifesto brushed aside the traditional forms of agency governance and required (with mixed success) the participation of the poor on three levels: (1) as members of the governing board, and thus as partners in the policy formations relative to the delivery of services; (2) as employees of the agency (giving rise to the "paraprofessional" in social services); and (3) as program participants (Office of Economic Opportunity, 1968).

The consequences of this increased governmental involvement on the federal level were, in some measure, to reduce the relative significance of the private social agency, to encourage evaluation of the role of the public social service delivery system, and to require the participation of the poor.

Although differences of opinion and acrimony attended the dynamic process of CAA board composition, and full compliance was rare, the die for more client representation was cast. This concern for participation was extended to and built into the Demonstration Cities Act of 1966, which established "model neighborhoods" in cities and local citizen councils to assist in the formulation of policy and the implementation of programs called for under that legislation. (Demonstration Cities and Metropolitan Development Act, 1966). (Moynihan 1969)

Relationships were profoundly affected by the consequences of citizen participation, especially the relationship between the service provider and the recipient. Previously the provider of services delivered those services without substantial client involvement and was largely immune from any critical assessment by either the community at large or, more significantly, the recipient of the service. The legislation and regulations since the mid-sixties have specifically attempted to structure a situation in which the ongoing feedback, of clients and public advocacy groups, both critical and otherwise, significantly shapes program policies and priorities.

Relationships between public and private agencies have also been altered. Private social welfare's portion of the total resources available for dealing with human needs decreased in relation to that of the public sector. However, many private agencies began to function according to a new set of publicly mandated rules. Federal intervention also provided many new devices through which financial and program participation could take place, so that a great wave of new and modified governing and advisory boards, as well as public commissions, sprang into being within the private social welfare enterprise. This has required a clearer definition of roles and responsibilities of board members and staff within those agencies. Where in the past the social agency relied primarily on a single mechanism, that of the governing board, the new public intervention into the social services system spurred the growth of advisory boards and encouraged open public hearings, sunshine laws, and public commissions.

The science and art of administration requires increasing attention to the interplay between the agency and its external environment in order to accomplish its funding and policy planning objectives. The two principal mechanisms utilized to facilitate this interplay are the governing board and the advisory board.

Governing and Advisory Boards—Mandate

The central distinction between a governing board and an advisory board relates to their authority. A *governing board* is legally charged with the direct control and operation of a single institutional unit. By definition, a governing board holds final administrative authority even though the authority to manage the operation of the agency may be delegated to an executive (Trecker, 1950).

The authority of a governing board rests in three key areas: The first area, the development of policy, is concerned both with the current operations of the board (which includes all aspects of program implementation, program client eligibility criteria, staffing, etc.) and, more importantly, with that aspect of planning which concerns itself with policy formulation which determines the future goals and objectives of the organization. The second aspect involves control over the fiscal management for the agency. Not only is the governing board legally accountable for the financial management of the organization, but it is also responsible for budgetary planning and fund-raising efforts. Finally, governing boards are responsible for the development of personnel policy, including procedures for the hiring of all agency employees and for their performance evaluations. A social agency board which does not have authority over each of these aspects of agency policy formulation and operation is not an autonomous agency capable of implementing its own decisions.

The *advisory board* system provides many advantages for today's complex community agency. The advisory board may report to the agency executive, a governing board, or a funding agency. Ideally, it brings into organized working relationships those persons and interest groups who can contribute to the development of agency program. As contrasted to the governing board, the advisory board has only the power to influence. Its ultimate authority rests either with the wisdom which it brings to the operating agency, or in its capacity to influence the political systems in which the services are being provided. Advisory groups make possible *ad hoc* efforts, such as the recruitment of professional expertise for special assignment, and facilitate the involvement of persons who would not be available for a continuing obligation as a member of a governing board. More importantly, it provides an arena for client participation in those public agencies where formal control of services cannot be lodged in non-governmental organizations.

Networks of advising or governing boards are found in both the public and private sectors. In the private sector, governing boards of traditional private agencies have the authority over their services. In this situation, the private agency determines the nature of services that it will provide according to its own resources, priorities and philosophy. It seeks to develop its own policy, provides its own financial support, and hires its own staff to conduct the programs. Most often members of the boards of such private agencies are selected on the basis of the specific financial or programmatic contribution that each member can make to the services targeted by the organization.

Another form of governance is related to the services of a publicly funded private agency, in which certain advisory participation of consumers is mandated. For example, much of the current day care programming is funded through a private agency, but these programs require an advisory group of parents to make suggestions relative to policy and scope of programming. Similar advisory functions are carried out in senior centers, nutrition sites, and other programs provided for older adults. A substantial number of these private agencies have been formed to implement federal human service policy.

The third locus of operation for such boards are those public agencies mandated by federal legislation to ensure varied citizen participation within the public agency itself, usually in the form of advisory councils or boards. Public involvement is increasingly common in virtually all human services: aging, mental health–mental retardation, children and youth, education, and community action and development. In these situations, the functions of advisory boards would appear to be clearly delineated. The public agency remains the agency of operation and authority, maintaining to itself the final determination of whether it will in fact accept the advice of its advisory bodies. In practice, however, it is often difficult to deny the advice of the various bodies attached to service delivery programs, and at the same time maintain credibility in the political arena.

It is not axiomatic that governing boards have greater impact on agency policy and operations than advisory boards. In some measure, the potency of a board stems less from its legal status than from its style of operation.

Board Functions

Perhaps the best way to view the board is as a policy planning and budgeting mechanism for the agency which on regular occasions performs facilitative, developmental, or implementation tasks. The Perenthal Model of Planning, developed by Professors William E. Perry and Seymour J. Rosenthal, specifies steps in the policy planning continuum. Although few governing or advisory boards take "time off" from day-to-day business to engage in long-range planning, it remains a vital board function. The planning model appears in Figure 5-1.

The function of the board is to assess the nature of problems on an ongoing basis, and to set goals for resolving these problems. The board should then develop program strategies consistent with the goals of the agency, and assign priorities. When the board considers constraints, it will be led to those goals which can be achieved in a given political and economic environment. High-priority goals which cannot presently be addressed represent "next steps" in the board's project development activities. Clearly an agency board (whether advisory or governing) must

Figure 5-1. The Perenthal Model of Planning*

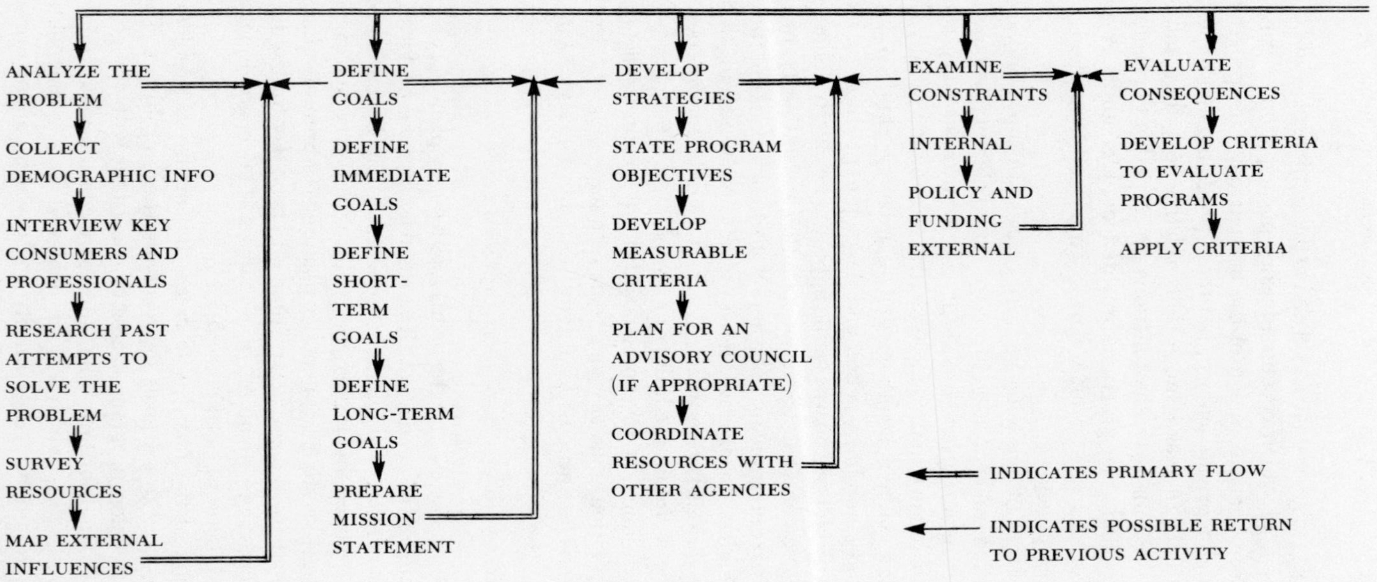

*In the Perenthal Model, Professors Perry and Rosenthal have drawn up other models as well as their own experience in attempting to provide their students with a workable guide for analyzing and applying a planning process. SOURCE: William E. Perry and Seymour J. Rosenthal with Alex Urhanski, *Social Planning Workbook: A Guide to the Planning Process* (Philadelphia: Temple University Center for Social Policy and Community Development, School of Social Administration, 1975).

develop the competence and capacity to evaluate its own effectiveness and staff input is essential. Without this feedback the board can remain dangerously ignorant of agency performance and its value to its client.

The evolution of public social policy during the past fifteen years has given increased visibility and impetus to the policy planning functions of boards. Beginning with the Model Cities program, federal requirements have continually addressed the process through which goals and priorities are established. This concern has resulted in technical processes which now form an integral part of the development of local and state plans in many of the human services. Further, the availability of public monies for an increasing range of social services requires today's boards to set priorities more carefully.

Key among the activities of the board, one which cuts across all the deliberations stated above, is the necessity to manage the external environment of the agency. Boards must be a major force in dealing with the issues of constraints, organization and mobilization of resources, and preparation of the environment so as to promote the goals of the organization. In this way, the board creates the conditions which permit staff the authority, the latitude, and the resources to implement the policies and programs as defined by the board.

The management of the external environment has grown more complex for human services agencies as the interaction with and dependence upon governmental resources has increased. This complexity extends to executive, legislative, and judicial spheres of external authority. The creative executive fully utilizes his or her board to further the ends of the agency in relation to such authority. Relationships with funding sources, legislative bodies at local, state, and federal levels, and judicial bodies which are in the process of determining issues which have an impact on agency practice require an agency strategy involving both executive and board in a cooperative effort to influence policy so that it is consistent with agency mission.

In addition to its policy-planning function, the board is also responsible for the maintenance of the organization. Such *organizational maintenance* can be defined as the development of resources, the identification and building of constituencies, accountability to the consumer system (which includes information-sharing), and maintenance of fiscal integrity.

The development of resources often grows out of the policy-planning functions of the boards, but can also be applied to general fund-raising efforts, interagency strategies, and the linking of financial and human resources to the agency.

Constituency-building is vital to organizational maintenance. Without an informed and supportive constituency, the success of the work of the board and its executive staff is in question. Of prime importance in the building of constituency is the capacity of the board to identify a constituent series of interest groups rather than a single constituency. Closely related is the responsibility of the board to broaden its base of representation and to provide for the orderly infusion of new leadership into the organization.

The board must also establish mechanisms which ensure accountability to its consumer population. These mechanisms enable the board to inform its various constituents about its problems, goals, activities, and future plans. The board's consumer constituency is of prime concern and requires an advocacy stance on the part of the board: the priorities of the consumer should be a primary concern of the board. Another aspect of organizational maintenance is the matter of fiscal accountability. Ultimately, the board cannot delegate its fiscal management responsibilities. The board therefore must have both a clear understanding of its fiscal role in receiving the financial support necessary to fulfill its programatic and financial commitments.

Board-Staff Relationships

Board-staff relationships are shaped not only by the apparent differences of roles and responsibilities but also by their relative power and differences in their orientation and values. Ralph Kramer has addressed this issue in terms of ideology, status, and power in board-executive relationships. He points out that, in spite of the fundamental employment relationship (in the case of governing boards), the professional literature suggests a more or less equal partnership through which balance is maintained through "exchange" relationships. In the exchange, the executive requires the sanction and support of the board. The board members gain prestige and a validation of their position of community leaders from this relationship to the executive (Kramer, 1969).

Kramer's work provides evidence that some board members tend to be more conservative and less committed to client self-determination than agency executives. However, it does not follow that these board values dominate agency practice. Because of the full-time presence of the agency executive, the "exchange" relationship, the selective raising of issues by executives, and the preoccupation of most agency boards with day-to-day business, agency mission and practice tends to represent a blend of executive-board priorities. An enormous range of board influence and styles are possible in its interaction with the executive and staff.

One way of viewing the style of boards in relation to staff is to consider its overall discharge of responsibility as being (1) controlling, (2) facilitating, or (3) laissez-faire. Control represents those actions of the board which seek to manage the direction and the resources of the organization. Facilitating is a function of the board which seeks to link and maximize the application of resources to areas given priority by the board. Laissez-faire applies to the tendency of the board to serve as a rubber stamp for staff initiatives or to expeditiously achieve compliance with federal regulations. Although each board represents a mixture of these styles, it is critical that boards identify their mandate and function if they are to gain sanction and authority.

There are a variety of ways of defining the board/staff roles and relationships. The initial distinction most often found in the literature suggests that the board is responsible for establishing policy and the executive and staff for implementing that policy. Having said that, however, a great area of ambiguity still remains in terms of how policies are established and the extent to which implementation is the sole prerogative of the executive and staff. It has been suggested that policy formulation and planning are joint responsibilities of the board and professional staff, policy determination is the responsibility of the board alone, and policy execution is the responsibility of the executive and staff (Sorenson, 1950). Perhaps the board/staff relationship can best be defined through looking at the alternative levels of control which the board exerts in the establishment and implementation of policy. At one end of the continuum the board maintains tight control of all facets of policy and program planning and implementation. In this unhealthy situation the board is essentially functioning as the executive in refusing to delegate proper responsibility to the staff. The board can also define all aspects of policy and program planning and implementation as its purview, but then proceed to carve out understandings with staff on an *ad hoc* basis as to how responsibility will be shared for the implementation of program activities. Still a third alternative is that in which board and staff struggle together to define clearly what specific roles and responsibilities each will assume and essentially to divide up the organizational turf so as to ensure the board's preeminent role in the establishment of policy and to protect the discretion of staff in operations. An illustration of the work product of one such struggle in which the authors participated appears in Figure 5-2 (Rosenthal and Young, 1976).

At the other end of the continuum is the situation in which the board serves merely as a rubber stamp for the staff or constitutes a legal fiction which exerts no control and assumes no responsibility for either setting or implementing policy. This too-common situation derives most often from one of three causes: (1) the formation of a board solely for purposes of compliance with federal regulations, where neither the board nor the executive is committed to the concept of a "working board"; (2) a general incompetence on the part of the board to fulfill its role; or (3) the clever maneuvering of the executive, who would prefer a board to serve as a rubber stamp, rather than provide substantive leadership.

Figure 5-2. Roles and Responsibilities

BOARD		STAFF
1. Overall: Sets policy and determines programs		1. Implements policy and programs
2. Hires executive staff and screens all community contact staff		2. Hires program staff
3. Approves and has input into budget		3. Develops budget
4. Monitors and evaluates goals and programs		4. Provides information on program progress to administrative staff and board
5. Sets program priorities		5. Develops proposals
6. Provides approval and advice regarding programs		6. Utilize professional knowledge in making judgments
7. Maintains linkages into community	BOARD DELEGATES RESPONSIBILITIES TO STAFF	7. Maintains linkages into community
8. Provides fiscal management Develops dollar resources Initiates planning process which includes development of alternative funding sources		8. Inform and assist administrative board and staff in availability of dollar resources
9. Educates staff		9. Educates board
10. Evaluates executive director		10. Evaluates staff

Board Composition

The initial section of this chapter indicated that historically the voluntary social agency board membership was essentially drawn from the leisure class and the private sector. Little thought was given to the board member as a representative of a constituency. Indeed over 80 percent of the organizations in a study conducted in 1958 (Trecker, 1958) had no written statements of qualifications sought in board members. The best that could be found was a general statement of qualifications. It was rare for any organization to spell out precise, written qualifications as to exactly what kind of persons were wanted to perform important tasks. Of key impitance to the definition of a properly constituted board is the notion of "representativeness." Whereas a position on such boards was once based on one's position in the economic structure, boards are increasingly being shaped to represent the agency's constituency, that is, to ensure that each board member represents individuals (such as clients) or institutions with whom the agency must relate. The representativeness of boards is the essential issue to most private agencies today. For the public or private agency carrying out governmental functions as a contractor or subcontractor, board composition is very often mandated through written guidelines that have been developed to ensure representativeness in connection with these public programs.

Representativeness is not a clear concept, and most boards today embrace at least two distinct concepts within their representational scheme. Alexander and McCann point out that the adjective "representative" and the noun "representativeness" carry different meanings. They suggest that the first of these is a socio-political idea and refers to the *authorized functioning or acting by one person in behalf of another or others*. The second comes from a statistical reference and has to do with the *quality of being typical or typifying a class*" (Trecker, 1950).

However defined, representativeness has become an accepted goal for most social agencies, boards, and executives. The authors have observed four dominant rationales today for the selection of board members, which happily converge with most federally mandated requirements. They include: (1) the degree to which the person being selected is representative of the group being served and therefore can provide significant insights into the consequences of board policies upon that group; (2) the degree to which the person being selected is representative of primary external agencies to which the board must relate on an ongoing basis; (3) the degree to which the person being selected possesses the specific skills necessary to advance the agency's development, for example, expertise relating to both organizational maintenance (accounting, legal, etc.) or policy-planning functions (program expertise, medical, social planning, etc.); and (4) the degree to which the person being selected is politically important or has access to additional resources which the agency may wish to tap. These interest groups represent a blend of potential board members and place the organization in a position to both manage and be responsive to its service network environment.

The principal consideration in shaping board composition among these interest groups flows from the nature of its purpose, mandate, and functions. If the agency is a public service agency or commission far removed from direct client service, it may wish to select a high proportion of representative professionals who can provide advice on the merits of a certain kind of a programming system. If the agency is directly involved in a consumer relationship, the agency will desire to see its board more representative of the community itself, so that it can maximize community acceptance of its policies and programs.

Administrators need to be sensitive to the consequences of "overweighting" the agency board toward a given constituency. An overweighting of consumers on the board may create hostility both within the board itself and in the community, should the consumers be seen as less than representative by the community itself. Further, most clients of public services do not possess the technical expertise or the access to resources which is vital for the maintenance of the organization. On the other hand, an overweighting of professional interest on the board may assure a perpetuation of professional interest which may not be in the interest of consumers. It is logical and fitting that the shifting patterns of board composition should reflect changes in policy and programmatic mandates. The board must remain constantly sensitive to these changes and guard against the dictatorship of one group of representatives over another. Balanced representativeness is vital for the long-term survival of the agency. It is a joint responsibility of both the board and its chief executive to ensure that representativeness be maintained.

Training

Board members are made, not born. One's position in life, whether rich or poor, does not necessarily provide the competence and capacity to serve on a social service agency board of directors. Too often agencies are satisfied just to recruit willing board members; more often than not willingness is not an institutional criteria for good board membership. To meet this problem boards and agency executives are increasingly turning to formal training to develop a more appropriate and responsive board.

Initial orientation of new board members is now a common practice in many human services agencies. It is most effectively conducted with a balance of old and new board members. Interestingly, the orientation process of similar agencies (e.g., Community Mental Health Centers within a state or city) is being coordinated through training institutions so that the common purpose agencies can effect training more efficiently.

Although the orientation process is fundamental it is but the bare beginning of educating effective board members. With regularity, agency boards need to develop training efforts which sharpen board awarenesses and skills and make them more aware of the ultimate purposes and goals of their activity. Training need not be removed from decision making; ideally, the relationship is symbiotic. The entire policy-planning function of the board requires the initiation of processes linking training with problem-solving. Also, new funding possibilities often emerge in an agency which require additional board understanding and creativity.

Training is not to be underplayed since (1) it is through this vehicle that increased knowledge is provided about the roles and the responsibilities that exist between agency staff, and (2) the training process provides a period of time wherein board members can develop strategies together which are not necessarily related to the agency's ongoing operational decision-making. Thus, training provides both the content and the process to ensure a more effective and collegial board.

Board Structure

The structure of the board, like its composition, must be responsive to the mission, priorities, and programs of the agency. Most boards of directors will require standing committees that are responsible for organizational maintenance activities, such as program planning and evaluation, personnel (including staff recruitment, hiring, and performance evaluations), and fiscal management and control. A board will often delegate certain policy and program planning and development functions to either standing or *ad hoc* committees, particularly where no executive committee exists. Such committees are considered standing committees in that they have a permanent position in the board structure and its delegation system. In addition, many boards empanel *ad hoc* committees from time to time to carry out intermittent agency responsibilities.

Mitton (1975) describes a "Matrix Organization" through which board structure ensures committee participation of each board member in at least two roles, corresponding to board policy-planning and implementation functions. This matrix created functional committees corresponding to agency services, and ensured that each such "functional" committee included representations from the finance, service appraisal, personnel, management audit, and policy review committees. Metropolitan Development Act, 1966).

Where boards are particularly large and unwieldy, a small working executive committee is employed to facilitate speedier decision-making. This represents an acceptable and desirable approach to good management. Most often such committees include representation which bears a close relationship to that of the board as a whole, and are empowered to make such decisions as the board itself is entitled to make, subject to the subsequent ratification of the board. Caution is required to ensure that a small group does not make all decisions for the organization, thereby usurping the role of overall board membership.

The authors have observed that the tendency for executives to dominate decision-making is more pronounced among the less experienced consumer-oriented boards. However, the issue here is in developing "creative tension" between the board and its executives. On the one hand, the board does not want to alienate its members by making decisions out of context of the larger group. On the other hand, it becomes impossible on occasion to move the agency forward if every aspect of decision-making requires the participation of the full board. As with many administration mandates, balance is all. This points again to the need for an appropriate structure within the board to assure that committees (both standing and *ad hoc*) are sufficiently responsible to the total board to ensure sanctioned decision-making in the appropriate place.

In the final analysis, the ultimate test for determining the appropriateness of the board structure is whether (1) the constitution of the board permits it to carry out its business from both management and programmatic points of view and (2) the committee structure is responsive to the policy and organizational maintenance priorities of the organization.

Summary

Most executives of social welfare agencies are aware of the need to take initiative in improving board performance. Most board members are similarly aware of the need for self-evaluation and improvement. The authors would like to suggest a brief checklist against which board accountability can be measured. Minimally, it requires a clear understanding of and strategy in relation to agency mandates, mechanisms for the delivery of mandated services, capacity of the agency at both board and staff levels, and a climate conducive to mission accomplishment.

Although the legal accountability of the governing board separates it from the advisory board, each has the responsiblity to purposefully plan for, negotiate, and influence the affairs of the organization. Minimally, either type of board must be so structured as to set goals, assure that those goals are addressed through appropriate implementation strategies of the agency, and assure that they are met through the evaluation of desired outcomes. In determining the sufficiency of an agency board in relation to this mandate, it can be considered accountable if:

1. *It is acting responsibly*
   Has it developed a clear statement of mission?
   Has it structured itself consistent with that mission?
   Has it provided ongoing knowledge and skills to board members which keep it up to date?
2. *Agency staff is competent*
   Has it clearly established minimum qualification required of staff?
   Has it overseen the development of clear and accurate job descriptions for agency staff?
   Is the supervisory structure sound and rational?

Has it provided for staff development and in-service training to keep staff up to date?

3. *Agency services are appropriate, efficient, and effective*
Has it developed a logical link between mission, goals, and program/services strategy?
Has it developed procedures to guarantee ongoing monitoring/evaluation of service utilization, quality, and impact?

4. *Community, neighborhood, and clients are properly educated in the use of agency services*
Has it ensured not only the appropriateness of its services, but also their availability and accessibility?
Has it developed appropriate methods for information-sharing as to how to utilize agency services?

5. *It is organized so as to anticipate and react to the future*
Do overall planning processes provide for long-range as well as short-range goals/strategies?

If either an advisory or a governing board meets the above tests of accountability, it has recognized several competing spheres within which accountability is relevant. These spheres are political (how much for what results), bureaucratic (meeting of guidelines within fiscal constraints), professional (increasing response-capability/allocations while extending services), and neighborhood/consumers (those who need help or those whom the community wants helped).

References

Advisory Committee on Citizen Participation and the National Social Welfare Assembly. "Citizen Boards in State Welfare Departments." Committee Bulletin 154. New York: The Committee, Dec. 1950.

Alexander, Chauncy A., and Charles McCann. "The Concept of Representativeness in Community Organizations." *Social Work* 1 (Jan. 1956): 34-48.

Cohen, Wilbur J. *The Secretary's Letter*. Vol. 2, no. 3. July Washington, D.C.: 1968.

Community Chests and Councils of America. "Boards and Board Members of Health and Welfare Agencies." Bulletin 179. New York, 1955.

Demonstration Cities and Metropolitan Development Act of 1966. (Public Law 89-754). S. 103(a)(2).

Engel, Robert L. "A Study of the Representativeness of the Governing Boards of Seventeen Voluntary Health Associations in the Detroit Metropolitan Area." Master's thesis, Wayne State University, Detroit, 1954.

Fairlee, John A. In Seligman and Johnson, eds., *Encyclopedia of Social Sciences*. Vol. 2. New York: MacMillan, 1958.

"Fifty Million Volunteers: A Report on the Role of Voluntary Organizations and Youth in the Environment." Prepared in connection with Human Environment. London: HMSO, Feb. 1972.

Kramer, Ralph M. "Ideology, Status and Power in Board-Executive Relationships." In Ralph M. Kramer and Harry Specht, eds., *Readings in Community Organization Practice*. Englewood Cliffs, N.J.: Prentice-Hall, 1969.

Mitton, Daryl G. "Utilizing the Board of Trustees: A Unique Structural Design." *Child Welfare* 53, no. 6 (June 1975): 345–359.

Moynihan, Daniel P. *Maximum Feasible Misunderstanding*. New York: Free Press, 1969.

Office of Economic Opportunity. "Organizing Communities for Action." Washington, D.C.: GPO, Feb. 1968.

Perry, William E., and Seymour J. Rosenthal (with Alex Urbanski). *Social Planning Workbook: A Guide to the Planning Process*. Philadelphia: Temple University, Center for Social Policy and Community Development, School of Social Administration, 1975.

Piven, Francis F. In Hans C. Spiegel, ed., *Citizen Participation in Urban Development*.

Rosenthal, Seymour J., and James E. Young. "Financial Training Program for a Governing CMHC Board." Unpublished, May 1976.

Sorenson, Roy. *The Art of Board Membership*, forword by Harper Sibley. New York, N.Y.: Association Press, 1950.

Trecker, Harleigh B. *Citizen Boards at Work*. New York: Association Press, 1970. Quoting Advisory Committee on Citizen Participation, Community Chests and Councils of America, Inc., and the National Social Welfare Assembly, "Citizen Boards in State Welfare Department," Bulletin 154 (New York: The Committee, Dec. 1950).

————. *Social Agency Boards: An Exploratory Study*. Connecticut School of Social Work, University of Connecticut, 1958.

Vinter, Robert D., Jr., and William F. Bussiere. *"The Characteristics of Social Agency Board Members."* Springfield, Mass.: Springfield College, 1954.

Wilensky, Harold L., and Charles N. Lebeaux. *Industrial Society and Social Welfare*. New York: Free Press, 1965.

PART III.
TECHNICAL
ASPECTS OF
SOCIAL
ADMINISTRATION

VALUES AND TECHNOLOGY: FOUNDATIONS FOR PRACTICE

Scott Muir Wilson

6

The amount of information required by administrators appears to be increasing exponentially. In addition to the quantitative problem, the administrator must make qualitative decisions about the type of knowledge essential for effective administration. Professor Wilson calls attention to the argument about values versus technology as foundations for administrative practice in the social services. After presenting the relevant issues, Wilson identifies a broad array of functional knowledge and skills which combine both the ideological and technical components inherent in the administrator's function.

Professor Wilson suggests a variety of means administrators can use to acquire the necessary competence in their agency. He then presents his concept of graduate education in social administration and concludes that the employment of social work graduates is the most cost-efficient alternative for assuring the performance of administrative technology while simultaneously retaining a sensitivity to social work values and administrative advocacy. This concern links directly to the theoretical content presented by Professor Slavin.

A revolution of unknown proportions is dawning and is altering society as we know it. In the last great transformation scientific and technical knowledge were applied to improve industrial processes, and the resultant far-reaching changes in social relations were largely unplanned. In the current revolution the objects of science and technology are precisely social processes, institutions, and people.

The systems sciences, the management sciences, and the information explosion open new vistas for social management and control. Some see in

these possibilities the acme of rationality and efficiency, a kind of technological utopia that blots out the last vestiges of man's irrationality and
capriciousness. Other see in them a monstrous system of "total administration" that cancels out man, not through terror and brutal authoritarianism,
but through gradual subjugation in the reasonable name of efficient problem-solving (Gruber, 1974, p. 625).

The societal dilemma posed by Gruber is replicated in microcosm in the
field of social welfare. The administration of social welfare services balances
precariously between values supporting social change and betterment,
client orientation and quality of care, on the one hand, and the growing
acquiescence to pressures to mount a technocratic armamentarium in
social welfare organizations whose effects on those values are not yet clear.

In one sense social service administration does not qualify as a microcosm of the larger society, and this limitation serves to enlarge the potential
impact of the dilemma Gruber describes: the social welfare field is in the
early stages of its experience with systems and managerial technologies.
Shapira is only slightly outdated now in saying that "the single most
conspicuous feature of the systems producing welfare services is their lag
behind other production systems in the use of modern technology of
management and production skills" (Shapira, 1971, p. 59). In attempting to
close this gap quickly the social service field runs the danger of adopting
any technical, managerial innovation uncritically; technical means can
become viewed as ends in themselves.

This chapter is concerned with the impact of technical "accountability
demands" on the social services administrator; it suggests alternative
means to balance conflicting value and accountability demands.

Accountability Pressures on Social Administrators

Administrators face increasing pressures in terms of their own and their
organizations' functioning because of the revolution of rising technical
expectations to which Gruber sees social institutions being more and more
exposed. But before we move to a focus on executive action, it is necessary
to describe the pressures themselves. Three levels of consideration are
central to this task: the societal, political-economic level; the level of
organizational definition and understanding; and the level of conceptuali-
zations of administration in the social services field itself.

SOCIETAL PRESSURES

The administrator of a non-profit social service organization has long known
that the "bottom line" social requisite for social services organizations is the
production of quality services which show results. In the past administra-

tors could respond accountably to a funding source with data on service activity (number of service units provided, number of clients seen, and so forth), while only indirectly hinting at successful service outcomes for clients. Current indicators, as in the 1975 Mental Health Act Amendments or the management-by-objectives thrust in regulations of Title XX of the Social Security Act, are that not only will goals have to be increasingly stated for service outcomes, but evidence of goal attainment will be required to document a fuller sense of accountability. While this type of requirement is consonant in spirit with social service values, the act of documenting "success" in social service provision necessitates staff resources and expertise beyond the current capacity of most agencies.

In addition to outcomes data, social service organizations are being asked to produce more and better data on service activities, on citizen involvement, and on community impact, and to document that all of the above are being done at high levels of efficiency. At the same time, as any administrator knows and as a Brookings Institution study as early as 1972 documented (Schultze et al., 1972), economic resources to support these expanded activities are declining in real dollar terms.

One line of argument in the face of this broadening gap between demands and resources is that social services must utilize the technical and managerial techniques developed to enhance control and efficiency in the profit-making sector. Some of these technical means for monitoring and accountability maintenance appear to have clear transportability to the social welfare sphere (for instance, computerized accounting and information systems), but the economic cost is such that a real choice between computer dollars and service dollars may have to be made by the administrator.

Other aspects of "technological transfer" have somewhat more dubious potential for social service organizations. The experience in the social welfare sector with the Pentagon-spawned Program Planning and Budgeting System (PPBS) showed it to be less than the panacea it may have orginally seemed (for examples, see Patti, 1975; Wildavsky, 1969). Management information systems are a central aspect of the monitoring and accountability demands being placed on the non-profit sector. Whether computerized or not, these systems offer the administrator and other agency staff the potential means for organizing and collecting large amounts of program-relevant information. However, the implementation of these systems is not without some peril (Massy, 1976; Fein, 1975; Hoshino and McDonald, 1975). Narrowly conceived systems are often utilized solely for "reporting out" purposes, with little or no use built into them for agency staff. Costs in staff time and other resources must often be subtracted from the "bottom line" of service provision.

The foregoing "tools" are increasingly common attributes of pressures exerted by funding and monitoring sources and a more demanding public for documentation of more efficient expenditures in the social welfare field. Accounting data such as cost units, time accounts, and cost-benefit ratios are other elements of societal demands with which the social services administrator must contend. The question is not whether the executive should contend with these increasingly technical demands, but how best to contend with them while maintaining a balance with service values and priorities.

ORGANIZATIONAL DEFINITION AND UNDERSTANDING

Modern organizational theory promotes an understanding of organizations, social welfare agencies among them, which if anything exacerbates the difficulties of the administrator's task. The reassuringly prescriptive nature of earlier "process" (classical and bureaucratic) or behavioral (human relations) schools of organization theory, in which the executive had only to plug in the appropriate structures or procedures or rewards, has given way to essentially non-prescriptive systems and contingency approaches.

Systems thinking requires that the administrator consider and analyze all system actors, processes, and boundaries before taking action. The contingency approach suggests, as Mullis puts it in simplified form, that "the correct organizational structure and management plan is dependent on the situation" (Mullis, 1975, p. 31). The interdependence among variables is maintained as in the systems approach, and additional stress is placed on the situational requirements of a given point in time. Thus the administrator is faced, at least in the thinking of current organizational analysts, with the need to constantly re-evaluate a bewildering array of organizational variables for their relevance in changing situations. The comfort of tradition, or even the maintenance of procedures that worked in the past, may be found to be the elements that are inhibiting current operating efficiencies and threatening the ability to maintain convincing accountability to external or internal publics.

Operations research tools such as linear programming, systems modeling, and mathematical models developed in response to the needs of more complex organizational settings, have produced quality products in resource-rich and basically controllable settings, but these are conditions which are not characteristic of most social service settings.

A more conceptual approach to understanding and then acting in the midst of administrative complexity is taken by Lindblom (1970) in distinguishing "root" from "branch" approaches to administrative decision-making and action. He rejects the root or rational model approach as too far removed from the "muddling through" reality of most administrators' lives.

He attempts to develop a theory of "branching" behavior by which the administrator is seen as moving incrementally with pragmatically limited knowledge to make a decision or take an action. The administrator's organization is, then, almost totally involved with a focus on marginal movement concerns. While this view may be descriptive of much of the reality of administrative and organizational life, as a prescription it places severe limits on the active role of values as guides to action. No balance is afforded the social welfare administrator between value-based demands and even incremental demands for technical accountability.

Demands for accountability within social service organizations, from clients, from staff, and from boards arise in addition to external demands, with unionization being only one among many factors impacting on how the administrator's role is conceived and carried out.

CONCEPTIONS OF ADMINISTRATION IN THE SOCIAL WELFARE FIELD

Perspectives on social administration itself have broadened in concert with greater system awareness and systemic demands on the social administrator. Hanlan (1970) distinguishes three types of administration of the social services which play out the characteristics of the role in the context of increasing pressures.

The first type he labels Social Work Administration. The knowledge base flows from social casework and groupwork and the assumption of a client pathology model is common. The goal is enhancement of client social functioning. Interventions of the social work administrator follow social work practice methods and stress the human relations approach to organizational management. The "closed system" nature of this view of social services provision should be apparent.

Hanlan's second type is called Social Welfare Administration. While assumption of a client pathology model may be operating here, Hanlan sees the interplay between social work and social science knowledge as the key attribute of this type. The goal of enhancement of social functioning is more broadly cast within social and psychological theory moving beyond direct practice applicability to include social welfare and administrative theory. Administrative interventions are more related to social science management tasks than is true for the social work administrator. While this type is more open to external influences it still maintains the client–social worker–agency connection in the foreground, and relegates other external influences to the background.

The last type Hanlan describes is Social Administration. This type reflects the thinking of several British authors (Titmuss, 1968. pp. 13–24; Donnison, 1962; Rodgers et al., 1968; Slack, 1966). Hanlan's social administration "moves further away from American social work's emphasis on residual functions and the concomitant stress on a model of individual achievement-failure. Social administration moves toward the opinion that knowledge and skills of the profession are interrelated not only with the social sciences but also with the values, priorities, and resources of the larger social institutions" (Hanlan, 1970, p. 47). Social work is viewed as a sybsystem of social welfare, which, in turn, is a sybsystem of the larger social, political, and economic institutions of society. The systems approach taken by social administration views individuals—and social work—as at least heavily influenced if not largely determined by the larger societal context. The goals of social administration flow from this view: the enhancement of social functioning through the creation of new societal resources for distribution. A fully "institutional" function, in Wilensky and Lebeaux's terms (1965, pp. 138–140), is intended.

Awareness of the somewhat "captive" position of social service organizations within broader social contexts produces an administrator who is not the expected bureaucratic monitor, but his opposite—in Hanlan's words an "administrative activist." In accepting the goal of creating new societal resources in its broadest sense, the social welfare organization becomes almost purely a means. The social administrator is guided primarily not by his agency's needs, but by client needs. Specifically, Hanlan says, these interventions "might be described as those of a middleman between the upper reaches of policy-making and the firsthand implementation of policy" (Hanlan, 1970, pp. 48–49).

Hanlan's presentation of Social Administration is displayed at length here because, as a basic definition of the field phenomenon of social service administration, this type is the only one with clear potential for bridging the dilemma Gruber stated at the beginning of the chapter. This perspective on social administration is both consonant with social work values and responsive to the realities of the social, political, and economic marketplaces in which the social welfare field functions or malfunctions, including a broad and proactive stance with regard to accountability demands. Two primary and synchronous roles for social administration are proposed: expertise in "working the system" of larger societal institutions to further the creation of new social resources (including the technical capacity to define and maintain accountability); and an advocacy stance determined by consumer or client needs. The system manipulator-advocate role for social administration does not, as Hanlan says, "imply a specific political ideology but rather [indicates] direct administrative action, initiative and leadership by social work executives" (Hanlan, 1970, p. 50). This "dual perspective" on the functional expertise of the social administrator again puts more pressure on the role; the expectations are broader in terms of system relatedness, and the multiple role-set is enlarged over that of the more limited and isolated "social work administrator" of the past (see Spencer, 1959, p. 9, for an example of the latter figure).

Accountability Attributes of the Social Administrator

In tying together the diverse pressures on the social administrator evolving out of societal, organizational, and role prescription demands of increasing magnitude it is important to focus on their impact on the operational functions of the practicing social administrator. These forces can be shown to produce an expectation of a broad array of functional knowledge and skills either directly a part of the administrator's own work or under the administrator's supervision.

A combination of two commonly accepted approaches to conceptualizing the administrator's role-set provides a convenient way of framing both personal administrator skills and organizationally defined levels of function. Parsons (1960, pp. 60–69) distinguished three functional levels in organizations at which administrators must perform: the institutional level, which Selznick views as the locus of leadership activities (1957, p. 36), and which show an emphasis on connecting the organization to wider policy, resourcing, community, and inter-organizational issues: the managerial level, which stresses control and creativity within the bounds of the organization; and the technical level, which keys on the technical means for producing organizational and social products. In a second approach Neugeboren (1971, p. 36), among others, identifies the three skill areas central to the administrator's performance as conceptual, technical, and interpersonal. Conceptual (or analytic) and interpersonal skills as concepts should not require further definition; Neugeboren defines technical skills as "fairly specific and distinctive knowledge and skills associated with [a] particular task area" (1971, p. 41). Examples are in the areas of public relations, personnel management, budgeting, and similar task areas.

A combination of these two approaches produces a nine-cell table which assumes that aspects of the three personal skill areas are to be found necessary at each of the three functional levels of focus—institutional, managerial, and technical. While this table could be used to explicate the full array of administrataive functions suggested in the preceeding discussion, its use is limited here to a focus on elements of administrative expertise centered on accountability functions. The complex of skills and tasks given in the body of the table are examples of operational demands that may be placed on any practicing social administrator. It should be observed that technical components and value-rated components are developed in an inter-related fashion, and not as separable elements. Conceptualizing agency goals as abstracted from societal values, for example, is played through the technical means for creating measureable outcome objectives by which the relative attainment of the goals can be documented. A management information system is seen not just as a means for exerting managerial control but, in keying on staff and client-defined data needs, relates to both practice and advocacy concerns.

Implementation of means for accountability to a "public will" and information to relevant publics is an organizational responsibility of the administrator. This includes interacting between a board or other governing body and the staff, and representing the agency in the community and before funding and regulatory bodies.

The administrator carries a leadership role in securing resources; in setting an organizational tone between the conflicting requirements of standardized controls and individualizing flexibility and creativity (or the degree of bureaucratization in any part of the agency); in creating and maintaining work standards; in creating and meeting a budget; in creating personnel policies; in goal formation or "enterprise determination"

Examples of Administrative Expertise: Accountability Activities

LEVELS	PERSONAL SKILL AREAS		
	Conceptual	Technical	Interpersonal
Institutional Level	Relate agency's goals to broader social goals, indicators.	Awareness of legislative, judicial, executive policy.	Build political support for agency goals.
	Identify external conditions which will mandate agency accountability.	Financial and social trend analysis abilities.	Build board roles in promoting accountability.
	Identify informational needs of various publics.	Ability to analyze accountability trends.	Personify agency goals, in terms of personal practice.
	Conceive of advocacy system, viewed partly as an accountability mechanism.	Identify, structure accountability supports in environment.	Motivate staff, client and community involvement in advocacy system.
	Create bridges between agency practice standards and broader standards of service.	Structure, build advocacy system. Relate standards to practice realities.	Promote staff openness to externally evolving standards.

	Conceptual	Technical	Interpersonal
Managerial Level	Guide agency's social problem definition consistent with its goals and practice capacities. Rationalize the administrative decision making process. Convert agency goals into MBO system which is meaningful to agency's practice. Identify decision criteria whereby internally motivated change is required. Identify planning and communications systems to be used for accountability purposes.	Analyze impacts of alternative types of problem statement. Oversee design and management of financial management procedures. Oversee design and management of management information system. Identify forms and procedures for handling accountability communications and planning systems. Create mechanisms for generation of management objectives in agency.	Involve board, staff, clients in problem definition process. Create and maintain reward system consistent with managerial and people needs. Motivate and organize staff and other inputs into MBO system. Involve agency system actors in dealing with financial issues, in sharing managerial responsibility.
Technical Level	Oversee operationalization of goals into measureable objectives. Identify technical staff competencies needed and necessity of reliance on outside resources. Understanding of research methods—quantitative and qualitative.	Understanding of direct and indirect indicators of client progress. Select viable technical means for maintaining accountability. Promote design and maintenance of a practice monitoring information system.	Involve staff, clients in defining measureable objectives. Support staff in building technical competence into practice roles. Motivate involvement in personnel and peer review systems.

(Spencer, 1959, p. 26); and in determining the success of the organization's activities.

The leadership areas require that the administrator have, or acquire, an extensive accountability technology. Accountability technology is built out of contributions from several sub-specializations. These include: (1) financial management and budgeting skills—on-going operations and grants related; (2) personnel management skills; (3) systems monitoring and reporting skills; (4) assessment skills (the ability to develop data within the operating system to answer specific questions about organizational processes, inputs, outcomes); (5) program and personnel evaluation skills; and (6) the ability to relate each of these discrete skill areas to "bottom line" service concerns and priorities. None of the first five areas of skills can be divorced from the service context of the social welfare agency. This fact enhances the crucial importance of the "interfacing" understanding that the accountability technologist must have of practice modes, including theoretical and functional aspects. Acquiring these skills in the agency, in a way which is congruent with practice values and advocacy concerns, is the challenge to the social administrator.

Alternatives for Acquiring Accountability Technology

The social administrator can consider a number of means for acquiring or developing these skills in the agency.

Training of current administrators. Under the supportable assumption (e.g., Lewis, 1975, p. 615; Mullis, 1975, p. 31) that many current administrators have not received extensive and recent training in accountability technology, a first alternative is new training for current administrators. This approach is necessary but far from sufficient to meet the mastery demands of the technology. Most administrators need training in basic understanding of the technologies, with perhaps some in-depth training in selected aspects of it. Given the continuing nature of on-going demands on the executive's time and skills, time for new training will necessarily be too limited to gain a user's knowledge of much of the required technology.

This approach is weakened, too, in its implicit assumption that only formally designated administrators or managers can accomplish management/administrative tasks. In fact, all staff members of social welfare organizations can profitably be seen as both administering and managing certain functions. The delegation of administrative/managerial accountability functions simply formalizes and recognizes current capacities for what they are.

Staff training. While having technical capacities to at least the level utilized in current job roles, staff will tend to need reinforcement in applying their technical capacities to broader functions. A social work supervisor accustomed to compiling service statistics will need some training in maintaining unit costs and cost-benefit figures on those services. While this approach is extremely useful in spreading administrative and managerial burdens among staff, and acts to relate these more abstracted functions closely to service provision considerations and perspectives, it is another example of "necessary but not sufficient." Practice staff are hired primarily for practice skills, and are not easily convertable into a group of accountability technicians without great cost to clients, to worker self-image and personnel, and to the agency's service capability.

Hiring accountability experts. A third alternative open to administrators in meeting demands for accountability is to hire specialists to take on parts of the overall task. These would include accountants for financial management and budgeting; lawyers for legal interpretations and for some aspects of personnel management; systems specialists for linear programming functions; computer specialists for programming of agency data into machine-ready formats. Within a relatively narrow range of skill, these individuals would offer the administrator the highest level of skills of any of the alternatives given here. A key drawback involves the high cost of these professionals and the narrowness of their impact on broad organizational needs. Their lack of service-relevant knowledge may produce problems in their attempts to interact with service provision staff. Given the shrinking social welfare dollar, the costliness of over-specialization at the possible expense of service availability can be questioned.

Use of contracted services. A fourth alternative calls for the administrator to rely on contracted services from private vendors, a practice that is gaining some currency within the social welfare field. Again, the quality of such services might be expected to be high, and knowledge of social welfare provision may also be present, at least for such vendors who specialize their services to the human welfare field. Problems with this alternative include the high cost factor and the lack of control over or immediate relatability of these now external activities by the administrator to changes in agency conditions or operations. Where stability and resources are assured, the contracting approach makes more sense; most social welfare organizations, however, seem not to be blessed with these conditions.

Hiring recent social administration graduates. The last alternative considered here through which the practicing administrator can expect to augment agency capacity to respond to technical operational demands, while maintaining a balance with service values and priorities, is that of hiring recent graduates of a master's level social service administration educational program. The remainder of this chapter is devoted to describing what the practicing social administrator can expect of individuals with this training, and to supporting the contention that this alternative best fits, as a priority approach, the broad-based technical skills needs of the administrator's organization.

What the Practicing Administrator Can Expect of Social Administration Graduates

In this section, a number of elements of the preparation of social administration graduates will be presented. The argument here is that, cumulatively, these elements provide potential administrative staff members who are uniquely valuable to the needs for balance and communication between technology and values of the practicing social administrator.

TRAINING AT THE "BALANCE POINT"

The first, and a key, element is that social administration students in schools of social work are trained precisely at and around the juncture of the competing value and technological perspectives Gruber describes. Both course content and practice work experience stress each of: (1) social work practice method and the values underlying method; (2) technical aspects of the social administrator role in depth and at least introductory exposure to technical aspects of other social work professional roles; and (3) the understanding of means for integrating value and technical elements.

Curriculm sequencing involves, at the outset, common orientation to: (1) the educational curriculum, taking into account the varied backgrounds of entering students; (2) the social work value and skill foundations to which education for social administration will be geared; and (3) the advocacy/manipulator perspective of the social administrator. A grouping of required, introductory-level courses is viewed as necessary to set the "educational climate" for the entire class of students. Student interactions are facilitated, and a productive sense of a class "cohort" built if students are grouped in their initial educational focuses. The emphasis on foundation-building within the classroom context is strengthened, as is the stress on conceptual skills.

Courses during the first semester, given Council on Social Work Education directives, are likely to include content on social welfare policies and services, social and psychological theory as these apply to social work practice, and research methodology. Further courses dealing with organizational theory and with issues and theories in social service delivery provide effective foundation content for administration students, the first dealing broadly with organizational behavior and the second reinforcing the direct-service base of social work practice in ways meaningful to students who will wind up administering such services.

It is particularly important that the advocate/manipulator perspective be apparent in each of these courses as a foundation concept which can be carried into subsequent course and field work. The policy course, for example, can take as a central theme historical and current instances of policy-formation instigated through advocacy and systems manipulation on the part of those in the social welfare field.

A further aspect of this element involves the sequencing of interpersonal, policy-related, and technical content. While the chart suggests balance between these three content and skill areas, it does not indicate when the content is developed. The clearest rationale supports an emphasis on technical managerial skills such as fiscal management (accounting, budgeting, forecasting), personnel management, program evaluation, and the creation and maintenance of management information systems in later semesters of course work, once the various contexts and rationales for the use of these skills have been examined. In general, the policy and interpersonal areas can be seen as moving from the more generic to the more specific: for example, from national health policy to organizational benefit systems; and from general theories of human interaction to creating effective task teams.

IMPORTANCE OF EDUCATIONAL FOCUS
ON TOP ADMINISTRATIVE POSITIONS

A second element supporting the value of the training of social administration students for practicing administrators concerns the level of administrative work for which students are being prepared. Three distinct, although somewhat overlapping levels of administrative practice in the field can be identified: (1) top administration, including such job titles as executive director, administrative director, or administrator; (2) middle-level management, including such positions as assistant director, administrative assistant, program director, program coordinator, division chief, or social service director; and (3) line supervision, assistant supervisor, or team leader. The entire thrust of this chapter is aimed at education for the assemption of middle and top administrative positions. The supervisory level is de-emphasized because of its primary (and limiting) clinical involvement. It is recognized, first, that the vast majority of students do not graduate from school and move directly into top administrative positions (Macarov, 1977); depending on past experience, a student's first job after graduation tends to be middle-management, supervisory, or direct practice (Biggerstaff, 1978). However, educational programs cannot focus only on "next steps"; *career* education is requisite for an educational program that will have impact on the practice of social work, and this involves training for future jobs. Underlying this rationale is the proposition that an educational focus on a higher level of administrative work will lead to higher levels of expectation on the part of students and, subsequently, higher actualization in terms of moving into top and middle administrative positions. The thrust is developmental: students in class and field settings should consolidate their current skills in being exposed to increasingly higher levels of administrative concerns—beginning at direct practice and moving through supervisory and middle-management to top administration—while they are being challenged with issues and skill requirements they will address fully only when holding a top management position.

A second rationale involves education's responsibility to train new generations of students to meet needs in the field—to fill past gaps in social work education. David Macarov points to the lack of education for top administrative roles in social work in a recent article (Macarov, 1977).

In a shorter time perspective, an educational emphasis on top administrative roles tends to de-mystify management for students, providing them a greater ability to move into high-level jobs when they are ready or as opportunity allows. Also, it is the contention here that all jobs in the social welfare field contain management responsibilities. Exposure to ways in which top administrators consider management issues should pay off in students' ability to connect management aspects of whatever job they hold to parellel agency-wide concerns; the results should be more effective practice by graduates as they move up through job levels and a more critical understanding of the ways in which management concerns are shared and acted on by all staff in an organization.

Most pragmatically, students who are exposed to top administrative work in the classroom field practicum are more effective in working with and supporting top executive staff in an agency during field placement; the "mind set" of the administrator is less foreign to the student, and a broader basis for exchange between the administrator-field instructor and the student is created.

RELATING ADMINISTRATIVE CONTENT TO PLANNING AND ORGANIZING ROLES

A third element concerns the extent and means for distinguishing purely administrative concerns from social planning and community organizing content. Gummer (1975) and Neugeboren (1971). among others, argue the continuum nature of the policy-planning-administration process, and feel that these three "specializations" cannot be treated apart from one another. Sarri (1976) does not deny the sometimes considerable overlap or mutual concern among the three specializations, but argues that greater clarity of the distinctions among them is achieved by forcing them apart in a curriculum. Slavin (1977, pp. 253–255) provides similar arguments for the distinction, based on an agency practice model.

The thrust of this chapter, particularly given the time constraints of a two-year curriculum, is toward an emphasis on the distinctive aspects of the administrative specialization, both in terms of unique technical expertise and in the nature of the systems manipulator/advocate role described earlier. A number of means can be suggested by which overlaps and common concerns of the three specializations can be addressed:

1. A common "core" of classes in the first semester of the program in which overlaps and distinctive concerns of each specialization are addressed. Foundation courses in social welfare policy, in social and psychological theories of behavior, in organizational theory, in theories and issues in service delivery, and in research methodology are effective vehicles for this purpose.

2. Joint field placements, combining students from two or more of the specializations in job roles within the same agency, provide a particularly effective means for students to "co-learn" the realities of overlap and distinctions of their primary roles as played out in the contest of a particular field setting.

3. A joint "professional seminar" as a practice course in the final semester, focussed on problem-solving in practice, allows students from the three specializations to act out their distinctive contributions and approaches to problem definition and solution, while experiencing aspects of mutual concern and skills.

PRACTICAL EXPERIENCE BACKGROUND

A fourth element supporting the coherence of social administration graduates with the needs of the practicing administrator involves the work experience in social welfare organizations these graduates have attained. First, administration students are accepted into the program only after having completed two years of full-time employment in a direct or indirect service-providing capacity in a social welfare organization: references for these students must indicate that they have been able to perform successfully in their job capacities, and in the broader contexts of the organization—bringing in value content, interpersonal skills, and technical capacities.

Second, students undergo three semesters of field practicum experience, placed directly under the supervision of a top-level or high mid-level administrator in a social welfare organization. The experience itself has great power in terms of students' "role modeling" of operational administrative behavior. The experience is enhanced by forcing students to deal simultaneously with the educator's insistence on rationalty, on idealism, and on long planning horizons, and with the pragmatic and immediate problem-solving pressures which force behavior on the practicing administrator approaching Lindblom's "muddling through" concept (1970).

It seems particularly true for administration in the social work field that skills learned in one practice setting can be transferred to other settings. A three-semester placement in one practice setting provides an advantage in allowing the student the opportunity to receive a fuller and deeper orientation to the agency and to have time to engage a number of professional tasks in depth. The first field semester is differentiated from those in the second year by allowing for a full orientation to the agency, and by the possibility of assigning the student to work directly with agency personnel other than the executive director in specific tasks. The orientation is aimed particularly at: (1) the policy system of the agency (e.g., legislative, economic, inter-organizational); (2 the agency's target population; (3) the services of the agency; and (4) the structure and processes of the agency itself. Students who lack direct social service experience can gain greater first-hand knowledge through working closely with the agency's "front-line" staff. Similarly, structured experiences with several levels of staff, taking on roles at each level, can provide the student with experiential knowledge of the practices of the agency which are major concerns of the administrator which the student is learning to become.

Summary

The practicing social administrator is faced with increasing pressures to maintain his or her organization's capacity to provide more and better services in the context of professional values, while at the same time employing increasingly specialized technologies aimed at accountability in an era of tight resources. Of a number of alternative means by which the practicing administrator can move to address these often conflicting demands, most are viewed as producing parts of the necessary capacity, but as entailing costs if relied on for a major part of the response to accountability demands. The employment of recent graduates of social work schools' administration specializations is presented as the most cost-efficient alternative for upgrading important aspects of administrative accountability technology while promising to retain a sensitiveness to social work values and an administrative advocacy stance.

References

Biggerstaff, Marilyn. "Preparation of Administrators in Social Welfare: A Follow-Up Study of Administration Concentration Graduates." Paper presented at Annual Program Meeting, Council on Social Work Education, New Orleans, March 1978.

Donnison, David V. *The Development of Social Administration*. London: Bell, 1962.

Fein, Edith. "A Data System for an Agency." *Social Work* 20 (Jan. 1975): 21–24.

Gruber, Murray. "Total Administration." *Social Work* 19, no. 5 (Sept. 1974): 625–636.

Gummer, Burton. "Social Planning and Social Administration: Implications for Curriculum Development." *Journal of Education for Social Work* 11 (Winter 1975): 66–72.

Hanlan, Archie. "From Social Work to Social Administration." In *Social Work Practice* 1970. New York: Columbia U. Press National Conference on Social Welfare, 1970.

Hoshino, George and Thomas P. McDonald. "Agencies in the Computer Age." *Social Work* 20 (Jan. 1975): 10–14.

Levinson, Daniel J., and Gerald L. Klerman. "The Clinician-Executive Revisited." *Administration in Mental Health* 1, no. 1 (Winter 1972): 64–67.

Lewis, Harold. "Management in the Nonprofit Social Service Organization." *Child Welfare* 54 (Nov. 1975): 615–623.

Lindblom, Charles. "The Science of Muddling Through." In Fred M. Cox et al., eds., *Strategies of Community Organization*. Itasca, Ill.: Peacock, 1970.

Macarov, David. "Management in the Social Work Curriculum." *Administration in Social Work* 1 (Summer 1977): 135–148.

Massy, Patricia G. "On the Line with MBO." *Public Welfare* 34 (Summer 1976): 44–48.

Mullis, Scott S. "Management Applications to the Welfare System." *Public Welfare* 33 (Fall 1975): 31–34.

Neugeboren, Bernard. "Developing Specialized Programs in Social Work Administration in the Master's Degree Program: Field Practice Component." *Journal of Education for Social Work* 7 (Fall 1971): 35–47.

Parsons, Talcott. *Structure and Process in Modern Societies*. Glencoe, Ill.: Free Press, 1960.

Patti, Rino. "The New Scientific Management: Systems Management for Social Welfare." *Public Welfare* 33 (Spring 1975): 23–31.

Raider, Melvyn. "An Evaluation of Management by Objectives." *Social Casework* 56, no. 2 56 (Feb. 1975): 79–83.

Rogers, Barbara N., John Greve, and John S. Morgan. *Comparative Social Administration*. New York: Atherton, 1968.

Sarri, Rosemary C. "Administration in Social Welfare." *Encyclopedia of Social Work* 1 (1976): 42–51.

Schultze, Charles L., et al. *Setting National Priorities: The* 1973 Budget (Washington, D.C.: The Brookings Institution, 1972), pp. 394–409.

Selznick, Phillip, *Leadership in Administration: A Sociological Interpretation*. New York: Harper and Row, 1957.

Shapira, Monica. "Reflections on the Preparation of Social Workers for Executive Positions." *Journal of Education for Social Work* 7 (Winter 1971): 55–68.

Slack, Kathleen M. *Social Administration and the Citizen* London: Michael Josephs, 1966.

Slavin, Simon. "A Framework for Selecting Content for Teaching About Social Administration." *Administration in Social Work* 1 (Fall 1977): 245–257.

Spencer, Sue. *The Administration Method in Social Work Education*. Project Report of the Curriculum Study, Vol. 3. New York: Council on Social Work Education, 1959.

Stamm, Alfred M. "NASW Membership: Characteristics, Deployment, and Salaries." In *Personnel Information, vol*. 12, no. 3. New York: National Association of Social Workers, 1969.

Titmuss, Richard M. "The Subject of Social Administration." In Titmuss *Commitment to Welfare*. New York: Patheon, 1968.

Wildavsky, Aaron. "Rescuing Policy Analysis from PPBS." In *The Analysis and Evaluation of Public Expenditures: The PPB System*. Washington, D.C.: GPO, 1969.

Wilensky, Harold, and Charles Lebeaux. *Industrial Society and Social Welfare*. New York: Russel Sage, 1965.

FINANCIAL MANAGEMENT AND SOCIAL ADMINISTRATION

Roger A. Lohmann

7

Financial management is an area of central concern in administration. In this chapter Professor Lohmann presents a broad framework for this process as it applies to all types of human service agencies, including the voluntary agency, the public agency, and the multi-funded agency. Consistent with the philosophy of this volume, the author focusses on the active role of the administrator, who should seek maximum control over vital decisions in both the planning and the implementation stage since budgets are important control devices.

Professor Lohmann proceeds to discuss budgetting in detail; included are very practical aspects concerning not only the technical elements but also the political aspects inherent in this process. This overview provides what Lohmann calls a "concept map" of the subject.

A Concept Map of Financial Management

For many professionals in the human services, budget-making and the owner related responsibilities of financial management in social agencies have an air of magic and mystery about them. Because accounting, cost estimation, fiscal analysis, and some of the other skills involved are, by and large, outside the realm of experience of most human service workers, initial encounters with these topics are often forbidding and anxiety-producing. Yet every student of human services administration and every practicing professional preparing to assume a position of agency or program management responsibility must eventually come to terms with these topics. For the truth is that management knowledge cannot be considered complete without some knowledge of the workings of financial resources in organizations and of the decisions which regulate their movement.

For the benefit of readers completely unfamiliar with this subject, it may be helpful to visualize the subject initially as a unique *concept space*, composed of a distinctive set of concepts and their interrelated meanings. This chapter is devoted principally to setting out ("mapping") the outer limits of that space, and of exploring some of the essential landmarks and pathways therein. We cannot hope in such a discussion to explore all the subleties and nuances involved. (What map ever does?) The reader should expect from this discussion, however, a broad understanding of the importance of budgets, how they are constructed, and important relationships between budgets and other managerial concerns, both financial and non-financial.

Initiation Rites

For many practitioners, the seeming obscurity of financial subjects will in no way be diminished, and will possibly even be increased, by their first encounters on the job. The reasons for this are quite simple, and related to the reference above to mapping: Most knowledge of financial matters does not involve a "theoretical map" of inter-related definitions and propositions which most students of human behavior have come to expect. Instead, knowledge in this area involves a detailed, operationally defined, but readily learnable "model" which is mostly definitional in nature. For instance, a "balanced budget" means that the income or revenue items are numerically equal to the outflows or expenditure items. Why is this so? Only because that is the conventional usage. What difference does it make? Well, that depends upon how deeply you wish to pursue the matter. There are sufficient theoretical bases underlying most of the terms and concepts used in human services financial management. In most instances, however, students are well advised to deal with these as conventions unless they wish to pursue advanced work in this area.

Because knowledge in this area consists of a large and inter-connected set of working definitions composing a single model, most newcomers have difficulty, understanding financial management. Awareness of this difficulty, however, should be tempered by two additional insights: First, nearly everyone (at least in the human services) has experienced similar difficulties in their initial exposure. And, secondly, like learning to walk, drive a car, type, or swim, once the initial difficulties are overcome, one can by and large forget about the basics and concentrate on using the knowledge.

Financial Management

Initial exposure to this model involves accepting certain standard assumptions about the situational context of financial management and the regularities imposed by that context. For example, whether one is concerned with organized agencies per se, or with more or less free-standing programs, a common financial concept essential for management purposes is that of the *entity*, which is simply the unit for which financial records (accounts) are maintained. In all cases, management concern with control, planning, evaluation, and even basic record-keeping must take the entity, or fund, into account. Furthermore, when common-sense motions of program limits conflict with established fund definitions, the common-sense notions must give way to the legal and ethical demands of the latter. Therefore, the initial task for financial management is to establish which program activities (workers, job assignments, travel, etc.) are associated with which fund activities (income or revenue, and expenditures). Usually, examination of planning documents, such as budget proposals, and control documents, such as charts of accounts, policy statements, and agency guidelines, will establish these relationships, although in smaller agencies staff members may carry these items around "in their heads."

Another standard contextual assumption affecting financial management practice involves differences in the types of agencies involved in the delivery of human services. Human service agencies today tend to fall into three reasonably distinct groupings: Two types, the *voluntary agency*, organized as a not-for-profit corporation, and the *public agency*, supported by tax revenues, are well-established modes of delivering services.

Until recently, management of financial resources in voluntary agencies has been quite limited, both because of the small scale of operations and the resultant lack of managerial specialization, and because of the primitive state of their financial technology. At the same time, attention to financial matters in public agencies was often exclusive prerogative of accountants, budget analysts, and other specialists located outside the service delivery agency in another branch or unit of government. In either case, the result was much the same: Human services administrators needed only a very sketchy general knowledge of financial matters in order to perform acceptably, because the expected competence was relatively low level and complicated functions were performed by others. A major consequence of this pattern however, was that the planned management of available resources was seldom possible. Administrators instead usually confined themselves to "substantive" matters, checking with the financial experts when appropriate to see if they could afford what they wanted to do.

More recently, we have seen the emergence of a new form of "third-sector" agency, in which more active financial management is essential. Financed in whole or part by public funds, but organized legally as not-for-profit corporations, these newer agencies have legal flexibility, and often the practical necessity, of simultaneously pursuing several types of funding from different sources. As a consequence, these *multi-funded* agencies require competent financial management, simply to decide which activities relate to which accounting transactions, since those decisions have an impact on intelligent programming. For example, if two separate federal grants support client transportation, the administrator must decide whether a single bus can be used and the costs pro-rated to the different funds, or whether two busses are legally necessary.

We shall assume throughout this discussion that there are certain aspects of financial management common to all human service entities. However, for the reasons mentioned above, these activities are best developed in third-sector agencies. Further, in managing financial resources the administrator must consider several dimensions. First of all, there is the question of *survival*. In most instances, the continued existence of an agency or program is dependent upon continued fund-raising activities. If such revenue stops, the agency will not be able to continue. Secondly, there is the issue of *fiscal control*. Boards of directors, outside funding sources, and the community at large generally insist that there be sufficient control over the safe-keeping and expenditure of funds to minimize, if not prevent, loss, theft, or embezzlement. Furthermore, any effort to actively manage resources and direct them to explicit uses and agency purposes assumes some measure of control. The administrator of a small public agency who must get approval for every expenditure decision from a county clerk or city comptroller may have relatively little managerial control to exercise. Thirdly, the active management of the allocations process, both in putting together an agency or program budget and in implementing that budget, call for a large number of decisions about where to spend, and not spend, money. Human service administrators, if they desire to influence their program, should seek maximum control over such decisions, both in the budget planning and implementation stages.

Such control is most justified when the administrator links substantive, programmatic perspectives with the technical perspectives of accountancy. The fourth major concern, which can only emerge if allocations management already exists, is an explicit focus on planning and evaluation as these relate to allocations and control decisions. In other words, until some control is imposed on allocations decisions, it is fruitless to talk of the future-oriented problem-solving approaches of planning, or evaluative concerns, with the efficiency and effectiveness of program activities. Increasingly, it is apparent that some human services agencies can move beyond their narrow concern with survival and control and confront the issues of allocations management, planning, and evaluation.

The budgetary process, both within the agency and in larger budgetary systems, is the focal point of human services management. Budgets are aften said to be plans, and indeed they are. They are also important documents for the fund-raiser for no funding source should be expected to give a large sum of money without some detailed explanation about how it will be spent. Further, budgets are important control devices, an aspect of the topic that is often overlooked. And the act of putting together a budget requires allocational decision-making, and provides an opportunity for fiscal planning and the establishment of evaluative criteria. In sum, the budgetary process is critically important, because so many cross-currents of financial management converge on it.

Developing a Budget Proposal

The actual development of a budget proposal should always carefully consider the four issues noted above: fund-raising; fiscal control; the substantive and programmatic implications of allocation choices involved; and the opportunities for planning and evaluation inherent in the situation.

The development of an agency budget differs from the development of the federal budget or a household budget. The differences, however, are primarily those of scale and complexity. The essential similarities which may initially elude the novice will become apparent with experience.

There are three principle elements in budget development: identifying the key items of a plan or program which involve expenditure of resources, or which may; generate revenue; "pricing" these items; and building a consensus for the budget proposal. The first two are essentially technical skills involving analysis and arithmetic, the latter, a form of human relations. *All three* are essential for the successful budgtary enterprise. Because it is likely to be familiar territory to most human service workers, we shall begin with the consensus-building.

Buget Reference Groups

A budget is a set of numbers, together with identifying phrases, that sets forth proposed expenditures and revenue estimates. From a behavioral standpoint, however, that document is a medium for communicating the "real" budget, the understandings and working agreements negotiated between the budget reference groups. Several such "constituencies" are usually involved in any budget, and it is an important management task to identify them.

The test for identifying members of budget reference groups is relatively simple: Who needs to know anything about the budget under preparation, and what specifically do they need to know? The first question will identify the parties involved, and the second allows them to be grouped. Need, in this case, operates on two levels: Who *must* be informed if there are not to be serious repercussions for the budget or its developers? This is the obligatory level. A second level, that of professional courtesy, involves identifying those who may be completely uninterested in process or details, but who should at least be informed when the budget process is complete and the total amount of requested funds has been decided on. Such courtesies, it should be noted, can amount to more than a display of good manners, for they can keep open the possibility of active support, should it be required. If there are any questions about who should receive courtesy notification, it is wise to err on the side of generosity. By contrast, in determining what information to send this group, it is wise to err on the side of sparcity, since the budget developer, rightfully proud of his efforts, may be inclined to send much more information than may really be desired by such persons.

In cases where a large number of persons are included in the obligations group, or where conditions require discretion or special handling, it may be advisable to refine this list: For example, one may identify the true "insiders" who need to be informed of every detail: those who actually developed the proposal and perhaps a critical supervisor or two. In special cases, where the budget is a grant proposal and the agency has a strong and on-going working partnership with the funding agency, the monitor involved might also be included if he is not adversarial or threatening. A second category would be the "big decision" people—those who need to be included in major decisions about the focus of the proposal, total cost ranges, and the like. For example, if a grant would involve doubling the number of staff members in an agency, the agency administrator and the board of directors need to be told!

A third group would be those with whom "working agreements" are essential in order to carry out the proposed activity. Thus, if one must get "sign off" approvals from persons within the agency or outside, they should be alerted in advance that their cooperation will be needed. Similarly, agreements involving the leasing or use of other facilities outside the agency or, inter-agency cooperation should also be worked out in advance, even though such arrangements may, of necessity, be tentative.

One should not expect at the onset to work out a final listing of those whose aid is needed, for as the proposal takes shape, different ideas and assumptions will be added or dropped, making it necessary to modify the list of those whose support is essential. It is important to remember that the reason for identifying these reference groups is to build the largest possible coalition of support for the proposal, and success will be affected by the time available, the organizing skill of the proposal developers, and the interest of those approached.

Another group may need to be dealt with in the proposal development process—those who are opposed to your proposal for some reason. Here one must be quite hard-nosed: To get your budget approved, total commitment and love from everyone will not be necessary and are rarely possible. It is important, however, to minimize active opposition both during critical budget hearings and behind the scenes when decisions are being made.

When faced with active or latent opposition, a useful strategy is to concentrate on defusing active opposition. If your program is disliked in another part of the agency, or in another agency, but those opponents are, for one reason or another, not disposed to do anything about it, ignore them. Only if you expect active opposition—a petition, counter-testimony at a budget hearing, a behind-the-scenes effort to influence budget decision-makers—will it be advisable for you to act. Even then, the objective should not be to win them over, but only to isolate and defuse their opposition. This is not to suggest that it is unwise to concentrate on winning over your opponents at other times, and under other circumstances. However, direct confrontation is risky, (*they*, after all, might win *you* over!), and budget negotiations should always be undertaken with an eye toward minimizing risk.

What, then, does one actually expect from these various reference groups? Under ordinary circumstances, the answer is nothing much. Gaining their indifference or presumed support is usually enough. It allows the budget developer to indicate, for example, that a number of important persons have been informed of the proposal and without evidence to the contrary their support is assumed. There are many ways to communicate this information to funding sources without simply telling them. For example, letters of support in a grant application identify people who do not oppose the proposal and are willing to put themselves out to the extent of writing a letter.

In some cases, however, more active support from your reference groups may be necessary. You may need to make use of them, for example, to counter organized opponents at public hearings, in casual conversations, or through letter-writing campaigns. Ordinarily, however, such active involvement of supporters is a limited resource and sould be used sparingly.

Working Up the Proposal

The analytical and arithmetic task of working up an actual budget proposal—committing numbers to paper—should normally occur simultaneously with identification and encouragement of budget reference groups. This step normally causes the greatest panic among new human services professionals, primarily because of their fear of complex mathematical calculations. "I can organize the support, sure," a student once told me, "but support for what?" In truth, ability to add, subtract, and multiply is about all the analytical skill it takes to perform most human services budget work.

The first step in developing an actual proposal should always be the same: learn the rules you will be working with. In developing a grant proposal, get a set of guidelines and read them carefully;, particularly the budget sections, which typically list major relevant items to consider. If you are not working with a grant proposal, identify whatever other guidelines are involved. Note that many such guidelines are informal working agreements about what is and is not acceptable, and that process can only be mastered through conversations with veterans of the process. ("The county commission never approves salary increases of more than eight percent, under any circumstances.") In the case of such informal standards, learning is an on-going concern, and one must always be alert for new information.

The existence of informal guidelines should never be used to justify sloppy preparation or inattention to detail. Inattention and insensitivity to formal guidelines can be a very costly mistake where budgets are concerned.

Part of the guidelines may include specification of the format in which your budget must appear (expenditure categories, necessary sub-totals, etc.). If so, you need only become familiar with that particular format and adapt your figures to it. If no such format exists, however, you may have to develop your own. In that case, it is usually wise to review standard formats until you find one that best approximates your needs and then adapt it to your purposes. Remember, the logic of such forms is that they are "in balance": that is, whether or not revenues are explicitly listed, it is assumed that revenues will equal proposed expenditures and, that groupings, or sub-sets of items, will add up to the total figure. "Hidden," "Assumed," and "Obvious but unlisted" figures are all equally unacceptable.

The most difficult part of any budget, of course, is deriving adequate expenditure assumptions. Two considerations are particularly important here. First of all, estimates should always be of the "reasonable and prudent" variety—a fact which can often be demonstrated by citing evidence that the figures in question are based on "usual and customary" expenditures in the agency or community. Second, one should always be alert to particular funding-source expectations or guidelines which override what is reasonable or customary. Thus, if it is reasonable and customary in your community for paraprofessionals to be paid $1.50 for a particular job, one should not expect to include that as a cost item in a federal grant request, because federal agencies are legally required to pay federal minimum wage levels for all work.

Properly pricing budget items can be a problem in those cases where atypical circumstances in the agency raise agency-normal costs beyond what the funding source considers reasonable and prudent. Thus, many rural agencies have traditionally had difficulties justifying high travel costs to federal agencies that usually operate on an urban standard. Similarly, some urban agencies have difficulty convincing the same federal agencies that high clerical and other non-professional salaries are typical for their communities.

Keep in mind in pricing budget items that you will rarely be expected to project costs exactly; a 10 percent variance over or under is sometimes used as a guideline. Your estimates will improve with experience; if you do not have it, ask someone who does. Calculating expected paper and supplies usage, for example, can be a nearly impossible task for a beginner, while projecting such usage based on prior experience can be relatively simple.

A key consideration here is how much to "fudge" or "pad" budget estimates. Of course, everyone would like to believe this doesn't occur, or at least that they don't do it, but it is almost inevitable that some excess estimating will be built into every budget. One reason for this is that in estimating one seeks always to "be on the safe" side of estimates which could be slightly higher or lower. When all those margins of safety are added together, they constitute a sum which can, in itself, serve certain useful purposes. For example, when one is faced with unavoidable cuts in a budgeted amount, such "fudge" items are a logical first target. To anticipate the possibility of such cuts, therefore, and to build in some excessive estimates specifically for that purpose would appear to be prudent; however, such padding should not be excessive, for, if the budget is approved as is, the agency may not be able to spend the entire request. In that case, it is possible that the agency may have to explain those same padded funds at the next budget period.

The largest single item in most human service budgets, and typically the one in which relatively precise cost estimates are possible, is the personnel section. Usually there are two principle cost items covered here Wages and salaries of employees, and fringe benefits (often computed as a percentage of total wages and salaries). Sources for this information are multiple: if the agency has a salary schedule, budgets will need to be prepared in accordance with it. If not, the "usual and customary" criterion can typically be applied by using the salaries for comparable positions in the community.

Once this category has been detailed, it can serve as a check on other categories as well. By comparing the percentage of personnal to total expenditures for the budget proposal with comparable figures for a similar agency or program, one can sometimes tell whether the proposal is "out of line." It should always be kept in mind that there are no absolute standards for this type of comparison; and even if one is "out of line," there may be a good reason for it. Determining this figure in advance may simply be good preparation, in case questions of this type arise during budget considerations.

Target: Reference Group Consensus

Eventually, of course, the objective of budget preparation is to put together a budget which will be acceptable to the funding source. That, however, is a far-off objective which it may be difficult to gauge usefully in preparing the budget. Therefore, a more proximate objective is to build a favorable consensus among the reference groups. Such an approach leads very quickly to the recognition that some of these reference groups are more important than others. An important task, therefore, involves determing whose support is most essential. One important consideration is the relationship between these reference groups and the most important reference group—the funding source. One should know which reference group members think like funding sources, which of them communicate directly with funders, and which are of no consequence. The entire process should produce an expanding climate of positive opinion culminating with the endorsement by the funding source. Careful planning and encouragement of support, together with a proposal which is understood by reference group supporters, should maximize the possibility of success.

Presenting the Budget

To orchestrate this expanding consensus for your budget proposal you must be familar with the stages of consideration through which the budget request must move. Will the proposal move up an organizational hierarchy, being incorporated at each step with more and more proposals, and becoming, as a result, less and less visible? Or will it be presented on its own to a sequence of budget committees, boards of directors, and funding source representatives? Although the number and circumstances of such presentations vary widely, the purpose remains constant: to present the budget in a manner most likely to broaden consensus behind the proposal. In so doing, it is often necessary to present information, and then explain and defend it without appearing defensive or threatened.

Budget presentations also vary widely in their degree of formality. In public appropriations contexts, such as city council, state legislative, or congressional budget hearings, legally mandated procedures may be accompanied by elaborate ceremonies and rituals. In such cases, the presentor is well advised to become well-versed in advance on the protocol of such an appearance. In other cases, the circumstances of "presentation" may be considerably more informal—in some cases, simply mailing in the proposal or supplementing a written proposal with telephone conversations. In each case, however, presenting the proposal in a favorable light requires sensitivity to the surface differences of the situation. In each case the funding source will ask one basic question: Why should limited funds be used for this particular proposal rather than others?

Consequently, the circumstances of presentations tend to accentuate the importance of the rhetoric of budget-making. The budget presentor should always make the best possible case for approval of the request in the most effective, convincing manner. The strength of the case will, in most instances, be affected by three factors: (a) the formal rules of the budget process; (b) the informal situational norms involved; and (c) ethical and legal sanctions regarding misreprentation of facts and accountability.

Written budget materials should effectively communicate the need for the activity, the consistency between the need and the level of funding requested, the "fit" between the proposed funding and the "larger purposes" of the funding source; and the ability of the agency to carry out the proposed activity.

There is often continuity from year to year among budget officials, whether in public bodies, United Way budget committees, or federal agency monitors. Under such circumstances, part or all of the above "case" for funding may not have to be repeated year after year because the decision-makers involved know much of the case already and would only be bored by repetition. For this reason, *incremental budget-making* is the most widely used approach to budget decisions.

In truth, decisions about budgets are seldom made after dispassionate review of evidence presented in a scientific manner. Instead, decision-makers facing complex, difficult, and tedious decisions tend to resort to time and energy saving devices. Thus, an agency presenting requests year after year for the same program may find that decision-makers concentrate almost exclusively on the "increment" of increase or decrease of the proposal from the previous year, rather than the overall merits of the request. Such limited, focussed decision-making appears to be an inevitable response to the complexity of such situations, one that is functional for both decision-makers and those making requests. Decisions are thereby reduced to managable proportions, and decision-makers stand a better chance of accomplishing their task in the time available. From the agency standpoint it tends to reduce survival anxiety, since the principal issue is the increase or decrease in funding, rather than whether or not to fund at all.

On the whole, such incremental approaches are the rule, rather than the exception, in budgetary decision-making in all human services contexts— public appropriations, voluntary-federated, and federal grant decisions. In recent years, however, critics of such "incremental" decision-making have pointed to a number of inherent weaknesses in this approach. For one thing, as noted above, such decisions are inevitably weighted in favor of existing funding, and the question of whether or not previous performance warrants continued funding seldom comes up. Even if the question does arise, agency officials can often deal with it readily by promising to do better in the future. Further, it is argued, such decisions are inherently supportive of the status quo, and make change difficult. Similarly, it is argued that by approaching decisions in piecemeal fashion, the funding authority never comes to grips with molding or shaping the system under its ostensible control. Instead, it allows and even encourages drift and indecision.

Budget Systems and Budget Revolutions

Such arguments have given rise in recent years to a number of proposals for budgetary reform in the public sector. These proposals have been universally critical of several characteristics of traditional budget *formats* as well as the incremental style of decision with which they are associated.

One format characteristic which has drawn criticism is the so-called *line-item budget* still in use in many public budget settings. This is undoubtedly the most elementary form of budget presentation, listing only a brief descriptive term and a summary total of proposed expenditures for each department or major unit involved. Nearly all critics of this format point out the tremendous information loss involved in this style of presentation. Virtually nothing of the goals, objectives, programs, and accomplishments of major organizational units (such as a state department of public welfare) are conveyed by this type of budget. Further, none of the specific agreements, negotiations, or understandings which are reached in the budgetary process are reflected in this budget form, except as they affect the total of proposed expenditures.

Line-item budgeting may once have been a satisfactory form of budget presentation. When the public business was carried out in a direct, fact-to-fact manner, and when government units were sufficiently small to be directly accountable to legislative bodies, the shorthand notations of line-item budgeting may have been entirely satisfactory. Historically, such forms were often associated with a direct form of accountability in which the public bodies which approved budgets also approved monthly or quarterly lists of separate expenditures made under those budgets. (Many school boards and county and municipal governments still continue this practice today.)   With the growth of government, however, such procedures and the resultant information they yielded were replaced, leaving only the information-deficient line-item budget. The prospect of a present-day Congress or state legislature reviewing in detail thousands of such transactions involving billions of dollars is unthinkable. Yet, no fully adequate substitute for such detailed information and routinized accountability procedures has been devised.

One of the major difficulties in resolving this problem is the lack of an appropriate scheme for the classification of expenditures. If each purchase of fuel, payroll check, and travel reimbursement is not to be listed separately, some scheme for combining such separate expenses must be devised. One approach to classification has been the *functional budget* categories found in most federal grant application budgets and other types of project budgets. Classification of expenditures in this mode involves the use of such accounting categories as "personnel," "travel," "supplies," "office rent." While such an approach is integrated into most existing accounting schemes in the human services, it is not without its problems. The principle difficulty with this approach is that it yields relatively large amounts of information meaningful only in the context of fiscal accountability and expenditure control. In that sense it is definitely a step forward, but hardly an ideal solution to the managerial use of budgets.

Critics of functional budgeting have been expecially concerned with its inability to deal adequately with questions of purpose, goal attainment, and accomplishment of objectives. One can readily determine, for example, that an agency plans to spend $100,000 on personnel costs during the coming year, and yet have no idea whatsoever what the people hired will be doing. Thus, it is essential to recognize that functional budgets can never be interpreted in isolation. Without any accompanying narrative "work program" they yield only information that is narrowly fiscal.

Concern over the weaknesses of traditional budget formats and decision styles has led to several proposals for major reform of public budgetary practices. It should be noted from the outset, however, that most of these proposals involve modifications in the operation of entire budget systems, a task well beyond the means of individual agencies and programs. To the extent that such reform proposals are implemented, therefore, it is most likely that they will come down to agencies in the form of modified guidelines which agencies must adhere to in budget negotiations. Therefore, familiarity with the drift of such proposals is a matter of importance for human service administrators.

One of the most controversial proposals for budgetary reform has been the Programming-Planning-Budgeting System (PPBS) approach, first implemented in the federal government in 1965, and later abandoned. This approach is built upon economic analysis of program impact, using cost-benefit technology, and presumes to restrict budget decision-makers to the allocation of funds based upon their short- and long-term economic consequences. Even after its abandonment by the federal government, interest in this approach has remained high in many circles. To date, however, there are no fully operational PPBS systems anywhere in the United States. Despite this obvious failure there have been several discernable results of this movement: First, the debate over "comprehensive" versus "incremental" approaches to budget decisions has generated a range of new insights into the nature of budgetary decisions. Secondly, the "program budgeting" format of PPBS has generated renewed interest in the linkages between budgeting and planning, and particularly in formats for defining standard categories of service and their expected outputs or benefits. Recent audit guidelines by the American Institute of Certified Public Accountants for Voluntary Health and Welfare Organizations, and the elaborate UWASIS-II taxonomy of human services produced by the United Way of America are among the many concrete results of this interest. Thirdly, PPBS has sparked interest in a broad range of developmental work on the application of cost-benefit and other measurement approaches to the effectiveness of human services. Finally, the PPBS phenomenon has created a climate of opinion receptive to other new approaches to organizing the budgetary process. Two such approaches warrant additional discussion here.

One of these, Zero-Based Budgeting (ZBB) received considerable publicity following its endorsement by President Jimmy Carter during his tenure as governor of Georgia and again in the presidential campaign of 1976. While this approach offers some conceptually interesting possibilities, its superiority to traditional incremental approaches has yet to be demonstrated. In fact, there is some reason to believe that ZBB represents a formalized, rationalized form of incrementalism. The core of the ZBB approach involves formulation and consideration of "decision packages" which are sequentially redefined into ever more inclusive terms through the organizational hierarchy. It is, in most respects, a formalized version of the consensus-building process noted above. The single exception to this similarity between ZBB and incrementalism would appear to be the suggested "periodic" reassessment of the advisability of funding particular particular program packages (a "zero-base" approach). It should be noted that while such reconsideration of "base" as well as "increment" may be commendable, enforcing realistic (as opposed to pro forma) consideration of this question is likely to be as difficult under ZBB operating rules as it is for present decision-makers.

In other cases, it has been suggested that Management by Objectives is an appropriate antidote to the deficiencies of contemporary budgetary decision-making. Probably the most fruitful concept in the MBO approach for budgetary purposes is the measurement of objectives. A genuine revolution in human services budget-making could be accomplished if agency representatives and budgetary decision-makers could agree upon particular criteria for assessing agency performance and ways of linking those criteria to patterns of agency expenditure. However, conceptually attractive such an approach might be, it is not presently possible in an operational sense.

We have no choice but to classify budget-making approaches like ZBB and MBO as but unworkable ideas at present. If budget systems are to be changed for the better, however, these good ideas must be converted into operational realities.

Budgets in Fiscal Control

Once a budget has cleared the budgetary process, its management usefulness is not complete. Approved budgets are useful instruments for managerial control and direction of project activities throughout the fiscal period, if the administrator is aware of their potential. Indeed, human services might well take a cue from commercial enterprises, where managerial control is the principal justification for the use and development of budgets.

The elementary use of budgets in management control involves periodic comparison of budgeted projections on income and expenditure with actual figures, in order to identify areas of overspending in which problems may result, and areas of underspending, from which transfers of funds to other areas may be arranged. This usage of budgets involves two distinct levels of skill on the part of the administrator: first, a basic understanding of the operation of the particular accounting system involved, its chart of accounts, schedule of activities and events, such as monthly closings, postings, and completion of trial balances; second, the ability to make simple mathematical distributions, converting yearly budget figures to monthly or quarterly figures. In addition to such skills, the administrator must have access to certain internal financial reports—particularly the trial balances mentioned above. This may present some problems in organizations where the accounting staff is not accustomed to sharing such information. In most instances, however, it is relataively simple to establish a case for the managerial importance of this information. Assuming, therefore, that such information is available, the human services administrator should be able to keep an on-going check on the comparison of real and projected expenditures simply by comparing trial balances and budget projections.

It is a good idea when engaging in this practice to become familiar with the rules and regulations affecting internal transfers of funds. In some cases, for example, it is possible to transfer 10 percent or more from one budget category to another without approval of the funding authority, and to make larger transfers with approval. Thus, if it is determined that duplication costs are far exceeding estimates, while travel costs are well below estimates, a transfer between accounts may readily resolve any problems. One must be very careful, however, to determine the appropriate rules governing such transfers to avoid serious legal or ethical problems.

In cases where additional management control is required, some more elaborate extensions of the simple comparison of budget and trial balance can be worked out. One approach, for example, would be to break down the annual figures into detailed variable monthly or quarterly estimates, based on projected fluctuations in expenditure or revenue. If one simply divides each budget item by 12 or 3, this approach differs very little from that suggested above. However, if such estimates acutally incorporate assumptions about fluctuations, the usefulness of this approach will be in direct proportion to the level of precision in monitoring expenditures. (As an example, heating costs may be higher in winter and lower the rest of the year. Staff may travel more in spring and summer than in other seasons. Conference, travel, personnel, and consultation costs fluctuations may all be reasonably predictable.) In general, the greatest payoff from this approach can be expected when there are anticipated fluctuations in personnel expenditures, simply because these are the major items in most human service budgets.

In cases where approved budget funds may be released to an agency on a monthly or quarterly basis, or even as reimbursements for expenditures already made, it may be advisable also to combine this approach with cash-flow analysis which examines the rate of expenditures compared with available funds. It should go without saying that one cannot expend funds which are not actually available, and overdrafting agency checking accounts is at least as serious as overdrawing one's personal accounts.

In most instances, such regular monitoring of expenditures should enable the human services administrator to locate and even anticipate expenditure problems before they occur. Two additional steps need to be taken, however, to assure full-scale managerial control over the budget. The first is a "recap" session in which key agency administrators and staff members meet to review the implications of the approved budget, and adjust prior plans to the final outcomes. A key consideration for this group should be how realistic it is to assume that the agency will expend all of the approved funds during the fiscal period. If the approved budget calls for an increase in staff positions, for example, and positions must be created and advertised, and candidates must be interviewed, it may be several weeks, or even months, before the program can be "geared up" to full expenditure levels. Unless reallocated as outlined above, such funds will remain as surpluses at the end of the funding period—and conceivably reflect badly upon the agency with budget authorities. In many cases, anticipated surpluses of this type can be identified at the very beginning of the fiscal period and reallocated to other uses as they occur.

If the recap session is fairly thorough and no such reprogrammable items are identified, one can assume that the budget results are on target and things should proceed smoothly and according to plan. It is wise, however, to repeat an examination procedure of this type at intervals during the year. For example, the monthly comparison of budgeted and actual expenditures noted above for the responsible administrator might "flag" possible troublesome items for reallocation on a quarterly basis. In most instances, the earlier such variances are identified the more readily one can take action to correct them. In any event, one should usually be prepared to deal with most such matters by early in the fourth quarter of the fiscal year, since any shorter time frame may necessitate hasty and inappropriate actions.

In sum then, the key aspect involved in linking the budget with control procedures in human service agencies involves identifying relevant information sources, such as the trial balance, and fitting the timing of budget assumptions about projected expenditures with information about actual performance. While such an approach will not provide comprehensive or fully up-to-date control of expenditures, it does offer a significant level of management control over actual performance consistent with the limits of information processing and accounting technology extant in most human service agencies today.

Conclusion

Financial management in all human service organizations is a set of inter-related activities encompassing fund-raising, allocation decision-making, fiscal control, evaluation, and planning. Budgets are a critical element in all of these areas. Key elements in budget-making involve working out or identifying the plan or program of activities to be budgeted, identifying and pricing the key expenditure items linked with that plan, and building a consensus for the resultant budget proposal with important budget reference groups including committees, boards of directors, staff members, and relevent decision authorities. The actual task of working up a proposal involves identifying formal rules and guidelines, as well as unearthing informal understandings which bear on the matter. Once a proposal has been worked up, the details of presentation should also be carefully planned and executed. Whether it is "presented" by mail, in person, or at a formal public hearing, the rhetoric of the presentation and the impressions thus created are not matters to be left to chance. Once the budget has been approved, it can have further management uses in control of program expenditures, provided the administrator has access to information on actual expenditure patterns to compare with budget projections.

The suggestions contained in this introductory review of budget-making in human service agencies in no way exhaust the possibilities. This discussion is intended only to suggest the rough outlines of the "concept map" of the subject. As such, it should be seen as a prelude to career-long exploration and refinement of the knowledge and skills appropriate to this provocative subject.

Reference

Braybrooke, David, and Charles Lindblom. *A Strategy of Decision*. New York: Free Press, 1963.

Committee on Voluntary Health and Welfare Organizations. *Audits of Voluntary Health and Welfare Organizations*. New York: American Institute of Certified Public Accountants, 1974.

Gross, Malvern. "The Importance of Budgeting." Simon Slavin, ed. *Social Administration*. New York: Haworth Press, 1978.

Hyde, Albert C. and Jay M. Schafritz. *Government Budgeting: Theory, Process, Politics*. Oak Park, Illinois: Moore Publishing, 1978.

Lindblom, Charles. "The Science of Muddling Through." *Public Administration Review* 19 (1959): 79–88.

Lindblom, Charles. "Still Muddling Not Yet Through." *Public Administration Review* 39 (Nov.-Dec. 1979): 5–12.

Lohmann, Roger A. *Breaking Even: Financial Management in Non-Profit Human Services*. Philadelphia: Temple University Press, 1980.

Lohmann, Roger A. "Break Even Analysis: A Tool for Budgetary Planning." *Social Work* 21 (July 1976): 300–308.

Lyden, Fremont and Ernest Miller. *Programming, Planning, Budgeting: A Systems Approach to Management*. Chicago: Markham, 1967.

March, Michael and Edward Newman. "Financing Social Welfare: Government Allocation Procedures." *Encyclopedia of Social Work* 16th ed Robert Morris, ed. New York: National Association of Social Workers, 1970 426–43.

Novick, David. *Program Budgeting*. Cambridge, Mass: Harvard University; Press, 1965.

Phyrr, Peter. "The Zero-Base Approach to Governmental Budgeting." *Public Administration Review* 37 (1977): 2.

United Way of America. *UWASIS II A Taxonomy of Social Goals and Human Service Programs*. Alexanderia, Va: United Way, 1976.

Wildavsky, Aaron. *The Politics of the Budgetary Process* 2nd ed Boston: Little, Brown, 1974.

THE DESIGN
OF INFORMATION
SYSTEMS

Thomas W. Weirich

8

The design of a management information system is usually viewed as a technical problem. In this volume we wish to call attention to our view that every administrative process uses both ideological and technical data as a basis for decision-making. Dr. Weirich's essay focuses on the administrator's perspectives and the critical choices that must be made to achieve an appropriate, efficient, and effective information system.

The discussion complements Slavin's, Gummer's, and Wilson's essays as it argues that information systems must be understood within their organizational context. Accordingly, Dr. Weirich is concerned with (1) organizational politics and power, (2) resources, (3) ideology, (4) technology, (5) decision-making, and (6)innovation and change. This chapter reflects the author's extensive experience with the design, operation, and evaluation of management information systems in the public sector. Thus the discussion is of practical use for the administrator as it addresses both theoretical and operational aspects.

The age of the computer has finally reached the social services. Many agencies are struggling to implement viable data-processing systems, while many others are contemplating such innovations. Funders are asking for ever more extensive reporting, and the public is increasing its demands for accountability. The need for information is so extensive that it is clear that the automated information system will be a fact of life for future social service administrators. Whether this will represent a burdensome intrusion into the administrator's realm or a useful tool to aid in management will depend in part upon the administrator's ability to manage the information

142

system. This in turn will depend upon the administrator's understanding of the position of the information system within the agency context.

The purposes of this discussion are to present some of the essential administrative and organizational dimensions of computerized information systems, and to point out the special problems and prospects for the social services. Primary attention will be given to the administrator's point of view, based upon the premise that he or she will make the critical choices. This chapter will not be a technical discussion of computerization and computers, nor will it be a cookbook on implementation. The administrator can employ experts to cope with the technological aspects, but he or she must first be prepared to cope with the experts.

The main theme pursued here is that information systems must be understood within the context of the entire agency or organization. They are not independent operations, but instead interact with the other parts of the organization and its surroundings. The theme is clearly stated by Lucas (1975, p. 6):

> An information system exists within the context of the organization; the problems of information systems are not solely technical in nature. Though there are technical problems and challenges, we have always been more successful in solving these problems than in dealing with organizational issues. It is our contention that *the major reason most information systems have failed is that we have ignored organizational behavior problems in the design and operation of computer-based information systems*. If steps are not taken to understand and solve these organizational behavior problems, systems will continue to fail (emphasis in original).

The situation in the social services is perhaps more difficult than elsewhere, for an organizational perspective on services is not fully developed. A discussion is needed, then, of the organizational issues in social services and how these inform the problem of computerized information systems.

It should be said that most agencies already have information systems of some sort. Those hurriedly scribbled case notes stuffed into a bottom desk drawer for future reference, or the boxes of case narratives stacked along the wall, differ only in sophistication and order from a well-oiled automated system. Most agencies have the rudiments of a management information system which can be used as starting points for automation. The essence of a management information system is the regular collection, processing, storage, retrieval, and presentation of standardized information deemed important to the organization. Historically these processes have been done by hand, but are now being gradually assigned to computers. Man or machine, the acid test for any information system is the degree to which it is actually used.

This discussion will be arranged around six major issues: organizational politics and power, resources, ideology, technology, decision-making, and innovation and change.

Organizational Politics and Power

Political action occurs both outside and inside the social service organization. Two trends in the political context help explain the increased importance of information systems. The first is the rationalization of the decision-making processes in the public policy sphere. Planning, controlled program change, and evaluation are becoming more important and thus increasing the demand for extensive agency-level data. Program, Planning, and Budgeting Systm (PPBS), Goal Oriented Social Services (GOSS), and Zero-Based Budgeting are manifestations of the rationalization process, each representing a different approach to improved decision-making.

A second trend is the increased demand for accountability, in terms of both fiscal control and program effectiveness. After years of unquestioned growth produced few measurable results, the services are now being asked to account for money spent and to prove some impact is being made. This too requires the collection of agency-level information.

These external changes have created the need for agency-level information, and most service policies now require some formalized reporting. Since these information needs are continuous and regular, one-time sporadic reports are no longer sufficient. Permanent mechanisms are needed to supply data on regular schedules and in fixed formats, as well as for special requests. The tasks are growing too large to be handled by hand or with part-time clerical workers. As a result, social service organizations are searching for and implementing computerized information systems. And those that already have such systems in place are trying desperately to understand them. For most service agencies, all of this constitutes a major organizational change.

Since the establishment of an information system is a major internal change, it threatens organizational power structures, domains, and areas of autonomy. It will thus probably generate substantial amounts of resistance and possibly conflict. To overcome the resistances, the initiators of the information system will need an established and stable power base. The persuasion of an expert or an ideological argument will be sufficient in a few cases, but the exercise of formal authority will be required in most. The lure of additional resources or power may act as incentives for those outside formal authority structures (Lucas, 1975; pp. 16–19; Quinn, 1973, pp. 19–23).

One change in the power structure will be that information system opertors will become important and influential actors. Management will become dependent upon the operators for the production of reports which satisfy external requirements and, to the extent the information sytem contributes to administrative practice, will look to the operators for advice. Line staff will use the system for record-keeping, identification data, or possibly referral help. The information system operators thus become the center of an essential communications network. They also will acquire authority to dictate certain organizational behaviors, such as the questions asked of clients and the categories used to define problems. In one agency both supervisors and staff frequently asked the information specialist for advice on how to code client problems. Eventually the standardization of the information system was internalized, and the precoded numbers for specific problems replaced more qualitative descriptions in normal conversion; unusual problems became "Code 99s."

The implementation of an information system increases the power of some organizational members while it reduces the autonomy of others (Quinn, 1973, pp. 9–12). Program accountability, for example, is more clearly defined, and substantial amounts of information can be produced to monitor performance. Those receiving the data have a continuous and "objective" supply of information which can be used to influence decisions. Program units, therefore, become more visible and must become more concerned with satisfying established performance standards. In one project, for example, a housing unit reported a large number of requests withdrawn by clients. Upon investigation it was found that the unit head feared losing staff if her unit had a poor performance record. To avoid reporting unmet needs for unavailable housing (even in a poor housing market), the unit head informed clients that there was little hope of placement and asked if they would like to withdraw the requests. Reporting large numbers of withdrawals seemed less threatening to this administrator than establishing a record of extensive unmet housing needs.

At the client-worker level, the flexibility of interaction may be reduced, with less discretion allowed in what information is elicited from clients. A computerized data collection form can become a determinant of the course of an interview, and a precoded list of problems and services can become a framework in which needs and actions are defined. Classification can easily become an end in itself, at the expense of the unique characteristics of each client.

Professional social service workers will no doubt resist these kinds of intrusions into their practice domains, and will resent the conformity that is implied. Missing information and incomplete forms can become a chronic problem, and some workers will insist upon narrative descriptions instead of precoded categories. One demonstration project established a workers task force to increase involvement in system design and reduce resistance to the use of forms and codes. This seemed to improve performance of information system tasks and increase workers' understanding of the over-all purpose of the system. The dependence of final reports upon each form and each coded message was clarified. Although such involvement is no guarantee of successful implementation, it can improve both understanding and commitment. Not incidentally, it is also a way to co-opt an important power block within the agency.

Service administration is itself an exercise in negotiating the tension between autonomy and control. Constituent parts of an agency fight to protect and improve their positions, while administrators push toward centralized control. Professions defend their areas of professional judgement and discretion. An information system must be established and survive among these larger political issues, and is never independent of them.

Resources

Most social service administrators will realize that an information system requires extensive new resources, but some may not realize just *how extensive* the needs will be. Even in limited versions an information system is expensive. In one demonstration project, for example, a proposal for a complete system estimated developmental costs equal to the entire project's yearly budget, and this did not even include operating expenses. The proposal was politely rejected as fanciful.

An information system is labor intensive to develop and capital intensive to run. Planning, design, and implementation require costly specialized expertise. Few agencies have employees with the necessary skills, and trial-and-error development is out of the question. Outside technicians are thus the only answer. Since information systems for social services are not yet common, there are few real "experts" around. Experience with other areas, even in the human services, may not be directly transferable, forcing the administrator to choose a consultant with unclear evidence of competence. Even when a qualified consultant can be found, the social service administrator's inexperience with such technical work puts the agency at a disadvantage in specifying the terms of the work contract. One can easily be overwhelmed by the jargon, charts, and possibilities. Social service administrators will need some sophistication in the use of consultants, as well as an awareness of the potential and limitations of computers.

The operating technology for the information system is also expensive, requiring costly machines or machine time, specially designed forms, and various other supplies. Salaries must also be paid for the technicians who run and maintain the system, and for periodic updates of the system design. Often overlooked is the tremendous need for training, both during implementation and afterward. It is possible to contract the operation of a system completely or partially to an outside firm, including training tasks. Although this relieves the agency of some of the more technical problems the resultant loss of control may reduce the reliability and responsiveness of the system.

Since the need for new human and capital resources is so great, it is almost impossible to avoid increased spending. Most service agencies do not have a "surplus" for investment in automation, which means that present resources will have to be diverted or new funding acquired. Internal reallocations are likely to be challenged, since that would mean taking funds from direct services and increasing the administrative cadre. New funding means a change in economic dependencies, either intensifying the use of established funding streams or developing new ones. Collaboration with other agenies is one possibility, if agreement on a shared system design can be achieved. In one state a consortium of local agencies has been formed to share experiences and costs of information system development. Codes or procedures that have been tested in one locale are adapted to a new setting, avoiding both the pain and the expense of starting from scratch.

Many of the difficulties in obtaining the needed resources were experienced by one major demonstration project in social service integregation. Initial attempts at system development were made by middle-level management people, who experimented with forms, codes, and record-keeping. It quickly became apparent that the task was too large and complicated for the non-expert, and that outside help would be needed. The agency could not hire its own staff, however, and had to rely upon external sources of help. Since it was the local branch of a state-administered department, the agency sought help from its parent organization. A limited amount of technical assistance was obtained, but this was ultimately ineffective in implementing the system. A state-level office of data-processing already existed, and it was reluctant to set up a local independent operation. Furthermore, the assistance given was sporadic, diverted by other priorities, and not attuned to local circumstances and needs. Trying a different strategy, the agency issued a number of purchase of service contracts, funded through special project monies and agreements with local governments. A contract with a data-processing branch of a neighboring college failed because of lack of attention and a mismatch in needed expertise. An individual consultant produced a grandiose design for the project, too sophisticated and expensive for its use. The project finally hired an individual consultant through a series of personal service contracts which stipulated close working relationships with project administration. Although the project finally established control over system development, it could not obtain funding equal to the task of implementation, and the system suffered from many setbacks and delays. The lack of resources and an inability to control available resources were at the root of many of the project's information system troubles.

The balance between control and expense will be one of the most difficult issues confronted. Those rich enough might be able to hire a complete staff and lease all necessary equipment thus avoiding control problems. Others may be completely dependent upon outside resources for system operation. The most typical, and possibly most desirable, arrangement will be a mixture of in-house staff and outside contracts. A systems analyst with a small clerical staff, for example, could handle the operation, maintenance, and interpretation of the system, while processing and storage could be purchased from outside providers. In this way, an agency could derive the benefits of computerized information processing, without shouldering the burden of capital investment.

Ideology

Conflicting values can produce many problems with information systems in the social services. Information systems imply a certain ideology, a world-view containing attitudes and beliefs about the way things are or should be. It assumes a way of thinking and acting and an approach to problem solution that are basically compatible with the systemic approach. Its values and norms define desirable organizational characteristics and behavior. These values may conflict with those of the social service agency, especially that of professionalism, and lead to misunderstandings and resistance. Prominent values often at issue are clarity, uniformity, permanency, and openness.

CLARITY

A fundamental prerequisite of an operational information system is clarity. Organizational goals need to be clearly identified and operationalized into measurable objectives. Organizational activities need to be clearly defined and concise indicators of the extent of services must be established. Extensive numbered system codes for needs, services, and providers illustrate the need for detailed clarity. The implementation of an information system forces increased clarity in organizational characteristics (Quinn, 1973, pp. 12–16).

Social service organizations are typified by ambiguity rather than clarity. Goals are not always clear, and often consist of general value statements.

Objectives are difficult to specify and are seldom stated in measurable terms, some defy operationalization; and official goals may not even reflect the actual operating goals of the agency. Services are difficult to divide into measurable units because many categories overlap.

In addition, it is frequently unclear how the information system will ultimately be used, a situation that was evident in the demonstration project mentioned above. Internal reporting requirements and the procedures for report utilization were never specified. Months were devoted to the specification of problem and service codes, while the articulation of the information system's mission with the organization's goal structure was neglected. The project's information system consultant attributed this to a basic misconception of what the information system was expected to do. The project's administration really wanted an "information management" system, not a "management information" system. The administration was motivated primarily by its need to respond to accountability demands and its desire to reduce paperwork. The most pressing organizational problems were the overwhelming information *processing* tasks, not the reform of decision-making processes.

UNIFORMITY

If clarity is the primary conceptual expectation of an information system, then uniformity is the primary behavioral norm. To function reliably an information system must use a standardized language (i.e., definitions, terms, codes) and a routinized set of procedures (ef. Quinn, 1973, pp. 7–9). Furthermore, these must be employed consistently by all users; for without a high degree of conformity, the data will be unreliable, the system will have little credibility, and the products of the system will probably not be used (Lucas, 1975, p. 4). For the administrator this means an increased emphasis on organizational control of employee behavior, through rule-making, quality control monitoring, and enforcement.

A typical service organization, however, has high degrees of pluralism and non-conformity. Such diversity increases with the size of the organization, as the proportion of professionals and the number of specialty units increase. Each professional group and program unit develops its own definitions, language, and procedures. Underlying these are basic differences in delivery paradigms and professional orientations. Attempts to change these features to a single format suitable to the information system can generate strong resistance (Zaltman et al., 1973).

The demonstration project that has been serving as an example had two special problems in this area. First, the project had five geographically dispersed and historically distinct service centers. The management and staff of each center had unique characteristics (one center was dominated by mental health related people, for example, while another had mostly child welfare staff), and each developed its own orientation to the information system. System terms and definitions were interpreted differently, resulting in inconsistencies in the overall system. The second problem came with an attempt to integrate different professional groups into a single delivery structure. The groups held onto their service concepts and forced them into the information system. The most apparent results were separate lists of service codes for mental health and non-mental health activities, and a long list of mental health oriented diagnostic codes, many of which overlapped the more general service needs codes.

PERMANENCY

An information system requires a relatively high degree of organizational stability during its development and implementation. It also needs permanency to be economically run. The design stages are long and the programming is complex. It is extremely difficult to establish a system for an organization that is constantly changing its central features. Time must also be allowed for "debugging" and refinement. The investments made in development, hardware, and supplies need to be stretched over a lengthy period of time. Although most systems attempt to be open to changes, realistically flexibility, must be limited.

A social service agency, on the other hand, can be a very unstable entity, especially in the uncertain environment of the public organization. Basic structures and processes change over time, and new services and practices emerge in response to professional developments and community needs. Policies change, creating new lines of authority, demanding new forms of data, and reshuffling funding streams. Research and demonstration projects fare even worse, having far too short a life span. The administrator is faced with a basic dilemma between responsiveness to information needs and responsible information management. Uncontrolled program changes can make the information system useless, while over-protection of the information system can endanger program effectiveness and enforce program rigidity.

OPENNESS

A final value assumption of an information system is openness. The assumption is that data needed by the system is available and readily given. A "complete" system needs a complete data base, and arbitrary barriers which impede that completeness must be avoided. Openness, however, need not mean that information is accessible to anyone. Once stored, the data base is usually protected from unauthorized entry; but such protection is not assured. A contributor may fear that the information given in confidence will later surface in unanticipated and unwanted ways. (The controversy over data banks and individual privacy is not limited to the social services, as there is also growing concern over credit, health, and educational records.)

Privacy is a central value in most social service agencies. The client-worker relationship is strictly confidential and held to be immune from intrusion. The rights of the client are paramount, and any attempts to expose personal information are resisted. Thus, social service workers may interpret extensive data collection as an intrusion into their professional domain and a violation of the client-worker relationship. The bonds of trust between client and worker are threatened, as are the prerogatives of professional discretion. To defend against these possibilities the service worker may purposely omit or change information, with the result that information is incomplete and unreliable.

Organizational privacy can also be threatened, since the performance of subunits becomes more visible when an information system is implemented. Without an information system subunits can retain information that might reflect negatively on their performance. With an information system, however, such information *automatically* goes to people outside of the unit, to superiors and possible competitors. The information is available for evaluation of the unit and as the basis for action against it. To prevent such negative repercussions the unit may resist participation or even "fudge" its unit reports. The housing unit mentioned above would have been more comfortable if it could have kept its problems with the housing market secret, but since the information had to be given, the least threatening reporting code was used.

These value conflicts have not received much attention in discussions of social service information systems, partly because administrators have not been sensitive to their existence. With the realization that system implementation affects some of the basic value foundations of their agencies, perhaps administrators can more effectively prepare for and confront such problems.

Technology

Information processing technology can be truly dazzling, and the inexperienced service administrator can be overwhelmed by the parade of the latest gadgetry, independent of its utility. Indeed, the future will probably see the incorporation of automation into service administration in creative and productive ways. In the meantime, however, there are fundamental issues which need to be confronted. One of the most important is the basic incompatibility between the technologies of information systems and social services.

Information system technologies are highly determinant; they are exact, certain, and predictable (Thompson, 1967.) Their products are clearly defined, and the paths to their achievement are concise and reliable. Before a computer program can be run, the formats for all outputs must be specified in detail, each process and step must be precisely defined and interconnected with others, and the strict specifications for data input must be set. The complex electronics of the computer are intolerant; ask any beginner who has sat at a terminal trying to run the simplest of programs. Because of the interdependence of system parts, a small change at one point, such as a slight change in a data collection form, will have ripple effects throughout the system. Problems arise when such an exacting technology is joined with one that is almost the exact opposite.

Social service technologies are patently indeterminant. Goals and objectives are ill-defined, supported by low consensus, and sometimes conflicting. They change with the winds in the policy sphere, so that many administrators are reluctant to be tied to the specification required by an information system. Furthermore, regular reports can be all too revealing of agency performance.

The critical problem, however, is the extreme uncertainty of the connections between service goals and organizational activities. There are few proven solutions, and most delivery strategies are complex, changeable combinations of many approaches. Since indeterminancy makes it difficult for the information system to accurately mirror service delivery, problems arise in both design and interpretation.

This technological mismatch is especially apparent in demonstration projects. Here, change and development are organizational goals, and many projects emerge without any clearly defined delivery model. In this situation it is virtually impossible to design an information system that accurately catches the present project while it remains flexible enough for adaptation to future unknown changes. Some information system specialists recommend delaying design and implementation until an agency has stabilized and its delivery model has crystalized. Administrators know that this could be a long wait, and the more practical solution will be some concessions on both sides.

Decision-Making

One of the most frequently heard justifications for an information system is the potential contribution to decision-making. This justification stems from a basic value assumption, and the central premise of information systems—

rationality. People, management and workers, are assumed to be rational beings, solving problems and making decisions based upon facts, logical connections between means and ends, and expertise. The only limits to these processes are the lack of sufficient information and poor information—processing techniques. The establishment of an information system is intended to supply all of the needed data and to simplify processing, thus enabling people to make more rational choices. Indeed, the real zealots believe that *the* solution to poor decision-making is automation.

Contrary to this, however, most organizations and the people who run them are not perfectly rational. Their rationality is "bounded" by both internal capacities and external constraints (Simon, 1965; Thompson, 1967). Service administrators know that this is especially true of human service organizations (Hasenfeld and English, 1974). Decisions are often made on political grounds, for ideological reasons, out of tradition or habit, because of economic feasibility, from personal intuition or bias, or sometimes from simple expediency. Some decisions are never consciously made; things just seem to happen. Skilled administrators use an informal "intelligence" network as the source of much information, and no information system will replace these more qualitative inputs (Holland, 1976).

Thus, the rationalization of decision-making in the social services is still incomplete. Nor is it specified how information systems are to be integrated into regular decision-making processes, let alone if it can be done at all. Both management and workers lack experience in the use of information systems, and the sophisticated techniques and potentials are new and strange. Some speculate that automation is just too new in the field of social services, as service professionals have not come to understand how it can be made to help them. One consultant reported, "I spent months just holding hands and telling staff that it is not 'Big Brother,' it is not '1984.'"

Given the precarious nature of social service organizations' environments, the indeterminancy of their technologies, and the state of administrative practice, non-rational decision-making is both understandable and probably necessary. These circumstances, however, also force service administrators to be more realistic in their expectations of automated information systems. It should be clear that computerization is *not* a magical solution to the problems of decision-making, and computer printouts will not replace sound administrative judgment.

Innovation and Change

The organizational characteristics discussed thus far interact with the information system. To a very large extent they will determine an agency's ability to implement. Without sufficient power and resources an administrator will not be able to initiate and sustain extensive innovation. A hospitable ideological context will reduce resistance to the change, while skillful political action will be needed to negotiate specific strategies and conflicts. Finally, adjustments in service technology and decision-making styles will be needed to make an information system more relevant.

In addition, these factors must be combined at an opportune time and under the right conditions. For example, periods of external pressure for increased accountability may be a good time to seek additional resources for system support, while outside demands also justify change internally. On the other hand, institutionalization of an information system already designed may be easier during calm periods, when standardization is possible and few changes required.

Successful innovation will also depend upon the willingness of agency staff to cooperate. Since the reliability of the system rests upon the data collection efforts of staff, their performance is essential. Staff resistance can frustrate the fanciest of designs. Training is of course one change strategy, effective for educating staff in the potentials and limitations of automation and in learning required procedures. Early and continuous involvement in the design and refinement of the system will increase commitment to the project and reduce some of the mysticism of computerization. Contributions and criticisms from staff will help assure that the system will meet their needs as well as the administration's, and might reduce some of the more burdensome and unnecessary procedures. Administrators will also have to use consultants effectively, taking care to specify expectations clearly and monitor development. The organization of information system "task forces" at crucial agency levels, such as line staff, clerical workers, and managers, to review and help in design is a promising change strategy. At the same time, the danger of the information system becoming an independent end in itself should be avoided.

Ultimately, successful implementation will depend upon judgments by all participants, especially administrators, that the information system is worth the trouble (cf. Salasin and Davis, 1976). There has to be a payoff, or a yield. If the system actually helps people do their work, solve their problems, and make their decisions, then it will be appreciated and used. One of the best ways to increase support for an information system, to increase its usage, and to improve its performance, is to make it satisfy individual and organizational needs (Lucas, 1975). These needs should be identified at the very outset, and should remain in focus throughout.

At the present time the anticipation of real benefits from a computerized information system in the social services is problematic. A number of issues remain unresolved. First, the benefits for accountability and research purposes are the most apparent. Improved data bases and reporting will certainly help in the general evaluation and understanding of the services. On the organizational level the situation is less clear. There is no tradition of regular use of information system products, and the integration of a system into the everyday work patterns has yet to be accomplished. The benefits on the worker level, in case management for example, will have to be demonstrated and refined. The claims made for simplification of tasks and improved monitoring and follow-up will have to be sustantiated, and it is doubtful that the system alone will cause better service follow-ups if none were done before it.

On the management level, the utility of the information system for decision-making, evaluation, and planning is still unproven. Administrators and managers will have to "learn" how to use the system, especially if it is to be more than just a report-generating device. Such learning can not take place without an interest in and a commitment to improved information management. Thus the steady commitment and support of top administrators are essential. Starting with a survey of informational needs for management decisions, and a review of existing ways information is obtained and processed, the administration can carefully build a new system.

Conclusion

The theme pursued here has been that social service information systems have to be understood within their organizational contexts. Service administrators will have to consider organizational factors as well as technical ones in their decisions to initiate, implement, and routinize new systems. Information systems can be magnificent, but they are not magic. The service administrator need not be mystified by their hardware, for in the end it is the administrator's hard work that will determine the system's usefulness. Although the computerized information system can certainly contribute to decision-making, it is no substitute for administrative judgment.

References

Hasenfeld, Yeheskel, and Richard A. English, eds. *Human Service Organizations*. Ann Arbor: University of Michigan Press, 1974.

Holland, Thomas P. "Information and Decision Making in Human Services." *Administration in Mental Health* 4, no. 1 (Fall 1976): 26–35.

Lucas, Henry C., Jr. *Why Information Systems Fail*. New York: Columbia University Press, 1975.

Quinn, Robert E. "Computerization and the Integregation of Services: An Empirical Study." In *Services Integregation: Selected Research Studies*. Cincinnati:

Information Systems Center, 1973.

Salasin, Susan E., and Howard R. Davis. "Achieving Desired Policy or Practice Changes: Findings Alone Won't Do It." In *HEW Region III Evaluation Conference: New Perspectives, Summary of Proceedings,* Philadelphia, D.H.E.W., Oct. 19–22, 1976.

Simon, Herbert. *Administrative Behavior.* New York: Free Press, 1965.

Thompson, James D. *Organizations in Action.* New York: McGraw-Hill, 1967.
Margie Zaltman, Gerald, Robert Duncan, and Jonny Holbek. *Innovations and Organizations.* New York: Wiley, 1973.

A FRAMEWORK FOR PROJECT DEVELOPMENT

Albert E. Wilkerson

9

As public money has been increasingly available to social agencies for special projects, it becomes a priority task for the social administrator to perform the leadership function necessary in planning for and/or executing these special programs. Professor Wilkerson bases this discussion on his years of experience with special projects.

The author is clear in his priorities; he spends a major portion of this chapter on the context of and purpose for the project as it relates to agency function. In an historical overview, Dr. Wilkerson explores the social work profession's concern with environment and psyche, and its changing interests and priorities. He also examines assumptions and myths about cause and effect, about creativity and innovation.

And, finally, Professor Wilkerson addresses the nitty-gritty of proposal preparation and negotiation through a series of trenchant questions and guidelines. His final comments on the monitoring and evaluation of proposals are directly related to Hirschhorn's essay on evaluation.

The availability of project funds from governmental agencies and private sources has had a significant influence on the design, quality, and extent of social welfare programs during the past several decades. Neighborhood organizations, human service agencies, and educational institutions have been able to launch new and experimental programs and services that would have been inhibited by normal budget constraints. These programs are meant to reflect recognized social needs, interests, and priorities at the frontier boundaries of social welfare as an organized effort.

Such programs are visible statements of the values, beliefs, aspirations, and myths that characterize a society at a given moment in its history. The availability of the funding is an expression of a positive direction and goodwill on the part of government and of private resources. But they express, too, the paucity of public commitment and the handicaps of an underdeveloped social welfare technology, in a search for workable formulas that serve both individual strivings and the societal purpose for common good.

That these social welfare situations are not regularly built strongly into the mainstream of public policy and institutional functions indicates the existence of counter-values within our political and economic systems. That the funds for frontier programs are scarce and promote fierce competition reveals the ambivalence that Western society tends to have about human development, social experimentation, and equalitarianism. Within this context—humanistic, pluralistic, and ambivalent—the social work administrator has an opportunity through project development to extend services, create new services, and undertake training programs and research.

Project Development Shapes Agency Function

A project proposal is a program design with supporting documentation that establishes organizational credibility and makes a case for external funding. It sets forth what is needed, why it is needed, and how it is to be structured and implemented to achieve the desired outcome. Essentially, the components in defining and supporting a proposed service, training, demonstration, or experimental program are the same as those in any sound research plan. A project proposal, in addition to the design of format and execution, includes assumptions about the nature of the problem, theoretical and practice knowledge and their application in other approaches to the problem or task, a defense of the approach selected, a time-frame, arrangements for monitoring and evaluation, and a budget.

To pursue funds is tempting in times of either affluence or recession. The temptation to branch out into activities that seem avant-grade, particularly during a period of social reform, is strong. And the temptation for agencies to add a program dimension that deviates sharply from the criticized traditional helping methods is pressing. But a decision to design a new program should emerge not from these enticements but from the agency's purpose, current activities and capabilities, and clearly perceived future directions. The introduction of a new program, no matter how small, significantly alters the agency's basic program gestalt, the agency's view of itself, and staff attitudes and behaviors. A program created primarily as a response to the availability of funds or the popularity of a new cause gives evidence of a severe budget crisis, diminishing clarity of agency function, or weak administrative leadership.

Intellectual commitment and psychological involvement of the total staff is crucial, even if they are not to be engaged directly in carrying out the program. A new program requires special attention, nurturing, and agency resource priority if it is to succeed. To give it sustenance, it must be highlighted for a time beyond its actual merit. Preferential treatment is a natural source for staff resentment and hostility. These emotions are easily intensified when the project is manned by outsiders employed specifically for the project, when the methodology used in the project is foreign to the staff as a whole, or if the basic assumptions about the nature of the problem are contradictory to the agency's central belief system.

Sound agency decision to pursue funds and sound use of project funds require that the new program represent the begining of a new agency direction that is expected to continue over a period of years. It should be a clear clue that the agency is now putting into place a component, thrust, or point of view by which it is willing to be defined, shaped, and known functionally and ideologically. If the agency does not anticipate this shift in gestalt, the decision to launch the program was ill-advised. Projects that are one-shot efforts expire at the end of the budget period are generally a waste of money; and they can have detrimental effects on the staff if they are seen as an aborted effort in social planning and professional practice.

The administrator must also determine whether or not there will be sufficient staff competence to maximize the project's possibility for success. There is nothing more pathetic than a group of clinically-oriented social workers trying to do social planning and community organization tasks for which they are not equipped, or planning persons suddenly shifting to training clinical tasks when they themselves do not comprehend the frameworks and dynamics of the several helping processes. Such changes in professional function are not at all unusual during the present period, as social workers eagerly search for updating through new tasks and new methodologies.

Determinants of Social Problem Definition

How any given social problem becomes catapulted into major and professional attention, and what processes give rank order to social problem priorities, are interesting questions for more intensive social science study. In the meantime, it does seem clear that social work interests during the past several decades have closely followed those federal priority determinations to which project funds are attached. The announcement of a federal interest, supported by governmental programs and awards for projects, may be counted on to become an immediate priority in social work agencies and social work education. Alcoholism, day care, and mental retardation are examples of this phenomenon. On the other hand, mental health and child welfare are fields with which social work has long been concerned and which finally came into their own as national interests. Prison systems and juvenile correctional facilities have still not significantly attracted the attention of the human service professionals. Social work interest in rehabilitative processes for incarcerated persons will no doubt continue to be delayed until federal interest and stimulation have ripened.

Federal response to a particular social problem surely derives in part from a needs assessment and from the slow but steady influence of federal bureaucrats sincerely dedicated to social problem-solving. But in a pluralistic society these targets and priorities are set in the main through political responses to powerful external pressures, through the normal processes of political bargaining, and through sheer expediency.

The states, of course, follow in large measure the leads of the federal government in determining what social programs they will initiate or emphasize. The political history of each state and country, is also a determinant; localities create a certain climate for social welfare development around favorite problems (Elazar, 1972). The whims of state politicians and bureaucrats are immediately discerned through their selective responses to federal guidelines. This patchwork pattern and constantly shifting scene does not lend itself to building state or regional foundations upon which social welfare programs can be rationally developed with any satisfactory degree of stability and continuity. The ineffectiveness of social welfare perspectives and decisions on the state and local levels explodes the myth that these units know their needs best and will respond to them effectively when given the opportunity.

The civil rights movement, the impetus for the present reform era, has of course been a major determinant in defining social priorities, creating assumptions about the nature of these problems, and giving direction for approaches to solution. The initial focus on the American poor in general and the Black population in particular has spread, as expected in reform movements, to cover a wide range of rights, opportunities, and resources for a range of neglected and disadvantaged groups. Social programs, from the federal level to the traditional volunteer agency, to neighborhood and self-help activities, all quickly accommodate to the perspectives, goals, and methodologies either stated or implied within the social reform context. This dramatic shift in ideology and task assignments has proven to be both challenging and agonizing for the human services professions and society at large.

The Environment Versus the Psyche

Since the beginnings of the profession at the end of the last century, social workers have understood that political and economic policies and practices significantly shape the private destinies of large sub-populations in a pre-determined way. Thus, attempts have been made in turn to modify these systems by humanizing or softening those forces over which the individual citizen has little or no control. Changes have indeed been made; and social workers have played some part in them. But social workers and other helping professions also came to an early recognition that the personal history of individuals is a complex matter and that psychological develop-ment and established behavior patterns can pit one against himself even while the help he needs is being offered.

In retrospect, there seems no doubt that the social worker's need for, and fascination with, dynamic psychology too greatly influenced casework and group work methods and too narrowly defined the scope of social work practice. But it is easy to understand how this occurred. The client fre-quently comes to the agency already psychologically damaged by internal and external pressures. The person who has had little success has obviously not had a life experience in developing successful coping abilities. The circle of hopelessness, anger, and indecision has engulfed the psychologi-cal-self. This encasement in defeat is further complicated by the human tendency to act on impulse and emotion rather than on intelligence and common sense. Thus, no matter how much environmental the origin of the problem, the psychological overtones and damage may be considerable.

Given this set of circumstances, the social work emphasis on clinical approaches to human problems was related to two sets of practice experi-ences or perceptions of the "problem." On the one hand, it was clear that the client's feelings, attitudes, and behaviors had to be dealt with if he were to maximize his use of even the most concrete of social services, and that the task was to be approached within a psychological context not unlike problem-solving around intensely personal problems. On the other hand, the lack of available concrete resources at the point that the client is in need can cause unbearable professional anxiety. To manage this anxiety, social work then defined opportunity-development and resource-acquisition as further psychological and social tasks for the client, thus asking the client to do what the professional was himself unable to accomplish.

In defining essentially social needs in psychological terms, social work was caught "blaming the victim" (Ryan, 1971) when, like all other profes-sions and institutions, it was called upon to justify itself in the glaring scrutiny of social reform. No satisfactory justification can be given. One can only move from blaming the client to blaming the system. Thus, much of social work practice and social work education has returned to an environmental focus, to social policy-planning, to administration, and to resource development as the general framework and strategy for social work practice. The resulting socio-political approach to practice is based in large measure upon opportunity and social deviance theory, aggressive self-help techniques, and a variety of partially developed theories of social change. Both the goals and the methodologies of the "socio-political" approach are geared to working with massive social problems and with subpopulations that are "victimized" by social conditions. The approach is based in a new set of ethics, in conflict, and in power. Exactly how this broad effort is translated into working with a particular individual or family is still in the embryonic state of development.

Such major shifts can occur in social work thinking and practice virtually overnight. The social work administrator must stay keenly aware of the newly emerging directions, the current state of the art, and the surrounding muddy waters. The design of any social work program reflects such new directions, or defends a more traditional approach, or seeks a compromise between the two. The compromise is the most difficult to achieve because it deals with the unanswered scientific questions as to how the person in the social situation is shaped by the intricacies of one's internal and external environments, and how in turn he alters the nature of these environments.

Assumptions and Myths About Cause and Effect

A proposed project, like any other piece of agency program (derived from broadly based societal priorities, immediate community urgencies, and newly emerging professional slants), is screened through psychosocial or socio-political perspectives that reflect an academic view of "reality," or the nature of human growth and development within that definition of reality.

The resulting perspective provides the framework for the specific assumptions upon which a rationale for problem assessment (cause) and anticipated outcome (effect) are built. The program method is the means or intervention strategy by which the correction is made or the desired results sought. To state a social problem and its solution in terms of a cause and effect equation is inappropriate in the light of the complexities of individual and social processes, the inadequacies of social science data, and a process philosophy that is now characteristic of both the natural sciences and social science. Nevertheless, a social work program at this point in time is, in practical terms, a cause and effect statement; our limited knowledge provides the rationalization.

In order to arrive at "cause and effect," one must select one or more variables toward which the intervention strategy is to be directed. The selection of variables reveals immediately the project assumptions as to cause. In juvenile delinquency, for example, a social work program might highlight court expectations and limitations, parent control, school attendance and performance, changes in peer associations, family interaction and communication, improvement in self-image or mental health status, or improved social, educational, and career opportunities, or some combination of these emphases. Assumptions as to the cause of delinquency would thus cluster around a view of personality and developmental factors, concepts of family interaction, ideas about learning and behavior modification, or beliefs about the efficacy of aggressive environmental manipulation.

In making a social problem assessment, one is influenced by social science theory and research data, one's own experiences and biases, and in large measure by the prevailing social and professional myths prevalent at any moment.

Social and professional myths are expressions of the predominant social thought climate of the day. They may be created by the intelligentsia or may derive from what groups believe about themselves. But whatever their derivation, myths are powerful in shaping private and public behaviors and in giving form and direction to societal and professional activities. Such myths are not to be equated with fabrication; rather, they are substantial overdrawings on a basic value, belief, or truth which call for new goals.

In the field of criminal justice, for instance, there is currently a growing belief that an ample provision of concrete social resources such as adequate housing, educational opportunities, or job training and employment are key variables in intervention toward the objective of successful coping and good citizenship. This new myth replaces the old myth that criminal behavior results from a genetic defect or from a developmentally warped mind or constitution. A current companion myth states that the person who has experienced a particular problem and has dealt with it successfully, is best suited to help others with the same problem. The old myth stated that the former client is the least likely to be helpful because he does not fully comprehend the dynamics of the problem, is not trained in effective helping processes, is likely to generalize about experiences that were uniquely his own, and is likely to act impatiently with a person who stumbles along with a problem which he himself has conquered.

The myth comes close enough to reality to have enormous popular and professional appeal. Identifying with a new myth can make one believe that he is innovative and can be immediately contributive to professional and social development. In the long run, much of social work activity may be more a statement of values than it is a defensible cause and effect relationship.

On Being Creative and Innovative

The guidelines from federal and state agencies, as well as from private foundations, uniformly call for or imply a priority on the creative and innovative. While the challenge has ego-appeal and is particularly appealing in a period of social reform directed toward "change" on all fronts, the challenge can lead to several serious traps.

First, as has already been mentioned, is the trap of oversimplifying or overweighting either the psychological dynamics or the social impacts that shape the life-development of individuals, families, and groups, arriving quickly at direct cause and effect equations.

A second trap is the belief that new and different social programming, *per se*, carries the forces for positive social change. In pursuing change through innovation, the administrator would do well to reflect for some time on the meaning and implications of both terms. Innovation is a scarce talent. Only rarely does the innovator appear on the social scene, as one who fully comprehends the whole of a phenomenon, visualizes a shift in the whole, and sets the course in a different direction.

In social work, when one deviates significantly from recognized or traditional ways of intervention, one is building new practice theory. Instant innovation is prone to be grandiose and gimmicky.

Through a rationally conceived and carefully designed project, one can train a group of persons for more competent performance in role and task responsibilities, provide more effective services for a specific group in a particular place, test out or demonstrate a new framework for social service delivery or planning, or provide new and useful research data. But major structural changes in society or comprehensive planning or practice impacts on basic social problems such as poverty, racism, crime and delinquency, and public school education should not be the immediate objective of funded projects. The scope of such problems and the strength of a time-limited project effort are not congruous.

Exceptions to this rule are perhaps the federal projects of "national interest." The definition and implementation of the concept of child advocacy is an example. Even so, to be of effective impact on a national scale, such projects need replication, and the findings must be implemented through legislation and bureaucratic machinery. An agency should submit a proposal for this type of project only when it has an unusual competence in the subject or practice area and has contingency plans for funding on a significant scale should the federal funding not be continued.

"Innovation" or "creativity" should be interpreted to mean an avoidance of clearly outdated social assumptions, of a repetition of social programming or methodological approaches which have not produced substantial results, or of an organizational carrousel built for staff activity rather than client benefit. Innovation should mean, rather, a genuinely client-centered focus with a strong advocacy stance, a humane service delivery system, a minimum of red tape, and a staff capable of translating program objectives into client outcomes. The imaginative aspect might be in the project's streamlined simplicity.

Whether the program is simple or complex in its assumptions and process, the narrative should be written clearly and with the precision of a research report. Some guidelines state that professional jargon should be avoided. Taken too literally, this is not altogether good advice. The use of a discipline's technical terms for the sake of sounding learned, or to appear avant-garde, is of course ostentatious. It is appropriate, on the other hand, to use concepts and terminology that are acquiring uniform understanding within the profession and reflect the profession's development. Unless the project is so maverick that supporting data are substantially unavailable, the job of documentation is made more difficult by creating new terms to describe an already known phenomenon, task, or process.

Innovation and change will be the watchwords of social work for decades to come, in both counseling and non-counseling arenas of practice. But the extent to which the weight is on the side of informed professionalism, rather than on humanistic enthusiasm, will no doubt determine ultimately the validity of social work.

Preparing and Negotiating a Project Proposal

An agency need for outside funding might simply be for the expansion of existing services, or for the addition of a rather standard programmatic component to complement existing services. For example, a foster home service might need additional counseling staff to work more intensely with natural parents; a family service agency might wish to add a homemaker service; or funds might be needed to launch an inservice training program in work with the aged. In such instances, the proposed services or training curriculum might well be replications of programs already in successful operation in other agencies. Hence there is no need to describe them as new and creative; what is required, rather is a sense of solid capability. Yet, the assumption of change is still operative here, as in all human services efforts—the assumption that somebody will be better off as a result of the project.

The more maverick project should begin at the point where other services or training stop, thus pushing toward experimentation or establishing new social service boundaries. This might involve a new approach to a popular problem, or a response to hitherto ignored or grossly under-served individuals or groups.

Demonstration and service projects are more readily funded if the applicant anticipates a future funding plan of its own following the funded project period. Projects that have shown a significant impact should be built into the agency's budget by the time of the funded expiration date.

After the definition of the problem has been made (assumptions about the phenomenon) and the objectives (desired oucome) have been determined, the program methods (program format, content, personnel, and processes) should then emerge from the exact outer limits of what research studies and practice knowledge have revealed to date. At this precise point, the innovative can come into play.

The objective should state the specific and measurable outcome anticipated within the given time-frame. The verb in the statement of the objective must connote change from a prior to a subsequent condition. The objective must, therefore, articulate the changed status anticipated, not the programmatic solution. The program is the "how" by which one expects to reach the objective. One should be careful not to promise more than can be accomplished, or more than can be evaluated satisfactorily. Many sub-objectives can be stated as "anticipated by-products," thus avoiding the necessity for formal evaluation if the process and costs are beyond the budget's capacity. Some guidelines also ask for a statement of "goals" as well as "objectives." In such instances, the goals should be stated in broad humanistic terms beyond the capability of the project, but toward which the objectives of the present project move.

Developing a proposal is time consuming and costly. One should never develop a full project proposal before preliminary explorations with a potential grantor. The administrator should assign the task of proposal development to a staff member who has writing skills and is adept in the art of negotiating. The person given this assignment must be able to present the agency in the best possible light, maximizing the impression that the agency's experience, current performance and capabilities, perception of the problem, and projected methods are right for this task at this moment.

In all project development, the initial approach to a potential funding source should be made through a detailed letter or a mini-proposal statement, providing a sketch of the existing problem, assumptions about the nature of the problem, the immediate objectives, the methods to be employed, a plan for monitoring and evaluation, and a tentative budget. The mini-proposal serves to interest the funding source in the project and provides the necessary opportunity for program personnel to help shape the proposal within the intent, priorities, guidelines, and budget constraints of the grantor.

Some federal agency grant guidelines require a more formalized mini-proposal submission and preliminary review through a two-stage application process. The process involves a condensed preliminary proposal, similar in form to the final proposal; the final proposal is submitted only by invitation.

Throughout the weeks or months of the application and review process, frequent contact with the grantor personnel is helpful in the development of the proposal and in sustaining the grantor's interest and attention.

While proceeding with the program design and proposal development a number of questions must be raised. The answers to many of these questions can be used in the narrative to support the need, rationale, and programmatic content of the proposed project. Lee and Jacquette (1973) have posed a number of such useful questions. Among them are:

> Is there a demonstrable need for the project?
>
> Whom will the project benefit and how?
>
> Why aren't others now meeting the need?
>
> If others are performing a similar function, how does the proposed function differ, and why is the difference important?
>
> Is the action proposed adequate to the problem addressed?
>
> Is the time right for the proposed endeavor?
>
> Are the proposed facilities and staffing sufficient for the job?
>
> Could the project be carried out better elsewhere or by other persons?
>
> Will there be a measurable improvement if the venture is seccessful? Will harm be done if it fails?
>
> (In what way) is it new and innovative?
>
> Is the program consonant with the (grantor's) current program objectives?
>
> Does it address an area that should receive priority in consideration of (competitive) proposals.
>
> Will the project draw in (multiple) financial support?
>
> Has appropriate evaluation advice been sought?
>
> Where the project lends itself to statistical evaluation, has provision been made for recording and analyzing relevant data?
>
> Will the results be transferable to other projects and localities?

In the federal grant requirements for institutions of higher education, there is increasingly a trend toward mandatory collaboration between the institution and the appropriate state agency at the central office level. The general requirement is that a designated official read the proposal and, in some instances, make a response to it. The requirement serves not only to help focus the institution's program upon the specified needs of the state, but also to bring into closer coordination the purposes and activities of the federal and state systems.

Social agencies and institutions of higher education making application for federal funding through state agency channels should be thoroughly informed of the purpose and programmatic range of Title XX of the Social Security Act, and of the state priorities, needs, and service plans relating to the subject of the proposed project. Specific guidelines and application materials are prepared by the state, and the budget format and financial arrangements are frequently a matter for negotiation.

The format of the narrative should be designed so that the written material is clearly linked and flows logically from one section to the next. Some grant application guidelines provide a narrative outline. Others suggest a narrative format by stating the grant application review criteria.

For example, the guidelines for the child welfare social work training program within the Office for Human Development (1978) state that the narrative should be organized under the following headings:

    I. Project Title and Objectives
    II. Background and Importance of Project
   III. Research (or) Demonstration Methodology
   IV. Evaluation Plan
    V. Work Plan
   VI. Project Staff
  VII. Implementation Potential

The Law Enforcement Administration Agency (Pennsylvania Governor's Justice Commission, 1978) requires use of the following narrative format:

    I. The Problem
      1. Nature and Scope of the Problem
      2. Supporting Data
      3. Relation of Problem to the (State) Comprehensive Plan
   II. Goal Statement (s) and Measurable Objectives
      1. Goal Statement (s)
      2. Implementation Objectives
      3. Performance Objectives
 III. Project Activities, Timetable and Resources
      1. Overall Approach
      2. Phases and Timetable
      3. Staff and Organization
      4. Applicant's Qualifications
      5. Equipment
      6. Facilities
      7. Technical Assistance
      8. Continued Support

IV. Evaluation and Monitoring Plan
   1. Evaluation Activities, Data Sources, and Measurement
   2. Feedback of Evaluation Findings to Project
   3. Persons to Carry Out Evaluation
   4. Standards for Continuation

The National Institute of Mental Health, Social Work Education Branch (1978) on the other hand, suggests that the proposal narrative flow from a consideration of the following general review criteria:

1. Significance of the project goals to the state-of-the-art/field.
2. Appropriateness and feasibility of the content, methods, and organization of the project to specified project goals and objectives.
3. Appropriateness of plans for evaluating success in achieving the goals and objectives of the proposed project.
4. Competence of the project staff in the proposed areas of work.
5. Suitability of the facilities and environment for carrying out the proposed activities.
6. Adequacy of the budget projections and other resources for carrying out the proposed activities.

A growing body of literature, while still relatively small, is useful in guiding the applicant organization and proposal writers in the tasks of program planning, searching for potential grantors, budget preparation, program evaluation, and negotiating with foundations and government agencies (White, 1975; Baker, 1975; Weissman, 1978; Lefferts, 1978; Lauffer, 1979).

An excellent generic narrative format has been developed by The Grantsmanship Center (Kiritz, 1974) which is useful when the grantor does not specify an outline required by that organization.

Proposal Summary
   I. *Introduction* (A description of the applicant organization, geared to establishing credibility).
  II. *Problem Statement or Assessment of Need* (A conceptual, documented description and perception of the problem).
 III. *Program Objectives* (Measurable outcomes).
  IV. *Methods* (The programmatic format and content to achieve the objectives).
   V. *Evaluation* (A plan for assessing the program's effectiveness).
  VI. *Future Funding* (Anticipated plans for continuing the project after the grant expires).
 VII. *Budget* (Generally for both the fiscal and the projected period of the project).

When using this format, it is also helpful to include a section on Resources, which identifies in narrative statements what the applicant organization is investing in the project and what exactly it is requesting from the grantor.

Proposal development might be most productive when approached by a team of persons. In this way, the imagination and knowledge of several individuals can be brought to bear on the planning and on programmatic elements. Team members can assist further by writing drafts of various sections of the narrative. One person might prepare the background statement, another the statement of the problem, another the program method, and still another the evaluation design. When the team approach is used, the group should be kept small. The larger the group, the more likelihood there is of flights of grandiosity or spinning off tangents that vary considerably from the guidelines or that make the project too cumbersome. A coordinator must be responsible for the overall production of the narrative and accompanying materials and must provide the kind of editing that assures balance, specificity, continuity, and wholeness.

Several patterns of funding exist, with the grantor's contribution taking the form of: *cooperative or multiple funding* (combinations of grantor support), *cost sharing* in accordance with a formula or through a negotiated percentage), or *diminishing awards* (decreasing proportions annually). A Budget Justification generally is requested as a supplement to the budget. Here, one states in narrative form the relationship of each budget item to the implementation of the project. Cost effectiveness has become an increasingly important concept in the review process. As one federal agency states explicitly, ". . . the Fund is interested in encouraging more value for the same dollar, or the same value for fewer dollars" (Office of the Assistant Secretary for Education, 1979).

Persons preparing or negotiating proposals frequently ask about the wisdom of having political endorsements of their applications. Political endorsements may be influential if they are used with discretion. Used blatantly for pressure, they are no doubt offensive to the grant program personnel and professional reviewers. It is best to limit the use of political endorsements to those projects which have broad community significance in the geographical area of concern to the elected official. Such an endorsement can then be meaningful and credible.

The site visit by persons representing the grantor is an important part of the negotiations, since it usually suggests a positive interest. The site visit requires the respect of a certain protocol. At a minimum, this involves a mutually agreed upon agenda, a carefully planned and uninterrupted use of time, the participation of knowledgeable staff and resource persons, and an ability to read mood and respond to unanticipated reactions in a way that carries agreement forward. The site visit provides an additional opportunity to demonstrate that the applicant is informed, capable, and prepared to put the program into action as soon as it is funded. It is the agency in a dress appearance. It is not, on the other hand, a time to ask for programmatic consultation or to bring up agency problems not related directly to the proposed project.

A Note On Monitoring And Evaluation

Monitoring an ongoing project is a shared role for the grantor and grantee. Selection of personnel, approval of expenditures, assuring proper accounting and audit, and maximizing the possibility of achieving the objectives through program quality are central to the agency's monitoring responsibilities. The responsibilities of the grantor are predetermined and clearly stated in the policy manual or contract. The administrator must guard against the temptation to divert project staff and other resources as props for other agency programs that are sagging.

Program evaluation presents a major problem in project development. Here, only attention can only be called to several basic considerations of which the administrator must be keenly aware. The issue of the validity of social work activity across the board and the issue of the validity of the evaluation research studies on social work methodologies are both of critical importance to the social work profession; and both are far from being resolved (Piliavin and McDonald, 1977). Knowledge about these issues and awareness of the complexities in evaluating human services outcomes will at least prevent the applicant from promising more than can be studied or promising what can be delivered only with substantial research personnel and cost.

Evaluation of social work outcomes is as essential to the life of the profession as it is to the lives and well-being of the client population. As social welfare expenditures come to represent an increasing slice of the gross national product, fiscal and social accountability require and deserve more than programs which are basically expensive value statements or experimentation with one's idiosyncratic beliefs.

References

Baker, Keith. "A New Grantsmanship." *The American Sociologist* 10 (1975); 206–219.

Elazar, Daniel J. *American Federalism: A View from the States*. New York: Crowell, 1972.

Kiritz, Norman J. "Program Planning and Proposal Writing." *The Grantsmanship Center News*, Jan. 1974, 11–14.

Lauffer, Armand. *Grantsmanship*. Beverly Hills: Sage, 1979.

Lee, F., and Barbara Jacquette. "What Makes for a Good Proposal?" *Foundation News*, Jan.-Feb. 1973, pp. 18–21.

Lefferts, Robert. *Getting Grants*. Englewood-Cliffs, NJ: Prentice-Hall, 1978.

National Institute of Mental Health, Division of Manpower and Training Programs, Social Work Education Branch, under Section 303 of the Public Health Service Act., Program Guidelines., 1978.

Office of the Assistant Secretary for Education. Fund for the Improvement of Post-Secondary Education: The Comprehensive Program, Program Guidelines., 1979.

Office of Human Development, The Children's Bureau, Child Welfare Training Grant Program, under Section 426 of the Social Security Act., Program Guidelines., 1978.

Pennsylvania Governor's Justice Commission, Law Enforcement Administration Agency., Program Guidelines., 1978.

Piliavin, Irving., and Thomas McDonald. "On the Fruits of Evaluative Research." *Administration in Social Work* 1 63–70. (1977).

Ryan, William. *Blaming the Victim*. New York: Pantheon, 1971.

Weissman, Harold. "Toward a Psychology of Program Design." *Administration in Social Work* 2 (1978): 3–14.

White, Virginia P. *Grants: How to Find Out about Them and What to Do Next?* New York: Plenum, 1975.

EVALUATION AND ADMINISTRATION: FROM EXPERIMENTAL DESIGN TO SOCIAL PLANNING

Larry Hirschhorn

10

Social administration is increasingly involved with program evaluation. Professor Hirschhorn first examines the social and political background for this phenomenon. He then proceeds to discuss in detail the classical model of evaluation, based on experimental design, and addresses the limitations of this model. And finally he suggests new approaches to evaluation within the political and technical constraints of the service system.

Ultimately, Professor Hirschhorn's interest is in the utility of the evaluation process and the responsibility of the administrator to use it as part of an integrated communications system involving all the relevant interest groups in the social agency. This is compatible with Dr. Weiner's focus on staff development.

Introduction: The Growth of Evaluation

Social program evaluation has come into its own. Increasingly, private agencies, public services, and national, state, and local government departments are using evaluators to determine if social programs work. A mental health agency will evaluate its out-patient service; a delinquency program, the effectiveness of its job placement service; a hospital, the impact of its emergency room care on the early treatment of traumatic injury; and a school program, the effectiveness of an after-school program on poor readers. As the number, kind, and complexity of services grows and as services take a growing percentage of the public tax dollar, service professionals, directors, and the clients themselves want to know if programs actually work.

The new interest in evaluation is related to the tempo and character of social change and development in the United States. Three factors stand out as particularly important. First, there has been a decisive shift in the sources of funding for human services. Prior to World War II, most human services were funded by local charities, business groups, and consolidated United Fund campaigns. Private charity boards, composed largely of business and professional elites, distributed these funds to various social agencies in the local federation. The boards launched periodic audits of the agencies under them and instituted common recordkeeping procedures. But generally, such services did not come under the scrutiny of the general public. The professionals controlled the content and form of the service, while the business elites controlled the distribution of the funds. (Lubove, 1969, ch. 7).

The system of private control weakened considerably during the Depression, when it became evident that the private service system could not possibly support the thousands of unemployed men and women who desperately needed money and services to survive. But it was not until after World War II that a definitively public sector services system began to emerge. Legislative landmarks stand as indicators of this development. The passage of the Full Employment Act, the continuing modification of the Social Security Act to encourage more services spending at the state and local government level, the passage of Medicaid and Medicare, the expansion of welfare rights and welfare payments in the late sixties, the passage of the community mental health acts, the compensatory education programs, the Old Age American Act, and, finally, Title XX of the Social Security Act all increased the role of federal, state, and local spending for human services. (Gilbert, 1977).

This shift in spending has placed human services in the public eye. In particular, as the public budget has grown in relation to the private sector and the tax base, government officials at all levels are demanding that services be accountable to their legislative mandate and to the clients they serve. Thus, increasingly, agencies, public and private, must evaluate their services to prove to government funding sources that they are satisfying the conditions of their grant. Human services in effect have come into the public arena where fiscal politics and community conflicts lead to continuing challenges to the presumed impact and purpose of any particular service. Evaluation has become a particularly important tool in this new politics of taxes, budgets, and resource allocation.

Second, governments have increased their support for human services at a time when a "crisis" of the human services professions has been emerging. Since the mid-sixties, clients, educators, politicians, and even some professional groups have argued that the helping professions do not really know how to help. Thus, many argue that community health is not really improved by medical services. Doctors can give immunization shots to limit the spread of diseases with a clear etiology, and they can help people recover from acute traumas (e.g., auto accidents), but they can do little to limit the spread of the diseases of "modern civilization" such as heart failure, cancer, and suicide. (Cassel, 1975). Indeed, there is increasing evidence that the medical system can cause disease. Modern hospitals are hothouses for germs of all sorts and many an old person has gone into a hospital with one ailment only to contract another.

The same arguments have been applied to the mental health professions and schools. Thus, it seems that therapists can do little for "chaotic" families in lower-class communities when structural unemployment distresses mothers and fathers, leads to separation, and places great burdens on their children, who become "symptomatic" in the schools and in their homes. Similarly, therapists could do little to limit the recent decade-long rise in suicide among young people, (Eyer, 1977, p. 3). Here, the lack of jobs, the uncertainties created by the Vietnam War, the growing struggle between men and women over new roles within the family and on the job created stress which could lead to suicide. Conflicts of this sort can only be worked out at the social level by social programs and community mobilization activities.

Similarly, it seems clear that schools cannot properly teach children who live in disorganized communities, who are exposed to the mesmerizing influence of television day after day, and who have no hope of getting stable jobs, much less a good career, upon graduation (Coleman, 1966). Teachers have little to offer young poeple in these settings and consequently they cannot teach them to read, write, or figure. Instead, they become school policemen, ensuring that their children do not tear up the school in the difficult eight to fourteen years that they must spend there ("Study Funds," 1978).

The sources of this crisis of the professions are many and varied. Clearly, the general challenges to authority, the problems of structural unemployment, the decay of the work ethic, the break-up of the nuclear family, are all instrumental here (Hirschhorn, 1979). Together they undermine the once solid mainstreme of social life that provided the benchmark for "normal behavior." Human service professionals can no longer adjust people to the community because the community itself has been weakened. The center of community life no longer holds.

Under these conditions, human service programs begin to fail consistently and new programs, insofar as they do not confront and address the general dimensions of the current social crisis will also fail. Manpower programs do not give young black men jobs; integration does not increase the capacity of black children to read; and Medicare does not improve the health of old people. Thus, government granting officers, congressmen, clients, and taxpayers no longer trust the professional, or presume that professional conduct and professional skills can solve social problems. Consequently, they try to make the professional accountable to clearly stated goals and purposes. Professionals must come out of the privacy of their offices, schools, and associations and into the public light of social agency audits and social program evaluations.

Third and finally, management methods have changed in both the private and public sectors. On the one side, the computer and all its accountrements have given rise to total information systems. Increasingly, corporations construct integrated information systems in which marketing, financial, manpower, and inventory data are all correlated one against the other in "real time." Corporate managers can examine the critical underlying relationships between and within the different divisions and operations of the corporation. In this way they can allocate resources in a more timely and optimal way.

Much of the same thrust is evident in public service management (Lund, 1978). The utilization of computer systems has led to the construction of prototype integrated information systems in which financial data, cost data, outcome data, process data (e.g., disposition through the system), and follow-up are developed and integrated through standardized record keeping procedures and computer technologies. There is, it seems, an internal loigic to the development of such systems. While at first financial, personnel, and payroll data might be entered, management will later push for more systematic process, disposition, utilization, and outcome data. Such information not only provides management with greater leverage for controlling the work of the professionals and non-professional staff, but more importantly, it allows the manager to buffer the agency from outside pressures. The greater the range of data the manger can supply to funding agencies, city bureaucracies, community boards, clients, and the like, the greater is his or her power to defend the agency against political or financial attack. Similarly, the more complete the information system, the better able is the manager to develop proposals and requests for funding for new programs. The information system in other words increases the adaptability and security of the agency with respect to its setting.

Seen in this context, it is clear that evaluation becomes one critical link in the development of an integrated information system. Unless managers and professionals know what the impact of their work is on the clients and community they serve, they cannot develop a complete picture of the significance of their services.

In sum, then, there are three interconnected reasons for the growth of evaluation—the growth of public sector support for social services (and the

corresponding decline in the significance of private charities), the crisis of
the profession and the consequent failure of social programs, and the rise of
a new management information technology. These trends all reinforce each
other. Thus, for example, the crisis of the profession increases the already
strong demand for accountability to taxpayers and clients, and simultaneously leads managers to press professionals into cooperating with an
information-based accountability system. These three factors, then, establish a powerful momentum for the growth and institutionalization of evaluation in the social services.

The Theory of Evaluation Practice: The Classical Model

Administrators do not do evaluation; they hire the evaluators. Thus they
face the recurring and sometimes insoluble problem of managing and
administering a group of professionals who resist authority and insist on the
"collegial" model of work relations. Evaluators, like all professionals, have
developed their own world view and special language both to practice their
skill and to defend themselves against incursions. To be sure, the language
is not simply a protective device, a veil to disguise the monopoly power of
organizational resources. It reflects authentic intellectual and methodological developments. Yet the non-professional, non-evaluator will often find
it hard to crack the grammer. Private languages developed privately in the
annals and footnotes of scholarly journals take on a life of their own. The
non-professional is excluded from the discourse. The administrator thus
faces a potentially frustrating, if not dangerous, situation. He or she must
hire evaluators but will find it difficult to evaluate their work. If they
produce results and reports that appear to convey the obvious ("on
balance poor children from decaying neighborhoods have lower self-
esteem"), the evaluators can counter administration grumbling with claims
that "resources simply did not permit an effective quasi-experimental
design," or "differential attrition of high achievers precluded systematic
comparisons between the control and experimental groups." These claims
may be right, wrong, or beside the point. But the administrator must know.

In this section we outline the grammar, the theory of evaluation practice.
The section is divided into three parts. In the first part we examine the
classical theory of evaluation-experimental design; the second we briefly
discuss the problems of measurement; in the third we examine the evaluator's role in evaluation design.

CLASSICAL EXPERIMENTAL DESIGN

The paradigm of evaluation as an activity has thus far been based on the
model of classical *experimental design* (Riecken and Boruch, 1974, chs.
3–4). The roots of this model lie in the "scientific method," that is, the

careful testing of alternative hypotheses to determine the true cause of a particular event or outcome. Such an approach is applied regularly to test the impact of drugs. Thus, for example, a doctor reasons that drug X will lower the blood pressure of chronically hypertensive people. To test this hypothesis, he or she will *randomly* select from a group of patients in a hypertensive clinic for testing, will *randomly* assign a patient from this group to a "treatment" group or a "control" group, will give the drug to the treatment group, and, after an appropriate period of time, will measure the average difference in the blood pressure level between the two groups. If that difference is substantively and statistically significant, he or she will conclude that the drug has an impact on blood pressure. The steps in the procedure highlight the key steps in experimental design. They are: (1) Specify an hypothesis as rigorously as you can: "This drug lowers blood pressure in hypertensive patients." (2) Locate and define your relevant population group: "Use patients in the hypertensive clinic." (3) *Randomly* select your sample and *randomly* divide them into a treatment group and a control group. (4) Administer the treatment and specify how the outcomes are to be measured: "Give the treatment group the drug and plan to measure blood pressures after a theoretically determined period of time." (5) Compare the change, if any, of the treatment group to the change, if any, of the control group: "How did the blood pressure of the treatment group change after the drug was administered, when compared with the control group?"

The classical experimental design is based on four critical points. First, one must have a specified theory and hypothesis. Second, one must be able to rigorously specify how both treatments and outcomes are to be measured. Third, one must choose the population sample, treatment group and control group *randomly*. Fourth, and finally, one must determine the statistical significance of the difference between the two groups (e.g., could the difference be the result of a chance error in measurement, or in the operation of some unaccounted-for factor?) and the substantive significance of the difference (e.g., was the difference of much importance from the point of view of health?).

RANDOMNESS

The first two points are common to all scientific experimentation and thinking. The fourth simply expresses the requirements of statistical hypothesis testing. The third point, however, is the central one to the problem of experimental design. Unless one generates treatment groups and control groups from a population sample at *random*, it becomes difficult to make statistically meaningful statements about any difference that might be found. Assume, for instance, that the doctor in the above example "advertises" for people (within the clinic) who would like to try the new drug. He then compares the results of this treatment with a group of untreated patients whom he sees regularly in the clinic. He finds that the difference in blood pressure between the two groups is substantive and significantly different. Yet is this difference the result of the drug? It might not be. A *selection* effect may be operating here (Campbell and Stanley, 1963, p. 40). The people who volunteered for the treatment may be predisposed to "getting cured"—they may be ready to relax and the drug treatment may provide them with the excuse to relax, to feel less tense, and, thus, to lower their blood pressure.

Random selection, however, rules out this possibility. If we select at random from the relevant population and, in turn, randomly distribute people between the treatment and control groups, we ensure that, within the limits of unavoidable errors in measurement, *there will be no systematic differences between the treatment group and control group.* The proportion of relaxed patients within the treatment group will tend toward equality with the proportion of such patients in the control group, as will such factors as height, weight, and age.

Random selection thus emerges as the precondition for all meaningful statements of cause, effect, and statistical significance. Random selection does not solve *all* the problems of design. Thus, for example, we must be sure that the population from which we choose our sample (the clinic) is *representative* of the more general population in which we are interested (e.g. adult men or adult men and women) (Campbell and Stanley, 1963, p. 16). Thus, for example, if the clinic is located in a comparatively poor area and the drug shows no effect, it is still possible that it would show an effect when applied to higher-income groups. In other words, a confounding variable, the level of income, may affect the treatment of the drug. There is no rule for determining whether, in fact, the population is representative. We can either sample from the entire universe of people (much as the census bureau does, although this is expensive) if we have no theory to guide us, or we can decide, on the basis of theory, that in this case our population is representative, that there are no systematically confounding variables.

Similarly, particular historical events may affect the result. For example, a president might be shot between the treatment and the subsequent measurement. The shock of this event may overwhelm the smaller difference generated by the treatment and everyone's blood pressure, in both the control and the treatment group's, may go up by the same amount.

These are issues of *theory*; no design method can circumvent them. But, within the confines of these theoretical issues, randomization remains the fundamental design for ensuring control group and treatment group comparability.

QUASI-EXPERIMENTAL DESIGN

Unfortunately, in many social service experiments, it is difficult to randomize the control and treatment groups. A remedial reading program in a low-income area may be opened on a first come, first serve basis until all spots are filled. If after a period of time we want to compare the reading scores of those in the program with those not in the program, we face an insoluble problem. Those children who came first to the program clearly possess some characteristic not possessed by those children who did not sign up in time to be accepted. Moreover, it is likely that this characteristic is in some way associated with the ability to read, or the likelihood of improvement in reading. The children who signed up in time probably have parents who are concerned with their children's performance and are anxious that their children improve. Because they were interested in the way their children read, they were in touch with channels of information and rumor that informed them early about the remedial program. But research shows that motivated parents who create a climate of support for study in the home can decisively help the school performance of their children. Therefore, the program attracted children who were motivated to improve; most likely they would have improved in reading more than the control group even if the program had not been offered. The program simply crystallized an emerging difference between the two groups of children. We cannot simply compare the two groups of children; the *selection* effect confounds clearcut comparisons.

Similarly, many programs are based on universal eligibility criteria. A summer camp program for poor children in a particular neighborhood might be open to all children in families where the parents earn less than $7,000 per year. In addition, the camp is big enough to accommodate all the eligible children. If we then want to evaluate the impact of the camp on the "socialization" skills and motivation of the children who attended camp, we cannot compare them to those who did not attend camp, since all those who did not attend were from families with incomes higher than $7,000. Children from these families may very well have a higher level of socialization skill and motivation quotients and, in fact, may be improving (with maturation) at a faster rate than children from poorer families. In this case, we are likely to *underestimate* the program impact.

Finally, many programs face the problem of attrition and cross-group communication and "contamination." In a behavior modification program for obese people who want to lose weight, some 20 percent of the initial treatment group might drop out. We cannot then compare the remaining treatment group's weight loss with a control group, since we would be ignoring the treatment's impact on those who dropped out. Yet we cannot include the drop-outs in the control group, since they were clearly exposed to the treatment, and any comparison between the treatment group of those who remained with the control group will tend to *overstate* the impact of the treatment. Unless we carefully interview the drop-outs to determine why they left (e.g., did they leave because of the program or because of extraneous issues, like moving away?), we cannot determine the exact amount of overstatement.

Quasi-experimental design tries to address these issues (Glaser, 1973, ch. 6). It provides a set of techniques, approaches, and recommendations when the experiment cannot be based on pure randomization. We cannot go into the details of these techniques. Put simply, the evaluator has to estimate how the likely and measurable, systematic, and substantively significant difference between the treatment and control group's would have affected the measured outcomes *independent* of the treatment itself. In the case of our remedial program, we could use certain proxy measures for motivation (such as the absence of one parent in the home, the number of children in the family, and the income of the family) to "factor out" the impact of motivation on the difference in reading scores between the control and the treatment groups. We "co-vary" reading scores with measures of motivation. This does not result in a complete removal of the effect of motivation; statistical theory suggests that we will still be underestimating its effect. But, in the absence of randomization, it does give a better estimate of the "pure" effect of the treatment alone.

Other such techniques exist. Thus, where eligibility criteria are universally applied (as in our second example), we could use historical data from school files to see how socialization skills change with age and then compare this data to the group who went to camp. We could use, in other words, a *time series* of past data. Finally, some evaluations will use *matched samples*, in which randomization will be "mimicked" by selecting a control group that matches the treatment group along several important dimensions (Riecken and Boruch, 1974, pp. 97–115). There are critical statistical problems associated with this technique. Generally, we do not know if we matched along the most important dimensions. We might omit a factor that positively affects different people's responsiveness to the treatment. If the control has less of that factor, then we would overestimate the impact of the program. Thus, for example, if we matched the control group in the remedial reading program along the demographic dimensions of age, race, and income, but did not match along the dimension "number of parents in the home," and if we argue that the first to sign up for the program are more motivated to improve, and if we also argue that motivation is positively related to the number of parents in the home, then it is likely that a greater proportion of such children in the treatment group live in two-parent families than the control group. Thus, *independent* of the treatment, they would be more likely to improve in reading skills, and we would overestimate the impact of the program.

In sum, quasi-experimental design consists of a set of design recommendations and associated statistical techniques when complete and total randomization is not possible.

NON-EXPERIMENTAL DESIGN

Finally, evaluators will often use strictly non-experimental techniques to determine the relationship between treatments, services, inputs, and outcomes. In these situations, the evaluator does not conduct an experiment at all. Rather, he or she compiles data on treatments and outcomes and uses correlation or regression analysis to determine if any statistical relationship exists between the two. Thus, if a principal wants to know if the race of the teacher in a predominantly black school affects children's school performance, the evaluators will correlate reading scores with the race of the teacher, using statistical techniques to hold other crucial variables, such as the teacher's age, sex, and experience, constant.

The techniques for the procedure are well established; the problems are, as always, conceptual ones. Again, as in the case of matched samples, we do not know if we have identified all the other critical background variables. If we have left out some, then we are likely to either overestimate or underestimate the effects of race on school performance. If black teachers are also predominantly younger and less experienced, and if we neglect to include the factor of experience in our correlation, and if, in addition, it is good for black children to have black teachers, we will underestimate the impact of race on school performance. This is a classical problem in correlation (it is called the "specification" problem), and no amount of statistical footwork will solve it. Only clear theoretical thinking will suffice.

OUTCOME AND TREATMENT MEASURES

Finally, evaluators working with any of these methods: experimental, quasi-experimental, and non-experimental design, face the difficult task of *measuring* treatment and outcome (Riecken and Boruch, 1974, ch. 5). In laboratory testing, there are rarely such problems. We can measure the amount of the drug we gave and the consequent drop in blood pressure. But in complex social programs, we face more difficult measurement problems. In the summer camp program described above, how are we to measure socialization skills? Should we use behavior marks in the subsequent school year? Should we call on independent psychological raters to observe the children at play? Should we administer specifically designed and normed tests of socialization? If so, against what groups do we norm the test?

Similarly, we often face the problem of measuring treatments. In a non-experimental design problem, we might want to measure the impact of resource inputs on the reading performance of school children. We might feel intuitively that the condition of the school facility is important here. But how should we measure it? Should we use the age of the school building as a proxy variable? Should we (again) employ independent raters, or should we construct some composite variable that includes factors such as building age, maintenance expenditures, and square footage? Again, only clear conceptual thinking can provide the answer.

All methods of evaluation face the critical issue of time. How soon after the treatment do we decide to measure the treatment groups and control groups? Here we face a complex of problems. On the one side, if we measure the impact of the program immediately after it is administered, we may disguise the problem of *recidivism*. Children in a remedial reading program may improve for a year after they complete the program but may regress back to the level of the untreated group within two years. On the other side, it may take two years before the impact of the program will be apparent. If we measure the children's performance immediately after the program is completed, we are likely to underestimate the program's significance. Yet, the longer we wait, the less equivalent will our control and treatment groups be, since events after the program will not affect them equally. These are thorny theoretical issues, and, again, only clear theory can help the evaluator resolve them.

The classical paradigm of evaluation is based on the model of scientific experimentation, and it works best under conditions of complete randomization. Where randomization proves impossible, quasi-experimental design is appropriate. Where the evaluator cannot experiment, but wants to determine the relationship between service inputs and outcomes, non-experimental methods can be used. All of these methods, however, must be complemented by sound theoretical thinking if the difficult problems of measurement, the appropriate time-span, and the control of background variables are to be faced and solved.

THE LIMITS OF DESIGN AND THE EVALUATOR'S ROLE

The limits of the classical model place the administrator in a critical role within the evaluation process. Evaluators may understand *method*, but they rarely grasp the critical dimensions of *context*. Unless guided, they cannot determine which goals and processes should anchor any evaluation design. The central conceptual questions, treatment measurement, outcomes, appropriate time spans, relevant control variables, and appropriate causal links between program inputs and expected outcomes, cannot be answered by the evaluators alone. To be sure, good evaluators are trained to elicit answers to such questions. They understand the nuances of surveys and interviews. But unless the administrators can give clear and unambiguous answers to contextual questions the evaluation exercises will be fruitless and the results will be mistrusted by all parties.

Imagine that an evaluator is asked to study the impact of a "work-education council" whose function is to help a community improve the way in which young people make the transition from school to work. The evaluator might design a standard outcome study in which he or she measures the impact of certain council-sponsored program (e.g., job fairs or field placement programs) on youth "attitudes" toward their job prospects. Such a study however would in all likelihood be beside the point. The work education council has a broad *coordinating* mandate to help the community deal with a clearly complex and deeply rooted problem. The goals of the council are not to design "successful" programs for the short run. Rather, it is likely that labor market conditions will be the most significant determinant of youth attitudes. Instead its most important function should be to help schools, employers, parents, and other social agencies develop a long-term action plan that might *reshape* the school-to-work transition. In this context, the test of the council's effectiveness is in its *developmental potential*. The evaluator wants to ask if the council has the potential to change the behavior of other institutions through its activities, not if its specific activities impact on youth's transition from school to work. But measures of developmental potential cannot be looked up in a measurement manual or guide for evaluators. They can only emerge through a collaborative assessment of the council's activity in which the evaluator and the administrator are actively engaged.

Similarly, imagine the following problem. An evaluator is asked to evaluate the impact of a behavorial counselling program on the subsequent work histories of the clients of drug programs. Chances are that in today's economy the evaluator will discover that the program has "no effect." Work commitments remain as abysmally low after as they did before the program. But once again this finding may prove irrelevant. The administrator may know that the resources committed to the program are simply insufficient in light of the monumental barriers that drug offenders must face when they re-enter the job market. The administrator understands the link between resource investments and program outputs. The question then becomes what aspect of the program *can* be evaluated that will yield reliable and meaningful information for future program design. In a collaborative assessment the administrator and evaluator might decide that *intermediate* measures of outcome, such as the capacity of drug offenders to use referral services, would be the most appropriate in light of resource constraints.

The implication is clear. Every service program operates within a field of forces, opportunities, and constraints. Evaluators, whether inside or outside the agency, rarely understand the resulting context within which the agency must operate and develop its programs. Outside evaluators may be simply ignorant; inside evaluators may be too committed to one or another "ideological" view of the agency, views they pick up or are socialized to in the normal course of their work. Only through a careful collaborative study in which the administrator provides leadership in defining the appropriate context and the evaluator provides leadership in shaping the appropriate design can a meaningful evaluation emerge.

Evaluation as Planning

THE POLITICS OF SYSTEM INTEGRATION

Evaluation theorists distinguish between "outcome" and "process" evaluation: the former is centered on ultimate impacts, the latter on the flow and organization of inputs. In the classical view, process evaluation plays second fiddle to outcome evaluation. Outcomes are the queens in the deck; process measures are the humble low cards. But today there is increasing evidence that the roles are being reversed. We are beginning to understand that the structure and pattern of outcomes can be best understood as functions of the way in which inputs are "supplied" to, and organized within, the agency.

Today, the critical development in social agency administration is the emergence of *planning* as a systematic and comprehensive activity. Planners, administrators, managers, and information specialists have begun to "model" the links between resource inputs, resource flows, and service outcomes. We know that a particular service can be described as a system in which service facility *access*, client population *profiles*, client *utilization*, case *flow* from intake to disposition, case *outcome*, and, finally, community *impact* are all integrated through a complex set of rules, unspoken procedures, institutional norms, client behaviors, and professional practice. Thus, *outcomes*, the traditional focus of the classical paradigm, can be examined and understood only as one link in an integrated and ongoing set of activities that are restricted by a set of *constraints* and *parameters*.

Once we take this view, we see that outcomes can be changed in many different ways. For example, improved case flow can release resources for better services, services can be developed to better match the demographic profile, and improved impact through community education and consultation can ultimtely improve service outcome for individual clients. In this context, evaluation becomes one and only one link in a social planning process.

Thus, the critical question that evaluators face today is not how to design quasi-experiments, but, rather, how to develop planning processes that permit outcomes to be monitored within a conception of the service as an integrated system.

In confronting this task, evaluators will face two critical constraints: the technical and the political. Clearly, any service organization must solve important technical problems in developing a monitoring, modelling and evaluation system for the services it provides. In particular, it must solve the important problems of measurement and information system design. But, in the last fifteen years, there has emerged a rich and robust body of theory and practice that can provide at least satisfactory, if not optimal, solutions to these questions.

The political question is the more important one. Any time evaluators, administrators, and planners try to construct a monitoring and planning and evaluation system, they step on everybody's toes. Old line program administrators fear that they will lose responsibility and status, while professionals find that they must change their practices. In any "system," people have built up control of its subparts by *creating* scarcities of resources and information (e.g., only the program administrators know how to regulate case flow through intakes and waiting list policies in line with the professionals' vacation schedules, or only the professional knows what impact he or she is having on clients, if any). Any monitoring system, if it is effective, will willy-nilly expose these scarcities, and planners will soon suggest how service could be improved if they were eliminated. *System integration* must inevitably upset the applecart of status and privilege in the agency.

Let us take a simple example—the development of an outcome information subsystem for the evaluation component of the general monitoring-planning design. Imagine that a community mental health center wants to institute evaluation as a regular component of its management and planning activities. The community mental health center probably has done a few confined and "one-shot" evaluation studies of particular programs that it sponsors, but it is discovering that pressure from the government and community boards, as well as new opportunities in the "grants system," all make it important for the agency continuously to evaluate and monitor its activity.

As the director, the evaluator, and a committee of professionals examine the problem, they discover that any systematic and ongoing evaluation activity requires a substantial change in clinical record keeping. Clinicians fill out intake, process, and closing reports in idiosyncratic ways. On the one side, some of their language is very case specific, so that cross-case comparisons over time are very difficult to make, or, on the other side, their language is simply too general to be of much use to anyone who is not familiar with the case (e.g., the patient has a "developmental problem of adolescence," or an "acute neurotic reaction"). While psychology supplies therapists with a rich diagnostic language, a record system for ongoing evaluation requires, instead, a fairly general language to permit cross-case comparison, but a language specific enough to measure progress toward stated goals and improved patient functioning (Bonstedt et al, 1973).

Thus, the need for evaluation poses immediate political questions. How is that language to be developed, who is to participate in the development of the language, and how will the language be implemented. As directors, planners, and evaluators quickly discover, it is difficult to change record-keeping unless the professionals actively cooperate in the process. Strong armed enforcement such as a directive from the executive director stating that forms must be done in a certain way might win surface compliance, but the professionals will find ways to subvert the intent and potential impact of the new system.

This is a delicate and complex task, because any substantial change in recordkeeping that permits non-professionals to read and interpret clinical records weakens the professionals' power to impose their particular model of treatment. If the professionals already feel threatened, if there is a general suspicion in the culture that they are ineffective, they will dig in their heels and resist such changes.

The director, evaluators, and planners thus face critical problems of strategic implementation. To develop the recordkeeping system, they must offer the professionals incentives and rewards for cooperation. But to do this, they must understand the dimensions and content of professional resistance. And to understand this, they must be alert to the general social evaluation of professions, the "crisis" of the professions, and the likely evolution of professional work.

If the director, planners, and evaluators solve this problem, however, they may face other equally complex ones. An active community board will have to be consulted on these changes—to be sure, they are changes of sufficient magnitude that all interested and important parties must be consulted. But as the director and others present their approach to record-keeping, particularly as they outline the new language (for instance, a comprehensible "levels of mental health fuctioning" scale), community board members will, no doubt, agree with some of the projected changes and disagree with others. More importantly, the discussion might open up other issues, for example, whether clients should have an ombudsman in the clinic.

Systematic changes in the recordkeeping necessary to develop a planning capability involve clients in a political process of defining the meaning of mental health functioning in the particular community in which they live. The director, planners, and evaluators might try to limit the consequent discussions; they could be too open-ended and lead to questions concerning the fundamental viability of any mental health clinic within the particular catchment area. Thus, as soon as the agency opens up these issues, it opens up broad-range discussions on the meaning and impact of the service itself.

These particular questions are so comprehensive and dominating that they make the more narrow design issues of the classical paradigm of minor relevance. The politics of services and of service development and agency planning enter into the central stage.

INFORMATION SYSTEM DESIGN AND META EVALUATION

Generally, as soon as evaluation becomes part of an ongoing planning and monitoring process in which case *flow*, facility *utilization*, service *outcomes*, and community *impact* are systematically and continuously measured, the design issues recede into the background. It is not that design becomes unimportant, for the systematic measurement of outcomes and the periodic review of treatment groups in comparison with untreated people in the catchment area can prove helpful. But, more importantly, the evaluation process becomes part of an integrated *communications* system, through which a variety of groups, the administrators, the granting agencies, the professionals, and the clients, can intelligently discuss the relevance of the service to the needs of people. The critical issues then become: (1) How does one design such an information-communication system? How can the information have utility, timeliness, specificity, and comprehensiveness? (2) How should the information be cycled through a generalized planning process? When is information released, who has access to it, and in what form? Is the information used for developmental decisions, for the maintenance of minimal standards of service, for defense against hostile granting agencies, for continuing client pressure against incompetent professionals? (3) How does one "evaluate" this design itself? How does one know that the information-communication system is working or not? What are the criteria? How does one, in effect, construct a "meta evaluation" system? In short, within this context, evaluation becomes an *ongoing* activity integrated within a *planning process* based on a *communication-information system*.

Such an information system should allow the participants in the planning process to monitor facility utilization, case flow, service outcome, and community impact. The appropriate measures of indices of these service system outputs must, in turn, be developed through a designed discussion process. Finally, the evaluation process itself must be periodically evaluated by criteria developed to monitor the utility of the information and communication system designs.

In this context, evaluation moves far away from the classical paradigm of experimental design. Where classical design requires that communication between the experimental and control groups be restricted lest the two groups "contaminate" each other's experiences, the planning mode of evaluation maximizes the flow of information among all the interested parties. Similarly, while an evaluator working within the classical design will not modify the treatment before the final measurement of outcomes, evaluators working as planners within an ongoing monitoring system will (with the cooperation of the professional and clients) recommend treatment modifications when and if they seem necessary.

Ultimately the planning model of evaluation permits a broader conception of treatment modalities. Thus, for example, there is growing evidence that self-help groups are among the most effective ways in which dissatisfied people can change their life situations (*Social Policy*, 1976). Evaluators working within the classical model, with its emphasis on *individual treatment*, *restricted* information flow, and the *controlling* role of the evaluator, would probably overlook the implications and power of the mode of treatment. Today, more than ever, we need a broad and flexible approach to service delivery. There is a danger that the classical model will favor the increasingly obsolete service model based on the treatment of a single client by a single professional in a situation in which the professional has total control over the rules of the treatment.

Whither Evaluation?: Austerity and Its Consequence

There is little doubt that the "systems" view of services and the consequent development of planning and monitoring technologies will increasingly determine the context and substance of evaluation activities, for many powerful and interdependent forces push in this direction. The question, then, is not whether the systems view will predominate but, rather, what *kind* of systems view will predominate. Will the new systems view broaden the level of participation in the development of services, or will it lead to a "rationalization" of services based on top-down control? Will the information systems simply measure the most narrow features of work load and case flow (e.g., case closings per professional per year), or will they, in fact, measure the broadest, most multi-faceted dimensions of impact and outcome? The choice, in other words, is between technocracy or participation.

It is fair to say that evaluation stands at a crossroads. Will it take the classical path and fall into an increasingly technocratic mode of acting and thinking, or will it take the planning path and help to open up service design and development to all interested parties? Powerful forces push evaluators in the technocratic direction. First, in times of austerity granting agencies often insist on quick and measurable results, and as a consequence evaluators and administrators will try to provide *narrow* measures of outcome based on an *individual* treatment view of clients. *Broad* measures of community impact and involvement take longer to develop are "softer" in character, and ultimately gain their legitimacy from the level of community participation that went into their development. They are not, in other words, measures of ultimately "objective" conditions, but, rather, reflect the degree, quality and nature of the consensus concerning the import of the service among all the interested participants.

Second, the pressure for austerity complements the growing resistance to change on the part of the professionals. As we have seen, professionals feel threatened today. They are fast losing legitimacy in the community, and, to protect their hard-won status and rights, they are increasingly digging in their heels, forming unions, and attempting to limit, as much as possible, the degree to which other groups can change the way they treat clients.

Imagine the following scenario: Administrators who are faced with such professional resistance and are simultaneously pressured by the granting agencies for good results will insist, as a minimum, that professionals see as many cases as possible. They will monitor the professionals' use of their time, find inefficiencies, and change procedures so that case flow is increased. Professionals will resist (through their unions), and a new politics of *case load conflict* will emerge and push out the more productive politics of service *quality* and *impact*. In this framework, evaluators will be used by the administrators to monitor work load alone. Management information systems will be developed, but they will monitor only the most narrow features of the service delivery system. Information will become a mechanism of control, rather than a vehicle of participation.

Yet, in the end, these pressures and counter-pressures will not suggest new alternatives to the incipient "crisis" of the services themselves. The continuing failure of services reflected either in high drop-out rate of clients, repeaters, low community visibility, or contining community distress will be felt by everyone. This gap between stated objectives and performance within a framework of austerity will, thus, lead to declining morale on the one side and growing cynicism on the other. Administrators will view their evaluation reports as simply levers to pry more money from the granting agencies. They will not use them in any authentic service development process. This combination of cynicism, low morale, workload politics, and service failure will only insinuate the service crisis deeper into the fabric of community life.

No doubt there are administrators who want to use evaluators and evaluation for service development, there are professionals who can change their approach, and there are grants officers who want broad measures of impact. The above scenario was exaggerated to make a point.

Administrators, evaluators, planners, and professionals all stand at a crossroads. No less at stake than the character and potential of today's social agency. Increased accountability at all levels of service, funding, and planning, is fundamental for sustaining the democratic character of post-industrial society. We are too interconnected today to tolerate monopolies on decisions that affect us all. Administrators and evaluators must place appropriate limits around the classical evaluation model and must in turn develop a broad participatory planning framework in which *process*, context, and *system* become the key organizing terms. Only in this way can they surmount the dangerous and emerging reality of austerity, narrow measurement, and work-load politics. Only in this way can they help resolve the current crisis in social service.

References

Anderson, Wayne, and Bernard Frieden. *Managing Human Services*. Washington, D.C.: International City Manager Association, 1977.

Cassel, John. "Social Science in Epidimeology: Psychosocial Processes and 'Stress Theoretic' Formulations." In Marcia Guttentag, ed., *Handbook of Evaluation*. Beverly Hills: Sage, 1975.

Campbell, Donald T., and Julian Stanley. *Experimental and Quasi-experimental Designs for Research*. Chicago: Rand McNally, 1963.

Coleman, James. *Equality of Educational Opportunity*. Washington, D.C.: GPO, 1966.

Bonstedt, Theodor, et al. "Four Ways to Goal Attainment Scaling." *Evaluation*, Special Monograph no. 1 (1973): 1–28.

Eyer, Joseph, and Peter Sterling. "Stress Related Mortality and Social Organization." *Review of Radical Political Economy* 9, no. 1 (1977): 1–44.

Gilbert, Neil. "The Transformation of Social Services." *Social Service Review 51*, no. 4 (1977): 624–641.

Glaser, Daniel. *Routinizing Evaluation*. Washington, D.C.: NIMH, 1973.

Hirschhorn, Larry. "The Theory of Social Services in Disaccumulationist Capitalism." *International Journal of Health Services* 9, no. 2 (1979): 295–311.

Lubove, Roy. *The Professional Altruist*. New York: Atheneum, 1969.

Lund, Donald A. "Mental Health Program Evaluation: Where to Start?" *Evaluation and Program Planning 1*, no. 1 (1978): 31–40.

Riecken, W. Henry, and Robert F. Boruch *Social Experimentation*. New York: Academic, 1974.

Social Policy. Special issue on self-help, Sept./Oct. 1976.

"Study Finds One in Nine Students Each Month Is Victim of a Theft." *New York Times*, Jan. 7, 1978.

PART IV.
HUMAN
RESOURCES AND
SOCIAL
ADMINISTRATION

ROOM AT THE TOP: WOMEN IN SOCIAL ADMINISTRATION

Leslie B. Alexander and Toba Schwaber Kerson

11

In spite of changing public policy and professional rhetoric, Alexander and Kerson note that the proportion of women in administrative roles in social work has actually declined over the years. Their chapter is therefore of particular relevance as it not only presents data on women in management but also seeks to explain this phenomenon.

The authors suggest several strategies which can be used by executives in the social services to assure that women are employed in administration. These strategies are aimed both at women on an individual level, to encourage them to move into administrative positions, and at the organization, to make it more structurally conducive in relation to employing women administrators. Furthermore, it provides a good example of the role the executive can play as change agent.

In recent years, the social work profession has renewed its commitment to supporting opportunities for minorities and the disadvantaged. In particular, there has been concern about the recruitment and advancement of racial and ethnic minorities within the profession itself. Paradoxically, the low-status position of women in social work has not received similar attention. While the profession has tried to honor its commitment to other groups, the administrative roles of women in social work have actually declined in number over the past twenty years (Szakacs, 1977).

Although the future of women in social service administration is embedded within the larger nexus of the improved status of women in all major institutions of society, the focus of this essay will be more limited and will address three areas: the first describes the data available about women in management generally, as well as about women in social service adminis-tration;* the second describes two models, the individual and the structu-ral, which attempt to account for the paucity of female managers in social work and other occupations; the third suggests specific intervention strate-gies, derived from these models, which can be used by social service administrators in the promotion of equal and expanded opportunities for women within their agencies.

Equal opportunity for women has been depicted as "smart business" by a prestigious business journal (Boyle, 1973). Just as it is smart for business, it is also smart for social service administration. Not only has there been waste of female talent and skill in social work administration, but the lack of equal opportunity for women has also violated the ideological tenets of the profession. Although professional advancement and the occupancy of an administrative role are not synonymous, they are closely linked in social work. As Fanshel has stated: "Many social workers derive their greatest satisfaction from being involved in direct practice and feel most fulfilled in such a role. However, this is not to deny that a move to administration is commonly viewed as professional advancement in a conventional sense and that it certainly leads to higher salaries" (1976, p. 449).

Empirical Data on Women in Management

Currently, there are at least three major areas of research on institutional sexism: organizational recruitment, or the "in-out" problem; mobility with-in organizations, or the "up-down" problem; and the reward and control structures of formal organizations, including pay differences within job classifications, or the "equal-pay-for-equal-work" issue (McDonough, et al., 1979). Because the problems for women in social work are not in the recruitment area, only mobility and equal pay for equal work will be considered.

Women in social service administration face the same problems regard-ing mobility or the "up-down" problem as do female managers across the occupational spectrum. In 1976, for example, only 20.8 percent of the managers in this country were female (U.S. Department of Labor, 1977) a figure which has not changed appreciably since (U.S. Department of Labor, 1979). Furthermore, there is evidence that women managers are clustered in particular types of non-business organizations such as educa-tion, the arts, social service, and office management. If employed in business, they generally do not work in manufacturing (Kanter, 1977).

*In this chapter, the terms "administration" and "management" are used synonymously.

Women are virtually absent from management positions in large industrial enterprises. For example, a recent survey by Burson-Marsteller, a
public relations firm, of 1,300 of the nation's biggest companies, including
banks, utilities, and financial, insurance, and transportation companies,
revealed that women held only one percent of top-management jobs and
only 5 to 6 percent of middle-management jobs within these companies
(Fowler, 1977).

Ironically, even in areas where the workers are overwhelmingly female,
the managers are likely to be male. For example, while office workers are
largely female, office managers are more likely to be male (Kanter, 1976).
Although the data are limited to the 1960s, a recent study of the internal
labor market structure of the professions of social work, nursing, librarian-
ship, and school teaching, all of which are female-concentrated professions,
reveals a similar pattern: men are disproportionately represented in
administrative positions in all of these fields.

The study of status differentials between men and women in social work
is of recent origin. However, scattered empirical evidence in the 1970s on
the sexual distribution of administrative positions across a number of areas
within social work continues to reveal a low level of female participation.
An analysis of 1971–72 survey data of partial National Association of Social
Workers' membership indicates that about 37 percent of the men, as
compared with 18 percent of the women, were in administrative positions.
In other words, the proportion of men in leadership positions was about
twice that of women (Fanshel, 1976).

Similarly, the Williams, Ho, and Fiedler (1974) survey of a sample of all
M.S.W. graduates of the School of Social Work at the University of Texas at
Austin, and Knapman's (1977) study of a sample of M.S.W. staff from
twenty family agencies in Michigan, both reveal that women fare less well
than men in the promotion-decision structure of organizations. In the
Knapman study, in particular, results indicate that "fewer females were
hired initially at the supervisory level, females were promoted at a slower
rate than males, and there was a significant relationship between sex and
position level" (1977 p. 463).

An equally dismal picture is found in the federal and state welfare
apparatus. An examination of the Social Rehabilitative Service within
HEW revealed that only 10 percent of all women were at the high-paying
grades of GS14–GS15, whereas 43 percent of all men in the service were at
these pay grades (Mason, 1977, p. 164). Men are also overrepresented in
administrative positions in social work education. For example, in the
mid-1970's, 63 percent of the full and associate professors in schools of
social work were men. (Ripple, 1974). As of July 1975, men comprised 88

percent of the deans and directors of accredited graduate schools of social work (Kravetz, 1976, p. 423).

The Committee on Women's Issues of the National Association of Social Workers conducted a survey of 868 agencies, including federally funded as well as private ones (Szakacs, 1977). Only agencies directed by social workers were included, thereby excluding approximately 67 percent of the community mental health centers. Membership agencies of the Family Service Association of America, the Child Welfare League of America, the National Jewish Welfare Board, and some Community Mental Health Centers were included. The striking results were as follows: First, as of 1976, only 141, or 16 percent, of the 868 agencies were directed by women. Second, the number of female directors had decreased from the 1950's by 44 percent. Third, men were replacing women in administrative positions at the rate of 2 percent a year.

An extensive national study of juvenile correctional facilities, carried out under the auspices of the National Assessment of Juvenile Corrections at the University of Michigan, revealed much the same pattern. The study demonstrated that "executives are predominantly male in all program types. The few females are found only in coed or all-female programs . . . where they are still outnumbered by males" (Vinter, 1976, p. 57). "The only area of administrative practice where women seem to have made dramatic gains recently is within the national leadership of the NASW. Whereas in 1970, the national leadership in NASW was 25.3% female, in 1976, it was 50% female" ("Survey Indicates," 1977, p. 12).

As with mobility, the equal-pay-for-equal-work issue in social work is a direct reflection of that issue in management in general (Larwood and Wood, 1977).* There are clear salary differences between male and female managers. Only about 11,000 women managers in the United States earn more than $25,000 a year in comparison with 449,000 men (Hennig and Jardim, 1977).

Several recent studies tackle some of the complexities of the equal-pay-for-equal-work issue in social work. Kadushin's 1976 analysis of data from a 1971–1972 partial survey of National Association of Social Workers' membership addresses this issue, as does Gould and Kim's 1976 study of salary differentials between male and female faculty members in the United States and Canada. Both studies found a significant difference in mean salaries between men and women. Unfortunately, although recently published material about sex discrimination in social work reveals considerable

*For more detailed information about salary differentials within selected occupational groupings, see Martha Williams, June S. Oliver, and Meg Gerrard, *Women in Management: A Bibliography* (Austin, Tex.: Center for Social Work Research, School of Social Work, University of Texas at Austin, Jan. 1977).

concern about this issue, "awareness of the problem has not been matched by systematic efforts to evaluate and respond to the problem at the methodological and organizational levels" (Figueira-McDonough, 1979, p. 221). For example, Social Science models are available for improving discrimination studies in social work (Figueira-McDonough, 1979). Fanshel's recommendations are also pertinent:

1. We need studies of how the career patterns of men and women in social work develop over time and how personal choices and aspirations interact with the institutional realities. Longitudinal studies following cohorts of recent graduates of schools of social work would be useful in this regard.
2. We need to scrutinize the decision-making process through which social work jobs are filled. We may find that inequities based on the sex of applicants result from the operation of subtle values and orientations more often than they do from blatant discrimination.
3. We need information about how sex-based status differentials in social work compare with those in other professions (1976, p. 454).

Thus, despite the fact that the social work profession is about two-thirds female and that many of its pioneers and leading theoreticians have been female, the stereotype of the male manager prevails in social work. Two examples from the social work literature capture the prevailing sentiment.

It is when she becomes a supervisor with male subordinates that her troubles may begin. There is a norm still prevalent in American culture which says: "Women should not be in authority over men of roughly the same social class and age." Further, the next step up is likely to be blocked for the female supervisor, because of the notion that women are not good risks for top administration. The rationale goes like this: if they marry, they may quit; if they do not quit, they may have difficulty getting along with their husbands, since it is still thought that women should not exceed their husbands in status and authority. In addition, the active, aggressive entrepreneurial behavior needed to develop professional and community contacts and to gain access to men of power—both essential for agency survival—is often deprecated for women (Wilensky and Lebeaux, 1958, p. 323).

A more recent discussion of some of the roles into which some males in social agencies cast female administrators reveals the same pattern. For example, in the "man's world" of administration, the female administrator may be stereotyped as a "dumb broad". To quote:

Ms. D., a female executive of a social agency who routinely represents her organization in interagency negotiating sessions, frequently finds it necessary to oppose the males who represent other agencies. This opposition occurs as a result of Ms. D's appropriately representing her agency's divergent perspective on the common problem; however, the males intepret her response as being caused by her "being too stupid to understand the situation." Consequently in such meetings she is either ignored or placed on the defensive by a coalition of males who endeavor to trap her into saying innane things (Curlee and Raymond, 1978, p. 314).

Two Models for Change in Management

As suggested by Kanter (1976b, 1977b), the discussion of women's work behavior can be divided into two major categories. The first category, which focuses on the individual as the locus of change, subsumes much of the writing on character and temperament, as well as the psychology of sex-role differences. Because it is based on the individual, this model is limited to a micro-level analysis. The second model, the structural organizational model, assumes that change must take place within the organization itself. Therefore, this approach proceeds from an intermediate level of analysis. This model focuses on the ways in which different forms of work organization, as well as the conception and fulfillment of the roles within the organization, shape behavioral outcomes. Following is a description of both models.

INDIVIDUAL MODEL

As mentioned above, the individual model includes two separate but interrelated fields of study: the psychology of women and sex-role socialization. O'Leary's comprehensive review of the literature (1974) focuses on the external and internal attitudinal barriers to occupational aspirations in women. In terms of external barriers, she refers to attitudes towards women in management, the prevalence of the "male managerial model," attitudes towards female competence, and sex-role stereotyping.

Research on attitudes towards women in management, beginning with the classic study by Bowman, Worthey, and Greyser (1965), reaffirms the idea that it is the male rather than the female sex stereotype which coincides with the managerial model in the United States (see also Rosen and Jerdee, 1974 Curlee and Raymond, 1978, and Chernesky, 1979). In spite of the fact that recent research on female work commitment does not reveal any lack of sincerity or dedication on the part of women, this myth persists. There continues to be a societal bias against recognizing female competence (O'Leary, 1974).

Of all the internal barriers to achievement which have been discussed, one of the most popular has been the alleged "motive to avoid success" (Horner, 1968). According to this explanation, women's internal motivations require them to fail so that the closer they come to success, the more likely they are to fail. In recent years the validity and reliability of the research on female occupational aspirations has been questioned (Tresemer, 1975; Levine and Crumrine, 1975; and Putnam & Heinem, 1978). An examination of this literature on female occupational aspirations leaves the reader uneasy. As O'Leary says:

> The empirical findings represented in many of the studies do not provide data adequate to assess the validity of many of the hypotheses tested. The literature relevant to attitudinal barriers is insufficient in breadth and scope to bridge a number of obvious inferential gaps. . . . Attempts to empirically specify the relative impact of each of the factors identified as potential obstacles to occupational aspirations among women are needed (1974, p. 334).

In reviewing the research findings on sex differences, Lipman-Blumen and Tickamyer (1975) also raise a similar problem:

> The plentiful and varied sources documenting sex differences lead to a number of problems. Research findings involve different disciplines, differing methodologies, different questions and assumptions, all applied to different portions of reality. Almost any given result may be contradicted by other studies and models. . . . Researchers also often ignore the greater within-group than between-group variance that characterizes the sexes (p. 301).

These same authors also indicate that there is very little definitive knowledge about the causes of sex differences in work behavior. Thus, while women may in fact differ from men in terms of attitudes, temperament, interpersonal orientations, self-esteem, and so on, the quality of current data is questionable and inconclusive. Without better understanding of the societal causes of sex differences, individual approaches inevitably lead to the conclusion that "factors producing inequities at work are somehow carried inside the individual person" (Kanter, 1977b, p. 261).

Sole reliance on this individual approach leads to strategies which stress changing individuals, making women more like men, rather than changing organizations. A recent and very popular book, whose analysis is largely within this tradition, is Hennig and Jardim's *The Managerial Woman* (1977). Based on the life and careers of twenty-five women who by 1970 had reached top positions in business and management, the authors conclude that women managers must acquire the perceptions, knowledge, and skills of successful males. While the authors recognize that some of the negative socialization experiences women have suffered cannot be changed, they do feel that women can learn to aspire towards management careers and can adopt their behavior to this end. Although Hennig and Jardim do focus on specific structural variables like informal organizational networks, their major emphasis is focused on various forms of self-improvement and "shape-up" tactics*. While such solutions address the problem in individual ways, they do not attack the organization of the work situation or organizational climate directly. In fact, although such strategies probably boost morale and offer work for female consultants, sole reliance on these approaches has the potential to stereotype women managers.

STRUCTURAL MODEL

The second of the two models, the so-called "structural model," is elaborated in the recent writings of Rosabeth Kanter (1975; 1976a; 1976b; 1977a; 1977b; 1979).* Based on her research in one large corporation described in *Men and Women of the Corporation*, and on a number of separate findings in the social science literature, Kanter argues that work attitudes and behavior are a function of location within organizational and hierarchical structures. According to her argument, the variables of opportunity structures, power or dominance structures, and relative numbers of sex ratios within and across hierarchical levels are more important determinants of the organizational behavior of women and men than either sex or social role differences.

Looking at each of these variables briefly, the structure of opportunity, or growth and mobility, within organizations is determined by such things as:

> promotion rates from particular jobs, ladder steps associated in a position, the range and length of career paths opening from it, access to challenge and increase in skills and rewards, and as a variable matter for each person, the individual's prospects relative to others of his or her age and seniority in turn shaped in part by route into the job (Kanter, 1977b, p. 246).

Power refers to the ability to mobilize resources, and is determined by both informal alliances and formal job characteristics. According to Kanter:

> Factors include the routinization or the discretion embedded in the job, the visibility of the function, relevance of the function to current organizational problems, approved by high status people, the mobility prospective of subordinates, and as a variable individual matter, the existence of sponsors or favorable alliances with peers (Kanter, 1977b, p. 247–248).

The third variable, proportions, refers to the social composition of people in similar situations. "It is a simple quantitative matter of how many people there are of what relevant social types in various parts of the organization— e.g., the proportion of women, men, blacks, ethnic minorities. Being

---

*See Chernesky, 1979 for an updated review of additional literature on individually oriented strategies for women.

*For the relationship of Kanter's structural model to the work of other organizational analysts, see Kanter, 1977b.

'different' is a matter of how many similar people compose the work force"
(Kanter, 1977b, p. 248).

Kanter hypothesizes about the ways in which these variables behave
(Kanter, 1977b). In the case of the opportunity and power structures, she
also suggests possible measurement techniques (Kanter, 1979). She asserts
that it is women's relative disadvantage in regard to opportunity, power,
and relative numbers that leads to behaviors such as limited aspirations and
concern with co-worker friendships. These behaviors are also true for men
in similarly disadvantaged positions. In other words, what might at first
glance appear to be sex differences can, in fact, be accounted for by the
person's position in the hierarchy of power and opportunity. Powerlessness
and low opportunity comprise self-perpetuating circumstances that can
only be changed by altering structures which lie outside the individual.

Intervention Strategies for Social Service Administrators

This section describes interventions to be used by the social service manager in expanding and enhancing leadership positions for women in social
service. Although there is a great deal of overlap between categories, for
heuristic purposes the strategies will be described according to the individual and structural models presented above. Obviously, administrators
must intervene on both levels in order for the necessary changes to occur.

Before strategies can be delineated, it is important to picture the system
in which these changes are supposed to take place. Institutions and agencies have been administered in male-dominated patterns which are so
ingrained that it is assumed that they will be perpetuated. Old-boy networks abound in social service to the same degree that they exist in any
other enterprise. In addition, individual executives, be they male or
female, expect these patterns to be perpetuated simply because they have
always been that way or because of an individual stake in the current
model. A female administrator has as much reason to respect the status quo
as her male counterpart. People who have achieved what they want are
unlikely to encourage change.

In considering these strategies, it is also important to recognize that
almost all of the literature deals with changes which must be made by
women. Obviously, this problem is as much concerned with men as it is
with women and must be viewed in that way in order for real and lasting
changes to occur. Biases must be examined on the part of the institution
and the men and women who manage and staff it at all levels.

INDIVIDUAL STRATEGIES

At the individual level the administrator needs to provide opportunities for
individuals to become more aware of and have greater possibilities for

improving their status within organizations. A first strategy is conscious-ness-raising. Here the administrator provides structure and time for groups of women to meet and talk intensively about whether or not they would like to be managers, and why they have arrived at such conclusions (see, for example, Ells, 1973). Within this context, the individual is helped to confront her ideas about administrative aspiration. Does she want to succeed as an administrator. If she does not want to carry administrative responsibilities, has she been able to sort out the reasons? Is her level of aspiration related to her concept of herself as a woman or the stereotype of a woman's role in this society?

An example of a way in which to organize and maintain a consciousness-raising group is the following. Announce at a staff meeting that you think that consciousness-raising is an effective tool for making staff aware of the opportunities for women in management and elicit any concerns they might have about taking such a step. Name a specific time and a private meeting place for these group sessions. For instance, announce that you would like to begin with one group as a trial run and that you will give ten volunteers time off from 3:30 P.M. until 5:00 P.M. each Thursday to attend the meetings. You might suggest that the group would meet for ten sessions and that they can choose whether they would prefer to meet by themselves or with a consultant from outside the agency. At this same staff meeting, you can state that the group will be asked to help evaluate its effectiveness and its particular structure midway through the meetings and again at the end of the ten-week period. If the group finds consciousness-raising to be an effective tool in this area, the number of groups can be expanded, with the maintenance of ongoing evaluation procedures to ensure the continued effectiveness of the program. It is vital to remember that male staff need and can respond to consciousness-raising as much as female staff. Part of the evaluation process will be to decide whether these groups are most effec-tive as single-sex, mixed-sex, or a combination of single/and mixed-sex meetings.

An additional strategy on the individual level consists of facing the person with the dual concepts of job and career. One of the reasons women do not climb further on the administrative ladder is the fact that many only expect to keep a job until something better comes along, or until they marry, or have children (Hennig and Jardim, 1977). Instead of this job orientation, women who want to become managers must learn to think in terms of a career. If they take a particular position, they should do so because it is one step in a career line geared towards leadership and administration. This strategy requires that individuals learn to think in career terms before or as soon as they enter the field of social service. When the administrator wants to encourage individuals to work towards administrative positions, he or she must help inform workers about the differences between jobs and careers.

Another individual strategy involves the development of the informal networks which are at the heart of middle management (Hennig and Jardim, 1977). With the administrator's encouragement, individual women must establish informal networks in order to gather more information about the organization—information about personnel, the sources of agency funding, and, most especially, the ways in which the organization makes and carries out decisions. Only through such informal networks can the individual really understand the organization, the ways in which power is accrued, and the means of gathering some of that power for herself. Somehow, women tend to think that the good, honest, hardworking individual will win out, when, in fact, the individual who understands the place and use of power in the organization stands a far greater chance of succeeding. An individual way to power is through the establishment of one's own familiar network system.

Again, it is important to remember that the way in which the organization is administered will have a great deal to do with determining the possibility of establishing such informal networks. The administrator's task is to allow executive staff some access to ideas, and to establish an atmosphere of trust in which networks can grow and flourish. If all management is composed of males, or males and an occasional female who have controlled most middle-level decision-making for a long time, the administrator must deal with this factor as well as encourage the establishment of new informal networks.

This last strategy underscores the overlap between the individual and structural approaches. In addition, it demonstrates clearly the need for combining the two approaches for maximum effectiveness. If the administrator encouraged women who were considering or aspiring to middle-management positions to establish informal networks and did not deal with the rest of the middle-management staff about problems of accessibility, the strategy would only lead to frustration. If, on the other hand, the administrator talked to middle management about accessibility but did not really encourage the establishment of new and expanded informal networks, the strategy would soon be lost in the status quo.

ORGANIZATIONAL STRATEGIES

The kinds of intervention strategies suggested by the structural model include such tactics as a thorough review of job ladders and an effort to open up new ladders, joint performance appraisal systems between managers and workers, job redesign and the development of new jobs, job rotation, the use of flexible working hours, and several more strategies which will be explained in this section. These particular strategies address both the power and opportunity structure within organizations (Kanter, 1977b).

The first step in the organizational approach is for the administrator to survey the situation in his or her own agency in order to enumerate how many managerial positions there are, how many of these positions are held by men and how many by women, and how many women within the agency are available and capable of assuming managerial responsibilities. At that point, it is fruitful to develop a task force of staff members within the organization which will identify issues particularly salient to women. One class of issues involves the menial tasks: Who goes for coffee? Who takes minutes at meetings? Who types up notes when secretaries are unavailable? Who buys staff gifts for the sick or for celebrating? Other examples relate more to the structure of the agency. A study should be made of job ladders, of the ways in which staff advances in the agency, and how many of those who advance are men and how many are women. What are the recruiting practices of the agency? What is its affirmative action policy? These and the myriad organizational issues which will be discussed in this section can come under the aegis of such a task force.

Another strategy is to conduct an audit of the career patterns of people who are or who have been employed by the agency. It may be that what the agency has described as its job ladder and what actual career patterns reveal are not reflective of each other. If women come and stay for only a few years, then move on to better positions elsewhere, that is an important fact to note about mobility within the setting. If, on the other hand, women work at the agency, stay for many years, and never advance beyond line positions, that information is also important to the understanding of mobility within the agency. If both men and women are quickly moving into leadership positions, it is vital to note the reasoning behind these decisions.

In response to the investigation of career ladder and career pattern, the administrator must be prepared to open up new ladders which will provide more managerial opportunities to women. Creation of new ladders means essentially that the administrator must define and describe managerial tasks which need to be accomplished, understand what abilities are required for these tasks to be accomplished, and must find new ways for staff to reach these positions instead of following the traditional job ladders. Then, of course, the administrator must deal with other staff who have arrived at their positions through the traditional routes so that they will come to understand and accept the new routes.

Job ladders and career patterns can be understood more clearly in terms of the "flow" within the organization.* Thinking in terms of flow as well as

*For a more comprehensive elaboration of "flow," see Churchill and Shank, 1976.

ladder and individual pattern helps the administrator again to consider individual and organizational strategies simultaneously. To arrive at the flow in the agency, the administrator will need four kinds of information: specification of the "management ladder," a measurement of the current "management mix," specification of a "hiring mix," and specification of promotion policies. Management ladder refers to the hierarchy of management positions within the institution. Management mix indicates the number of men, women, and minority-group members in each level of management throughout the agency. Hiring mix means the number of persons from each population group to be hired into each of the management levels each year. Finally, promotion policies refers to the probabilities for each group being promoted, demoted, staying at the same level, or leaving the agency each year. This model will yield an explicit description of the flow within the organization.

In addition to the factors which comprise "flow," there are additional factors which will contribute a broader organizational appraisal.* One is the earning gap between men and women in a particular agency. Another is careful documentation of the reasons for leaving and the career patterns followed by women who sought other employment after working for the agency. The third factor is the recruiting procedure used by the organization. Where and how does it recruit? Are the same questions asked of new men and women? Is there an active search for women who are ambitious, career-oriented, and managerially inclined? A last factor is the opportunities for training within the organization. Are there such opportunities? Are they the same for men and women? Are the qualifications for the training programs equal for men and women? Perhaps most important, are there mentors available who can encourage women to climb the organizational ladder, and indeed to expedite that climb? Undoubtedly, another reason why women remain in non-management positions is that there are so few older women available to act as mentors to younger women.

Once the administrator has this kind of information, she or he can use specific strategies to improve opportunities for women in management. In order to help women make early career choices, especially when they have small children at home, the administrator can institute explicit rules and programs which will allow the women not only to work, but to acquire managerially skills. Many women who have come back to the field after raising families have achieved low-level managerial positions at which they function expertly. Because of the late date at which they have re-entered the work force, these women will probably not reach the high-level managerial positions which their competence would allow. If a way could be

*For a discussion of organizational appraisal, see Orth and Jacobs, 1971.

found to keep them focussed on their careers, and make it possible for them to function managerially when they are raising their families, both the individuals and the organization would benefit. One way to accomplish this is through "flex-time", which allows women some flexibility in work hours, thereby permitting them to build their careers as well as attend to their family responsibilities. With a flex-time approach, the individual qualifies as a full-time employee, with all of the requisite benefits, but has some flexibility in scheduling the particular hours to work each day. Many organizations with a heavy concentration of professionals have tried this approach and have found it to be easily accommodated and highly effective (Elbing et al., 1974; Golembiewski et al., 1974; Martin, 1975 Nollen and Martin, 1978; and Nollen, 1979). In fact, the kind of service an agency can offer is often enhanced by flex-time. Thus, this easy-to-execute administrative procedure could benefit social worker, organization, and clientele alike.

For example, many agencies would like to offer evening, weekend, or holiday service. A woman with a family may find it easier to work at these times because babysitting is more readily available. A woman with leadership potential would be ideal for those unusual work hours when supervision and the regulatory structure of the normal work week would not exist. Such a service would require independence and creativity, and thereby help to shape managerial skill.

Another managerial task, comfortably suited to a flex-time schedule, is the evaluation of an agency service. Most accountability studies are carried out with data available from agency forms. The staff member who carries out such accountability studies need not work regular hours.

Another middle-management task is inservice training. Such training is not carried out continuously, but often takes place in intermittent, yet heavily concentrated periods. For example, teaching of didactic material could be offered as a part of inservice; In a child welfare agency, for example, new theories concerning child abuse might be taught in this way. The inservice training specialist could make a thorough study of the new theories and could then present them to the staff. In the same way, when a new mandate affecting child welfare service is handed down from the legislature, the administrator would ask the inservice training specialist, working on a flex-time schedule to investigate the mandate, assess its impact on the agency, and report to agency staff.

Almost all agencies are interested in inservice training, evaluation of service, needs studies, program planning, marketing of services, planning and execution of special community programs, outreach activities, liaison, and many other tasks which are usually assigned to administrators and which can be accomplished by using either flex-time or part-time scheduling. In the case of evaluation, accountability studies, or even personnel audits, greater objectivity may be possible for part-time staff who know full-time staff less intimately and, therefore, are less influenced by the internal politics and personalities which can make inside evaluation difficult. Studies of work load, needs studies in the community, special liaison with community agencies or groups, and marketing or outreach efforts can be accomplished very well by part-time staff.

While the issue does not arise with flex-time scheduling, since workers receive the benefits and status of full-time employees, part-time employees have typically not been eligible for the standard benefit package in most settings. If part-time work is promoted as an important strategy for shaping female managerial potential, part-time workers must be eligible for standard benefits, such as maternity leaves, sick leave, paid vacations, hospitalization, and pensions. If they are not eligible, part-time work becomes exploited work: a source of cheap labor rather than a means for developing managerial potential. Parenthetically, the question of pensions, mentioned in connection with part-time work, is also an important issue for full-time female workers. Personnel officers within social agencies should encourage female employees to participate fully in pension programs. All too often, both women employees and management have not regarded pensions for women, particularly married women, as a priority issue.

An additional strategy is the provision of day care for young children so that their mothers can work and have their children near. If the agency thinks it is too small to maintain a day-care center or has too few mothers employed who would utilize this service, a consortium of local agencies can share the responsibility for one day-care center. This idea has been carried out successfully by large companies in other countries for many years. In addition, working mothers could be permitted to use their own sick leave when their children are ill. Provision of day care and the availability of flexible working hours of employment and part-time work are all specific ways to provide opportunities for women and to demonstrate the organization's commitment to the employment of women.

There are additional strategies to consider. The institution could develop a policy of promotion from within, and could encourage capable women to assume managerial positions as they become vacant. In addition, the agency could regularly post and disseminate information about opportunities for increased leadership responsibilities. Also, the agency could offer advice and counsel through the personnel department about job ladders and promotion. Finally, a grievance process could be instituted which would funnel complaints about discrimination.

One final strategy for change on an organizational level is the availability of training programs for management education. Training programs should be made available within and outside of the agency. Effective in-house training requires that the administrator create a positive atmosphere, one in which there is no resentment towards those receiving the training. Training outside the agency is easier to arrange, but is an individual rather than structural or organizational approach.

In order to offer an in-house training program, the administrator should have available special textbooks, readings, casebooks, and audiovisual materials. Videotape equipment is essential if women are to have immediate effective feedback on their behaviors and actions. If they are attempting to take charge during the role play of a decision-making meeting and their body messages belie their words, videotape will teach them about this discrepancy more effectively then any group leader or textbook. In addition to materials for special courses, journals, books, and government pamphlets dealing with management issues should be available in the organization library or reading room. In that way, all agency employees can read these materials and better understand the organization's commitment to opportunities for women in management (see Alpander and Gutmann, 1976).

Ideally, women managers or administrators should do much of the teaching. They will understand the subtleties and difficulties best. If that is not possible, women management consultants should be hired so that male managers can learn from them before training themselves. If women are available, they will be role models and mentors as well as trainers.

Reviewing the strategies described so far, it is obvious that both the individual and the organizational approaches must be used in order for appreciable change to occur. Needless to say, structural change is needed on more than the agency level; structural change must occur on the professional level, and the administrator is often in a position to expedite such change.

The first aspect of the profession in which structural strategies must occur is professional education. The administrator controls the exposure of the social worker to management tasks in several steps in the process. In allowing field placements in his or her agency, then designing those placements to meet what he or she thinks are the educational needs of the students, how often does the administrator say: "This student must have years of clinical practice before she is ready for any administrative responsibility"? Most management skills are distinct and different from clinical skills. What makes a good manager may be quite different from what makes a good clinician, although some individuals may possess skills in both areas. The administrator must be willing to train social work students, and particularly women students, in the administrative skills which are so crucial to management.

By the same token, administrators must be willing to hire young and inexperienced social service managers, both male and female. This support must come from administrators who understand the nature of management skills; by defining carefully what he or she consideres to be management tasks, the administrator can offer beginning workers with leadership potential position that carry managerial responsibility. The ethos of the practitioner's "doing her time" before she can assume administrative responsibility is harmful to the growth of strong leadership within the profession. Again, women more than men need to be encouraged and supported to assume managerial tasks as soon as they begin their work. Men seem to expect such responsibility, while women do not.

Finally, social service administrators must define both social service management and education for social work management for the profession. The administrators are the only social workers who know what the job requires. Out of their own experience, administrators must do appraisals of their own positions and other positions presently practiced or required by their organizations. Above all, they must encourage competent women to seek and accept administrative responsibility. In a profession whose majority is women, many highly skilled individuals are being passed over for administrative posts because they have not been taught to think they can or should be administrators, and because administrators have not encouraged them to work managerially.

Conclusions

This chapter is concerned with the underemployment of women in social service administration. After presenting empirical data on women in management, including social workers, the chapter describes two models for change which can be used to increase opportunities for women in social service administration. The first is the individual model, which places cause and responsibility on the individual. The second is the structural model, which states that change must occur on the organizational level. The third, and most important, part of the chapter uses the models to suggest specific strategies through which administrators can bring women into social service management.

Although these strategies are described as individual or organizational, it is only by using a combination of strategies that administrators can realistically promote equal opportunity for women. Without such strategies, social welfare institutions will remain unresponsive to the interests and concerns of female practitioners. Through their use, women will have more opportunity to move into administrative positions armed with expertise and motivated by opportunities for advancement.*

References

Alpander, Guvenc G., and Jean E. Gutmann. "Contents and Techniques of Management Development Programs for Women." *Personnel Journal* 55 (Feb. 1976); 76–79.

Basil, Douglas C. *Women in Management*. New York: Dunellen, 1972.

Belon, Cynthia J., and Ketayun H. Gould. "Not Even Equals: Sex-Related Salary Inequities." *Social Work* 22 (Nov. 1977): 466–471.

Blaxall, Martha, and Barbara B. Reagan, eds. *Women in the Workplace*. Chicago: University of Chicago Press, 1976.

Bowman, G.W., N.B. Worthy, and S.A. Greyser. "Are Women Executives People?" *Harvard Business Review* 43 (July-Aug., 1965): 14–30.

Boyle, M. Barbara "Equal Opportunity for Women Is Smart Business." *Harvard Business Review* 51 (May-June 1973): 85–95.

Brager, George, and J.J. Michael. "The Sex Distribution in Social Work: Causes and Consequences." *Social Casework* 50 (1969): 595–601.

Chernesky, Roslyn H. "A Guide for Women Managers: A Review of the Literature." *Administration in Social Work* 3 (Spring 1979): 91–97.

Churchill, Neil C., and John K. Shank. "Affirmative Action and Guilt-Edged Goals." *Harvard Business Review* 54 (March-April 1976): 111–116.

Curlee, Mary B. and Frank B. Raymond. "The Female Administrator: Who is She? *Administration in Social Work* 2 (Fall 1978): 307–18.

Elbing, Alvar O., Herman Gadon, and John R. Gordon. "Flexible Work Hours: It's About Time." *Harvard Business Review* 52 (Jan.-Feb. 1974): 18–33.

Ells, Susan C. "How Polaroid Gave Women the Kind of Affirmative Action Program They Want." *Management Review* 62 (Nov., 1973): 11–15.

Epstein, Cynthia K. *Woman's Place: Options and Limits in Professional Careers*. Berkeley, Calif.: University of California Press, 1971.

Fanshel, David. "Status Differentials: Men and Women in Social Work." *Social Work* 21 (Nov. 1976): 440–447.

Figueira-McDonough, Josefina. "Discrimination in Social Work: Evidence, Myth, and Ignorance." *Social Work* 24 (May 1979): 214–24.

Fowler, Elizabeth M. "A Survey on Women Directors." *New York Times*, Oct. 7, 1977, p. D5.

Frank, H.H. *Women in the Organization*. Philadelphia: University of Pennsylvania Press, 1977.

Glazer, Nora, and Helen Youngelson Waehrer, eds. *Women in a Man-Made World*. 2nd ed. Chicago: Rand-McNally, 1977.

Ginsberg, Eli, and Alice M. Yohalem, eds. *Corporate Lib: Women's Challenge to Management*. Baltimore: Johns Hopkins University Press, 1973.

Golembiewski, Robert T., Rick Hilles, and Munro S. Kagno. "A Longitudinal Study of Flex-Time Effects: Some Consequences of an OD Structural Intervention." *Journal of Applied Behavioral Science* 10 (1974): 503–532.

*An abridged version of this chapter appeared in Kerson and Alexander, 1979.

Gould, Ketayun H., and Bok-Lim C. Kim. "Salary Inequities between Men and Women in Schools of Social Work: Myth or Reality?" *Journal of Education for Social Work* 12 (Winter 1976): 50–55.

Hanlan, Mary. "Women in Social Work Administration: Current Role Strains." *Administration in Social Work* 1 (Fall 1977): 259–265.

Hennig, Margaret, and Anne Jardim. *The Managerial Woman*. New York: Doubleday-Anchor, 1977.

Hochschild, Arlie Russell. "A Review of Sex-Role Research. In J. Huber, ed., *Changing Women in a Changing Society*. Chicago: University of Chicago Press, 1973.

Hoffman, Lois W. "Fear of Success in Males and Females: 1965 and 1971." *Journal of Counsulting and Clinical Psychology* 42 (1974): 353–358.

Horner, Matina. "Sex Differences in Achievement Motivation and Performance in Competitive and Non-Competitive Situations." Unpub. Ph.D. diss., University of Michigan, 1968.

Howe, Louise Kapp. *Pink Collar Workers: Inside the World of women's Work*. New York: Putnam's, 1977.

Kadushin, Alfred. "Men in a Women's Profession." *Social Work* 21 (Nov. 1976): 440–447.

Kanter, Rosabeth Moss. "Women and the Structure of Organizations: Explorations in Theory and Behavior." In Marcia Millman and Rosabeth Moss Kanter, eds., *Another Voice: Feminist Perspectives on Social Life and Social Science*. Garden City, NY.: Anchor, 1975.

———. "The Impact of Hierarchical Structures on the Work Behavior of Women and Men." *Social Problems* 23 (1976a): 415–430.

———. "The Policy Issues: Presentation VI." Martha Blaxall and Barbara Reagan, eds., *Women and the Workplace*. Chicago: University of Chicago Press, 1976b.

———. "Some Effects of Proportions in Group Life: Skewed Sex Ratios and Responses to Token Women." *American Journal of Sociology* 82 (1977a) 965–990.

———. *Men and Women of the Corporation*. N.Y.: Basic, 1977b.

———. "Differential Access to Opportunity and Power." In *Discrimination in Organizations* ed. by Rodolfo Alvarez, Kenneth Lutterman and Associates. San Francisco: Jossey-Bass, 1979, pp. 52–68.

———. "Power Failure in Management Circuits." *Harvard Business Review* 57 (July-Aug. 1979): 65–75

Kaplan, Alexandra G., and Joan Bean. *Beyond Sex-Role Stereotypes: Readin Toward a Psychology of Androgyny*. Boston: Little-Brown, 1976.

Kerson, Toba S. and Leslie B. Alexander. "Strategies for Success: Women in So Service Administration." *Administration in Social Work* 3 (Fall 1979): 313–

Knapman, Shirley Kuehnle, "Sex Discrimination in Family Agencies." *Social W 22 (Nov. 1977): 461–465.

Kravetz, Diane. "Sexism in a Woman's Profession." *Social Work* 21 (Nov. 1 421–427.

Larwood, Laurie and Marion M. Wood. *Women in Management*. Lexington, Lexington Books, 1977.

Levine, Adeline, and Janice Crumrine. "Women and the Fear of Suc Problem in Replication." *American Journal of Sociology* 80 (1975): 9

Lipman-Blumen, Jean, and Ann R. Tickamyer. "Sex Roles in Transition: A Ten-Year Perspective." In Alex Inkeles et al. eds., *Annual Review of Sociology*, Vol. 1. Palo Alto, Calif.: Annual Reviews, 1975.

Malkiel, B.G., and J.A. Malkiel. "Male-Female Pay Differentials in Professional Employment." *American Economic Review* 63 (1973): 693–705.

Martin, Virginia H. *Hours of Work When Workers Can Choose: The Experience of 59 Organizations with Employee Chosen Staggered Hours and Flexitime*. Washington, D.C.: Business and Professional Women's Foundation, 1975.

Mason, Katherine M. "Welfare Sisterhood: A Bond between Worker and Client." In John Horejs, Thomas Lealz, and Patrick R. Connally, eds., *Working in Welfare: Survival through Positive Action*. Iowa City: University of Iowa, 1977.

McDonough, Peter, Robert Snider and Joyce P. Kaufman. "Male-Female and White-Minority Pay Differentials in a Research Organization." in *Discrimination in Organizations* ed. by Rodolfo Alvarez, Kenneth Lutterman and Associates. San Francisco: Jossey-Bass, 1979, pp. 123–157.

Nollen, Stanley and Virginia Martin. *Alternative Work Schedules; Part I: Flexitime*. New York: Amacon, 1978.

Nollen, Stanley. *New Patterns of Work: Highlights of the Literature*. Scarsdale, N.Y.: Work in America Institute, 1979.

O'Leary, Virginia E. "Some Attitudinal Barriers to Occupational Barriers in Women." *Psychological Bulletin* 81 (1974): 809–826.

Orth, Charles D., 3rd, and Frederic Jacobs, "Women in Management: Pattern for Chance." *Harvard Business Review* 49 (July-Aug. 1971): 139–147.

O'Toole, James, ed. *Work and the Quality of Life*. Cambridge, Mass.: MIT Press, 1974.

Putnam, L. and J. S. Heinem. "Women in Management: The Fallacy of the Trait Approach." In B.A. Stead, ed. *Women in Management*. Englewood Cliffs, N.J.: Prentice-Hall, 1978.

Ripple, Lilian, ed. *Statistics on Graduate Social Work Education in the United States, 1973* New York: Council on Social Work Education, 1974.

Rosen, Benson, and Thomas Jerdee II. "Sex Stereotyping in the Executive Suite." *Harvard Business Review* 52 (March-April 1974): 45–58.

Ross, Alice. "Sex Equality: The Beginnings of Ideology." In Alexandra G. Kaplan and Jean P. Bean, eds., *Beyond Sex-Role Stereotypes: Readings toward a Psychology of Androgyny*. Boston: Little, Brown, 1976.

Scotch, C. Bernard. "Sex Status in Social Work: Grist for Women's Liberation." *Social Work* 16 (July 1971): 5–11.

Simpson, Richard L., and Ida Harper Simpson. "Women and Bureaucracy in the Semi-Professions." In Amitai Etzioni, ed., *Semi-Professions and Their Organization*. New York Free Press, 1969.

Stamm, Alfred M. "NASW Membership: Characteristics, Deployment, and Salaries." *Personnel Information* 12 (May 1969): 33–45.

"Survey Indicates Social Work Women Losing Ground in Leadership Ranks." *NASW News* 22 (1977): 12.

Sweet, James A. "Recent Trends in the Employment of American Women." In Laurily Keir Epstein, ed., *Women in the Professions*. Lexington Book: Lexington, Mass.: 1975.

Szakacs, Juliana. "Is Social Work a Women's Profession?" *Womanpower*, Feb. 1977, pp. 1–4.

Tresemer, David. "Assumptions Made about Gender Roles." In Marcia Millman and Rosabeth Moss Kanter, eds., *Another Voice: Feminist Perspectives on Social Life and Social Science*. Garden City, NY.: Doubleday-Anchor, 1975, pp. 308–338.

U.S. Department of Labor. *Employment and Earnings*. Washington, D.C.: GPO, Oct. 1979.

U.S. Department of Labor *Employment and Earnings*. Washington, D.C.: GPO, Jan. 1977.

————. Women's Bureau. Washington, D.C.: GPO, 1975. *1975 Handbook on Women Workers*. Bulletin 297.

————. Women's Bureau. *Women and Work*. R. and D. Monograph 46. Washington, D.C.: GPO, 1977.

————Women's Bureau. *Women Workers Today*. Washington, D.C.: GPO, Oct. 1976.

Vinter, Robert D., ed. *Time Out: A National Study of Juvenile Correction Programs*. Ann Arbor: University of Michigan, National Assessment of Juvenile Corrections, June 1976.

Wilensky, Harold L., and Charles H. Lebeaux. *Industrial Society and Social Welfare*. New York: Russell Sage, 1968.

Williams, Martha, Liz Ho, and Lucy S. Fielder. "Career Patterns: More Grist for Women's Liberation." *Social Work* 19 July 1974): 463–466.

Williams, Martha, June S. Oliver, and Meg Gerrard, eds. *Women in Management: A Bibliography*. Austin, Tex.: Center for Social Work Research, School of Social Work, University of Texas, Jan. 1977.

THE
MINORITY
ADMINISTRATOR

Ione D. Vargus

12

As minority administrators are increasingly employed in the social services, it is important that all of us, non-minority as well as minority, become aware of the particular stresses faced by this group. Dean Vargus addresses the subject from two vantage points. First, she identifies the personal, professional, organizational, and societal expectations and the dilemmas that accompany them. She then discusses mechanisms for coping with these dilemmas.

While Perlmutter's essay identified a series of political and policy constraints which are externally induced, Dean Vargus is concerned with psychological and sociological factors. Although the author targets her discussion for minority persons who will assume administrative positions, it is relevant to all participants in the administrative role.

> We are training not isolated men but a living group of men—nay, a group within a group. And the final product of our training must be neither a psychologist nor a brickmason, but a man
>
> (DuBois, 1961, p. 72).

Introduction

Of all the professions outside of theology, social services and education probably have the largest number of minority administrators. In fact Hebert (1975) indicates his particular concern with the tendency in public administration for black administrators to be assigned exclusively to traditional social agencies. Although there may be more receptivity to minority administrators in the human services, the fact remains that administrators

216

face peculiar stresses and strains which are a direct consequence of belonging to a minority group.

There is a growing body of literature on issues, concerns, and problems that face minority administrators in public administration and higher education. Likewise, an increased number of conferences include workshops for minority administrators. The issues and problems are becoming more apparent.

The purpose of this chapter is to identify some of the professional and organizational dilemmas and expectations faced by non-white social service administrators. While the overall content of this book is useful to all administrators, the minority administrator faces unique problems in coping with the external environment, in working with staff, in developing resources, and in developing decision-making styles. Confronted with unusual psychological, sociological, and political problems, the minority administrator who takes cognizance of these difficulties will tolerate frustration better and should be challenged by skill needed in dealing with such problems.

The chapter is addressed to non-whites who serve as executives, subexecutives, and administrators of units. However, the discussion should serve to sensitize all administrators and boards to the unique roles, conflicts, and contributions of the minority administrator. The first section discusses personal, professional, organizational, and external dilemmas and expectations; the second section discusses coping mechanisms for handling the dilemmas.

Dilemmas

HIRING

The dilemmas for the minority administrator can begin at the point of being hired. It is only natural to believe that one is being selected for a position because of one's competency. But the non-white individual may need to go beyond that assumption to see if there are other variables which may bring more than the usual administrative pressures. As examples, social service organizations may be motivated to hire a minority person to show good faith in affirmative action, to meet community pressures for a minority administrator, or to recognize the racial composition of their clientele.

Resentment by others often accompanies hiring for affirmative action goals; and even if the arguments of "reverse discrimination" and "reverse bias" are not openly discussed, the feelings may be there. When hired because of community demands, the minority administrator may find that the expectations from that segment of the population are ones that cannot be met, often because of organizational constraints unknown to the community.

The person who is hired to administer to a particular minority segment within a larger population may be perceived as less than competent by his colleagues and even viewed with some suspicion by that population. If, per chance, the individual tries to break out of that role, he or she will be seen as rejecting the group for which he or she was hired to work.

There is a different dimension from those discussed above but one that is of concern to minority persons as they think of climbing the ladder. It is a sad, but true, phenomenon that minority executives often seem to gain leadership opportunities when an organization or agency has come upon hard times or has deteriorated almost beyond rejuvenation. Such, for instance, has been the case for elected minority officials in some cities and minority administrators of school systems and other public institutions. Social service organizations have also come upon hard times just when they seem to be more receptive to minority leadership and just when minority social work graduates have amassed the credentials for such positions. External problems may doom competent minority administrators to failure.

Nevertheless, even with all of the above, persons of color should be encouraged to take administrative jobs. They will do well, however, to recognize that there will be extra pressures and constraints from the moment of hiring. The repercussions may vary but they will be there. In addition there will be expectations that relate to the person, the role, the style of administration, and interaction within the organization.

SELF-IDENTITY

The extent to which an administrator identifies with his religious or ethnic background is not usually challenged. Passing notice may be made of the ethnic background of an administrator, particularly in parts of the country where ethnic neighborhoods are strong, and there may even be an automatic assumption that he will help his own. On the other hand, he or she may choose to highlight ethnicity or not as he or she pleases. But with a non-white administrator, the question of identity is raised immediately. Even white persons who feel that they have some knowledge of the minority experience may ask if the administrator is identified enough with his or her own group. Others may ask if he or she is overidentified. Pressures may come from either position. Here are two real life examples:

> A newly-hired Black administrator was often asked to eat lunch with the Black staff. Since the Black staff had gone out of the way to provide a comfortable adjustment to the city and the job, the administrator naturally responded positively to the friendly overtures. Some white staff "excused" this behavior on the basis that the administrator needed the psychological support and needed to do some political work. Other white staff felt that this

behavior was over-identification and favoritism. Only after a confrontation with white staff was it established that the Black administrator was responding normally to a reaching out by the Black staff without political or psychological overtones and that the luncheon conversations rarely related to aspects of the work situation.

As another example, a minority administrator was leading a discussion on racism for the staff. There was much divergence on the strategy for overcoming racism, and the administrator tended to side with some of the white staff (although for different reasons). The minority participants were actively engaged in the conversation. Later, a white staff member, who did not agree with the other white members, confronted the administrator with claims of being insensitive to the wishes of the minority staff, and implying in these claims that the minority administrator was not identifying enough.

Such, however, is the expected lot of a minority administrator. Expectations may range from those which suggest a color-blind attitude to those of strong identification. The point is that there will be expectations.

THE SUPER-PERSON

A common discussion among non-white administrators is the felt expectation that they are to be super-persons. On the one hand, they have been socialized from their early years to believe that they must be better in whatever they do. And they strive to do so. On the other hand, they resent the fact that this is necessary. Nevertheless, the minority individual may demand of himself or herself and others may demand of him or her, performance which would not be expected of a majority-group member.

LIAISON ROLE

Sometimes a minority administrator is hired with the notion that this will pacify minority staff, and there is often a subtle implication that such a person will buffer the complaints of the staff. When the staff continues to pursue grievances, the minority administrator may be regarded as ineffective, although this aspect of the job was never described or made clear.

An administrator hired without this expectation can interact more freely in regard to racial issues. This often results in more effective resolution of grievances or modification of complaints.

When the minority administrator voluntarily chooses to intervene, such action may come to be expected. In addition, it may have the effect of taking others who should be responsible and involved "off the hook." Thus a superior can claim commitment but may never really be tested due to the minority administrator's intervention. Therefore, judgment is necessary. It is only natural to want to intervene if you feel you have something to contribute and can reduce the problems of the minority group and the organization. However, rushing in to "save" the situation could actually decrease one's credibility, remove responsibility for action from where it belongs, and delay a confrontation that might come anyway.

KNOWLEDGE ABOUT RACIAL MINORITIES

This issue interlocks with the expectation that a minority administrator should be able to demonstrate more knowledge about minority group behavior. Since minority groups have often indicated that one of their own would have more knowledge and understanding, this is a justifiable expectation. It is a knowledge that too often leads to frustration, for the preciseness and accurateness of the understanding may be disregarded if it is not what white superiors or the larger society wants to recognize. The advice may help the institution to strengthen itself, but it may also be perceived as a threat or as requiring too radical an operational change.

The minority administrator is then faced with a decision as to how far to press for understanding of minority needs. As Floyd McKissick (1970 p. 14) notes, "No matter how much power Blacks think they have, when the power begins to irritate whites it will be withdrawn." Rowan's article (1976), "Is There a Conspiracy against Black Leaders," confirms this point of view. The administrator must then ask whether it is more important to keep the position and do what one can or institute an all-out campaign. The latter course may result in dismissal. The advocate role of social service administrators is increasingly espoused, but the issue is even more sensitive when it revolves around racial and ethnic concerns.

MINORITY-GROUP EXPECTATIONS

Minority professionals are often criticized for not helping their own enough and for being too conservative in their approach to problems. This criticism is particularly evident in writings by Black professionals (Hare, 4; Cruse 1967; Anderson, 1973), who stress that the person who has climbed the ladder must help others do the same. In forecasting the differences in style that would occur in the "Black Establishment," Bennett (1964 p. 78) noted "that Negro men of power are on trial, not for the battles they lost but for the battles they did not fight." The minority professional "must pay his dues." These dues are, of course, added to the other stresses he faces. Nevertheless, many minority administrators accept the responsibility.

The written attack on Black leaders and professionals has come primarily from other Black professionals, but minority communities also do not accept minority administrators without question. Since minority communities have not stressed academic and professional credentials, a myth abounds that the minority community does not demand accountability and competency from minority administrators. This is far from true. Minority communities understand that racism has prevented its members from gaining credentials others may possess; but, with or without degrees, the community wants and respects competent people. Because of the great needs of minority communities, the minority administrator's practice must excel; for these communities do not need slipshod or sloppy practices but the finest that the profession has to offer. The minority administrator can no longer expect to be spared public criticism in the minority community. Thus, while a community may continue to demand a person of color in an administrative role, it may ask for the ouster of a given minority individual ("Group Asks Ouster," 1976; "Fire Moore Now," 1976).

Herbert (1975 p. 559) notes:

> It is important to recognize that, as the number of minority professionals and administrators at all levels of government increases, the expectation of minority people for more responsive government will probably expand simultaneously. . . . The powers possessed by minorities employed in the public sector in most cases seldom are adequate to meet these expectations . . . . Where public agencies do not manifest a change in programmatic efforts which might be interpreted by minority communities as being more responsive to their needs, the tasks of minority administrators within those agencies, particularly at the local level, will become increasingly more difficult.

The non-white administrator of a social agency is viewed not only as an executive but as a community leader. The problems of leadership within the minority community have been a favorite topic of Black magazines and authors. White authors (e.g., Wilson, 1960, and Warren, 1965), have also given considerable attention to this area. While this chapter will not review the concerns, issues, and problems, it is sufficient to say the role is not easy. The point is that a minority administrator of a social service agency will be highly visible and expected to carry out social and community activities that go beyond his designated professional role.

INTERNAL MINORITY COMMUNITY

A minority administrator will need to be conscious of the reactions of minority staff members. Minorities live in a society in which the actions of a single person reflect on the entire group. Some minority staff will be wary because they believe that a white administrator is easier to deal with. Other minority staff may be concerned about the problems already suggested in this chapter and the effect of organizational racism on the administrator's performance. The staff may be fearful that the administrator will be co-opted, if he or she has a reputation for confronting racial issues or will be less aggressive than the situation requires if he or she takes a "color blind" stance.

If the administrator is clearly a "token" placed in a decision-making role, the staff may reject him. If the person is brought into the agency with no more credentials and qualifications than those of minority personnel already there, staff morale will be damaged. The greatest unpopularity awaits that minority administrator whose minority staff believes that he has been brought in to oppose or dismantle the special programs that have been established for minority consumers. The issue has been particularly notable in higher education where special programs for minorities have been established. Minority administrators appointed to coordinate or improve established programs are often regarded with suspicion.

On the other hand, the administrator may have to make difficult personnel decisions involving a member of his or her own minority group. Whereas a white administrator might fire a minority person and be called racist by the community it is not as likely to affect him or her to the same degree in the community. The minority administrator is more apt to be a part of the same community as the professional staff, and questions and comments will be raised regarding the situation. Although he may be tempted to explain his or her actions, the administrator is constrained for ethical reasons from discussing the situation. This absence of response may seem to confirm the inquirer's perception; if there is a response, it may implicate others. The administrator can minimize this complication by discussing the problem of community reaction with the about-to-be terminated employee. The problem is more exacerbated in smalltown minority communities where jobs are at a premium and where all professionals of the same minority group move in the same social circles.

At the other extreme is the situation in which a minority administrator may promote a minority staff member to an important position for which many are vying. Such a promotion will invariably be viewed as favoritism. Although showing such favoritism is as American as apple pie and white ethnic groups have been lauded for breaking into the mainstream by such behavior, it is viewed as wrong when practiced by minorities and immediately attacked as reverse racism or reverse discrimination. But the point here is that the if choice is an honest one the minority administrator need not shy away from such practices. In fact if he or she avoids promoting members of his or her own group, the minority staff may be critical.

INCONGRUENCE OF GOALS

Minority administrators are often hired by social service agencies and organizations whose clientele have become predominantly minority. While this is done with the expectation that the minority administrator will help the agency to deliver its services more effectively, the agency personnel and policies may continue to function without changing its operational behavior. Trapped by tradition, directed by a board that may not understand the need for new policies, staffed by personnel that have been socialized into specific but inappropriate social work methods, an administrator may find it difficult to bring about the very changes for which he or she was hired. In some communities, this has resulted in an agency's breaking away from its parent organization or sponsoring funding sources. Such action, of course, brings it own problems, and some organizations have not survived. A minority administrator who believes separation will enable her to deliver more effective services to the minority population should analyze the tactics of other agencies, whether successful or not. Since money is always of importance, Davis' book (1975) on fund-raising in Black communities should be consulted prior to any such decision.

Strategies for Coping

LIFE EXPERIENCES

Considering the additional stress and strain that a minority administrator faces, one might well pursue a different career. The job does have its rewards, however, particularly if one likes challenges, feels racially or ethnically identified, and wants to "pay his dues." There have been stunning examples of minority persons who, having attained positions of influence, have chosen to risk their positions and reputations by suggesting and enforcing policies beneficial to minority groups. While these policies are beneficial for all, for the first time the factors of culture, tradition, life styles, and history are consciously infused into policy so that it is more sensitive to the needs of minorities.

What does one do to overcome the strain and stress? Life experiences have often prepared the way. The social service administrator who has had experience on the front lines of service has already faced racial and ethnic problems. Calling on the reserves of strength and the tests of past experiences can help him or her cope with the new set of problems.

While the sociologist Kenneth Clark, (1979 p. 100) has noted that individual and collective racism is more sophisticated now, the problems of hostility, the super-person expectations, or the isolation of being the only or first minority may have been experienced in previous positions.

> A minority female was selected as the administrator for a large and prestigious organization which had never had a minority decision-maker. Initially she was overwhelmed by the questions from so many people, particularly the media, as to how she felt to be the first and how this would affect her. As she thought about it she realized that in her career she had had several occasions of being the first minority but without acclaim. She was then able to respond to the questions, indicating what she thought might be points of

stress but with anticipation that, as in the past, the interactions with others would be positive.

The problems are often not new ones, but they are not always anticipated and sometimes appear in unrecognizable forms in the new role. Thus, the administrator might ask, "Have I been here before and what did I do about it?"

INTERPRETATION

The minority administrator will always need to be engaged in educating others to the differences for minorities and therefore for himself or herself in the system. While this may seem to be an additional burden, one cannot expect an organization or institution to adjust itself or redirect its behavior when it does not know the problems to begin with. Therefore, when a minority administrator engages in behavior that an administrator might not ordinarily show concerning a racial issue, he or she might interpret to the staff or superiors why he has behaved this way, rather than assume that they will understand. This opens the doors for greater communication and for sharing insights, and can save the institution embarrassment. The top authorities or the board may not approve of the administrator's approach but at least they have been informed in case the administrator becomes embraced in conflict. Several minority administrators have attested to the fact that this kind of openness has raised the respect of their superiors in the hierarchy and, while the behavior may seem to be risky, that, indeed, it has led to even more security. If one reflects upon it, this makes sense. After all the person who is open and honest (but also skillful in approach) is more likely to be trusted.

SUPPORT GROUPS

This leads into another strategy for coping. Minority administrators may find it useful to join an organization composed of other minority administrators. Local ad hoc groups are springing up in many places. There is now a national group which calls itself Black Administrators in Child Welfare and another entitled The Conference of Minority Public Administrators (Robinson, 1974). Such groups offer support for the unique perceptions of the minority, and for differences in the delivery of services to minority clients. They act as a guide to younger and less experienced administrators and they allow for a safe letting off of steam. In addition, their objectives often include a community service component.

Another support group can be the minority staff of the agency. Although some of their apprehensions were mentioned earlier, the staff can offer psychological support in subtle ways. Such help is often quite intangible, but just the fact that they would understand the extra strains and stresses of the role can be helpful.

> For example, a minority male who was known to be aggressive on racial issues was elected to an administrative position. His former colleagues, who also had often been labeled as "militant," met with him to let him know that they recognized his difference in status. They realized that his concerns must now be much broader than racial issues, that he would have to be objective in his dealings with non-minority staff even if they did not agree. They mentioned that they expected to disagree with him on occasion and that such disagreement might be misinterpreted by others as being non-supportive. They indicated that when they had a complaint or concern regarding racial issues, they would discuss it with him prior to taking action. The new administrator felt very supported by this discussion.

Where an administrator might have to deal with organizational issues or community issues that have racial or ethnic overtones, the staff can provide diversity of opinion and broaden the administrator's perspective. Out of a sense of protection for the administrator, the staff may alert him to some difficulties that are brewing.

Some of the literature in business journals that explores the relationship between minority administrators and minority staff suggests that it is generally negative. Here it is important to recognize cultural differences as well as unique relationship issues. The fact that minority staff may more openly confront a minority administrator with criticism is not necessarily bad. It may be very helpful in the growth, development, and effectiveness of the administrator. If a minority staff member asks for specific help in a situation where he would never approach a white administrator or if the janitor engages in conversation these acts could be considered not as demeaning but as a compliment. These practices should be viewed in terms of how the administrator is approached and with what kind of attitude. They should not just be dismissed as a show of less respect.

AUTHORITY

A non-white administrator will find resentment and hostility from many white persons with whom he must deal including some of his own staff. Black (1976) reminds us of the "girdle of authority" that is possessed by a minority administrator. The social work practitioner is familiar with the concept of authority through specialized knowledge, but the administrator's authority is also gained through his position and role. Thus, others will defer to that authority, particularly in an exchange process where the administrator has something he can give or withhold. Even without exchange, the norms of organizations still operate to accord a measure of respect to those in the hierarchy. Thus in those situations in which the administrator believes that racism is operating, he or she may need to use authority to accomplish objectives.

NEGOTIATION AND COMMUNICATION SKILLS

Where conflict that has overtones of a racial issue occurs, special knowledge in negotiation must be gained. In an extensive study of conflict between Black protest groups and white-dominated institutions, Chalmers (1974) argues that "even a first examination leads to the conclusion that the union-management framework must be substantially modified before it can be applied to racial negotiations." Ackerman (1973 p. 94) concurs with this viewpoint as it relates to employees:

> A well-known characteristic of large organizations is that, unless somehow provoked to do otherwise, they tend to approach today's problems in the same way that worked yesterday, even though the context in which the new problems arise may be different.
>
> To illustrate, companies with strong unions and a long history of successful labor-management relationships develop routines for processing employee grievances that grow out of the union experience. If a complaint arises alleging plantwide discrimination, both union and management try to rephrase it in traditional terms; then they can handle it in their usual fashion.
>
> However, the minority employees may feel that their situation will not receive the special attention they believe it warrants if they rely on a decision-making process that has failed to satisfy their needs in the past. Consequently, they avoid the union and attempt to communicate directly with executives many levels above those managers normally responsible for employee grievances.
>
> The normal reaction in such instances is to rule the employees' tactic inadmissible and insist that they "play by the rules."

Chalmers calls attention to additional communication problems in racial negotiations. Among the underlying reasons for communication difficulties is the deep suspicion with which the opposing parties regard each; suspicion distorts signals and hinders communication.

Chalmers also points out the critical but unenviable position of a black administrator in racial negotiations. The varying roles that a minority administrator can play are not only complex, but can be rejected either by the protesting group or the institution for whom he or she works. Even if one shares the position of the protestors and effects modest change, this may be considered a hindrance rather than an achievement because the change is not perceived as radical enough.

Good communication and interactional skills are a must for administrators who work with community groups. During the 1960's one of the major problems of white administrators in business and higher education was the inability to know how to respond appropriately and adequately to minority communities (Vargus, 1977a; Sethi, 1970). Ill-worded and vague responses were often more infuriating than negative answers. The inability to respond effectively immediately (not necessarily by giving into demands) meant that the next time around there was a growing list of demands from a group. Most administrators were unaware that they contributed to this expansion. In response to a request for more specificity, a group would subdivide the demands making the list appear longer. An ineffectual response often pinpointed other problems that the group faced with the administrator.

While a minority community, although hopeful, does not really expect a white administrator to respond adequately, it feels even more disappointed if a minority administrator does not communicate effectively.

Thus, not only must a minority administrator be aware of negotiation processes, racial negotiations particularly, and have strong interactional and communication skills, he or she must also understand the ways in which he or she may be perceived. His or her very credibility is always at stake and while much of this may be unavoidable, one can at least keep from making gross errors.

Summary

This chapter is addressed to those minority persons who will assume administrative positions in social agencies. It deals primarily with psychological stresses and strains that, when applied to Black executives, have been called by Brown (1975) the "Black Tax." Brown believes that "to mask the forces of stress in their organizational lives can be psychologically lethal. There is nothing to be gained by denying the existence of danger." On the other hand, we would not want a student of administration to feel so overwhelmed that he or she would not pursue administration. Obviously there are a number of minority executives who deal with the "tax" daily.

This chapter did not address an equally important issue which needs to be addressed to the white-controlled institutions: how to find and keep minority administrators. Some useful ideas in this regard are suggested by Palmer (1969).

The introduction of minority personnel has been the catalyst for review of many procedures in the business world as noted by Beatty (1973) and Nadler (1969). The latter notes, "It appears that one by-product of hiring minority group members is the examination and often the reform of distorted or outmoded practices and issues." Vargus (1977b) finds that, in raising a number of questions related to problems confronting minority practitioners, social agency supervisors may need to redefine their practices. Hopefully, the organizational climate will change with the increasing presence of minority administrators so that a reader of the future might find this chapter obsolete.

References

Ackerman, Robert W. "How Companies Respond to Social Demands." *Harvard Business Review* 51 (July-Aug. 1973): 88–98.

Anderson, S. E. "Pitfalls of Black Intellectuals." *Black Scholar* 5, no. 3 (Nov. 1973): 22–31.

Beatty, R. W. "Blacks as Supervisors: A Study of Training, Job Performance and Employee's Expectations." *Academy of Management Journal* 16, no. 2 (1973): 196–206.

Bennett, Lerone. *The Negro Mood*. New York: Ballantine, 1964.

Black, Gorham, director of Region III, Health, Education and Welfare. Interview on Aug. 19, 1976.

Brown, Robert W. "The Black Tax: Stresses Confronting Black Federal Executives." *Journal of Afro-American Issues* 3, no. 2 (Spring 1975): 207–218.

Chalmers, W. Ellison. *Racial Negotiations: Potentials and Limitations*. Ann Arbor: University of Michigan, Institute of Labor and Industrial Relations, 1974.

——— and Gerald W. Cormick. *Racial Conflict and Negotiations: Perspectives and First Case Studies*. Ann Arbor: University of Michigan Institute of Labor and Industrial Relations, 1971.

Clark, Kenneth. "Contemporary Sophisticated Racism." in Joseph R. Washington, ed. *The Declining Significance of Race?: A Dialogue Among Black and White Social Scientists*. Philadelphia: Afro American Studies Program, University of Pennsylvania, 1979.

Cruse, Harold. *The Crisis of the Negro Intellectual*. New York: Morrow, 1967.

Davis, King. *Fundraising in the Black Community*. Metuchen, N.J.: Scarecrow, 1975.

DuBois, W. E. *The Souls of Black Folk*. Greenwich, Conn.: Fawcett, 1961. Orig. pub. 1903.

"Fire Moore Now: Union." *Sunday Sun Times*, Sept. 19, 1976.

First National Congress of Black Professionals in Higher Education. "Administration Workshop." University at Texas at Austin, April, 1972.

"Group Asks Ouster of RMSC Head." *Bay State Banner*, Aug. 12, 1976.

Hamilton, Charles V. "Race, Ethnic and Social Class Politics and Administration." *Public Administration Review* 32 (Oct. 1972): 638–648.

Hare, Nathan. *The Black Anglo-Saxon*. London: Collier-MacMillan, 1964.

Herbert, Adam W. "The Evolving Challenges of Black Urban Administration." *Journal of Afro-American Issues* 3, no. 2 (Spring 1975): 178.

———. "The Minority Administrator: Problems, Prospects and Challenges." *Public Administration Review* 34, no. 6 (Nov.-Dec. 1974):556–563.

Holsendolph, Ernest. "Black Executives in a Nearly All-White World." *Fortune* 86, no. 3 (Sept. 1972): 140–151.

Howard, Lawrence C. "Black Praxis of Governance: Toward an Alternative Paradigm for Public Administration." *Journal of Afro-American Issues* 3, no. 2 (Spring 1975): 154.

_____ and Joyce Roberson. "The Black Administrator in the Public Bureaucracy: Case Studies in Cross-Cultural Pressures." *Journal of Afro-American Issues* 3, no. 2 (Spring 1975): 219–235.

McKinney, Jerome. "An Overview of Black Perspectives on Financial Management." *Journal of Afro-American Issues* 3, no. 2 (Spring, 1975): 187–188.

McKissick, Floyd. "Preface." In Nathan Hare, *The Black Anglo-Saxon*. London: Collier, 1970.

Moore, William, and Lonnie Wagstaff. *Black Educators in White Colleges*. California: Jossey-Bass, 1974.

Nadler, Leonard. "Minority Group Employment: Unforeseen Benefits of Specialized Supervisory Training." *Personnel* 46, no. 7 (May-June 1969): 17–26.

Nelson, William, and Winston Von Heine. "Black Elected Administrators: The Trials of Office." *Public Administration Review* 34, no. 6 (Nov.-Dec. 1974): 526–533.

Palmer, Edward H. "Finding and Keeping Minority Group Managers." *Personnel* 46, no. 1 (Jan.-Feb. 1969): 13–17.

Perry, Lorraine R. "Strategies of Black Community Groups." *Social Work* 21, no. 3 (May 1976): 210–215.

Rich, Wilbur. "Future Manpower in Urban Management: A Black Perspective." *Journal of Afro-American Issues* 3 no. 2 (Spring 1975): 160–172.

Robinson, Rose M. "Conference of Minority Public Administrators." *Public Administration Review* 34, no. 6 (Nov.-Dec. 1974): 552–556.

Rowan, Carl. "Is There A Conspiracy Against Black Leaders?" *Ebony* Jan. 1976): 33–42.

Sethi, S. Prakash. *Business Corporations and the Black Man*. Scranton, PA.: Chandler 1970.

Smith, Calvert H. "In White Universities: Why Black Administrators Fail." *Black World* 24, no. 10 (Aug. 1975): 26–29.

Vargus, Ione D. *Revival of Ideology: The Afro-American Society Movement*. San Francisco, Calif.: R & E Research Associates, 1977a.

_____. "The Minority Practitioner." In Donald Brieland et al., eds., *Contemporary Social Work*. New York: McGraw-Hill, 1975.

_____. "Supervision in Social Work." In Kurpius DeWayne et al, eds., *Supervision of Applied Training*. Westport, Conn.: Greenwood, 1977b.

Warren, Robert Penn. *Who Speaks for the Negro*. New York: Random House, 1965.

Wilson, James Q. *Negro Politics: The Search for Leadership*. New York: Free Press, 1960.

ADMINISTRATIVE RESPONSIBILITY FOR STAFF DEVELOPMENT

Harvey Weiner

13

In order that the social service system achieve its objectives and fulfill its mission, it is essential that all members of the staff be involved and informed. Dr. Weiner identifies staff development as an administrative priority, not only as it enhances knowledge, but especially as it fosters work-group cohesion.

All too often staff development is pushed aside as administrators are involved with what they view as more important aspects of administration. Dr. Weiner presents the view that good administration requires clarity and commitment to staff development activities; he focuses on the structural, financial, and interpersonal commitments necessary for an effective program. For an ever-present problem exists in many social agencies where staff feel alienated as a result of impersonal and rigid attitudes and policies.

Dr. Weiner is seeking a humanistic approach to administration based on the premise that positive interpersonal relationships developed among staff will enhance and improve work with clients and promote more effective service delivery.

The purpose of this chapter is to present an administrative perspective on program and planning issues related to staff development. The focus will be on in-service training, supervision, and extracurricular activities which occur outside of the agency. Together, these form a continuum in regard to maximizing staff skill and knowledge in the interest of meeting program objectives. In addition to a discussion of administrative responsibility, a model of the planning and implementation of staff development activities in a large, multimodality drug abuse program will be presented. The administrative issues discussed will illustrate the use of staff development to enhance knowledge and skills while fostering work group cohesion, both of which represent important areas of administrative concern.

A creative, well-planned staff development program can also lead to improved staff morale and motivation. An administrative commitment to quality staff development activities can be the difference between a stultifying, bureaucratic, "this is the way we've always done it" approach and an open, creative endeavor in which administrators and line staff mutually strive for the most effective and efficient means of meeting program objectives. It is beyond the scope and intent of this chapter to fully explore the issue of staff morale. However, it has been the experience of the author that morale is the single most important factor in determining overall service quality. If staff feel that their personal needs for participation and their professional needs for growth are recognized and rewarded, they will bring a greater degree of enthusiasm and creativity to their work. The converse is also true. The depersonalized wasteland which has come to characterize certain social and health care agencies can be viewed, in part, as an outgrowth of the fact that staff in these programs feel depersonalized and alienated as a result of rigid bureaucratic attitudes and policies.

Staff development is an area of administrative responsibility that is sometimes honored more through "lip service" than through actual planning and program implementation. This often occurs with those who are new to administration, for the rationalization can always be offered that one is "too busy" with more important administrative matters. In reality, no administrator is too busy for anything she considers important. Administration like life, requires establishing priorities in the use of one's time.

Good administration requires a thorough understanding of program objectives, and clarity as to how staff development activities will relate to these objectives. Also needed is an understanding of the structural, financial, and interpersonal aspects of staff development, and the potential for conflict, as opposed to creative change, which may result from these activities. The following sections will present a discussion of these issues.

Objectives of Staff Development

The objectives of staff development are twofold, and both relate to the achievement of program objectives. Traditionally, staff development has been concerned with enhancing staff skills and knowledge. While this still remains the primary mission, a secondary purpose involves the use of these activities to foster improved communication and work group cohesion in regard to clinical, case management, and administrative issues. Central to this is the understanding by staff of program objectives and client population characteristics, subjects which represent excellent topics for initial staff development seminars.

Issues related to staff communication and interaction have become especially important with the decline of the traditional agency which employed only social workers. Increasingly, social workers are functioning in large, multidisciplinary programs or institutions where effective client care requires cooperation and mutual respect between professionals and non-professionals from a variety of backgrounds. Often there is a need to integrate the formal education of professionals with the real life "street" knowledge of non-professional staff (Weiner and Kleber, 1977). Also, social workers are no longer merely providing "ancillary" services. They are increasingly assuming supervisory and administrative positions in these multidisciplinary settings and must, therefore, be able to define clearly the objectives of staff development and the relationship between these activities and program objectives.

Issues related to work group cohesion pose the real administrative challenge in the planning and implementation of staff development activities. A well-planned staff development program helps develop a consensus treatment philosophy among clinicians, and reasserts the primary service goals of the agency. This will be discussed further in the section describing the program model.

After the administrator has defined the objectives of staff development in relation to program purpose, he needs to understand how structure can facilitate or impede the achievement of these objectives (Smalley, 1967).

Structural Considerations

Administrative responsibility in regard to the structural aspects of staff development refers to the planning and implementation of such activities through the purposeful use of staff, time, and available resources. Meetings, case conferences, seminars, workshops, and supervisory conferences need to be included in the rhythm of the work week and administratively sanctioned as a legitimate use of staff time.

The author has previously written about the relationship between program structure and function, and how the purposeful use of structure can facilitate the achievement of program objectives (Weiner and Schut, 1976). Administrators need to recognize that their own attitudes toward staff development will often be reflected in the kinds of structural arrangements made for these activities. In some agencies, no one person is given the responsibility for planning and coordinating a staff development program, and no regularly scheduled time is available for these activities. Staff development in such settings has a random, "hit or miss" quality, with no integrated plan or purpose. If administrators view staff development as a waste of time and only grudgingly allow occasional lectures, staff will be quick to perceive the futility of investing much energy or effort in these activities. Such administrators should not be surprised to find that their most creative and committed staff soon seek employment elsewhere.

An essential structural component involves vesting responsibility for staff development coordination in a well-defined position in the agency hierarchy, preferably with an person who is a part of top administration. This is important because it symbolizes the level of administrative sanction attached to staff development. Also, it allows for the exercise of authority necessary to commit agency resources (including staff time) to facilitate the establishment of a comprehensive program. Assigning staff development responsibilities to a person who occupies an obscure cranny in the table of organization clearly demonstrates that such activities are viewed as unimportant by administration.

Other examples of structural facilitation of staff development include establishing a professional library, providing leave time (and reimbursement, if possible) for professional conferences and college courses, and providing space and supervisory time for the placement and training of professional students. Some financial commitments are involved in these arrangements, as will be discussed in the following section.

Financial Considerations

The financial aspects of staff development refer to the use of money and/or other agency resources (including staff time) for these activities. While the allocation of some money is desirable, it is by no means essential. It has been the experience of the author that quality staff development activities can be organized with minimal investment if administrators encourage creativity and staff participation. For example, agencies with easy access to universities can arrange for faculty to visit for occasional lectures at no cost. If the agency provides student field placement training, professional schools will often reciprocate by making their faculty available for staff development activities. Similarly, private practitioners in the community can be asked to lead a case conference or lecture on treatment techniques. Also, clinical and administrative staff from neighboring programs can exchange visits to share expertise and stimulate program development.

Staff within the program can be encouraged to conduct seminars and workshops to share their experiences, and they can be asked to invite professional collegues for the same purpose. This can be particularly stimulating in multidisciplinary settings. A small amount of money set aside for honorarium fees to cover travel and lodging expenses provides access to a wider pool of professionals.

Student field placements present excellent staff development opportunities in that students often bring a fresh and stimulating perspective. Also, the cross-fertilization which occurs at interdisciplinary student-staff meetings often provides the impetus for a re-examination of existing program policies and procedures.

Other examples of how programs can commit financial resources to encourage staff development include offering reimbursement for college tuition, granting leave time and reimbursement for relevant professional conferences, purchasing books, films, and other training materials, providing two-way mirror and videotape facilities, and subscribing to professional journals for an agency library.

Structural and financial commitments are not enough, however. As in all aspects of social work, the crucial ingredient involves an interpersonal process.

Interpersonal Considerations

Although the stated purpose of these activities is staff development, administrators sometimes plan complete programs with little or no input from line staff dispite the fact that staff development activities are meaningful and relevant in direct proportion to the involvement of all staff in the planning process. Staff participation ensures relevance and, more importantly, demonstrates respect for staff competence and maturity.

An important interpersonal consideration is the willingness of top-level administrators to participate personally in staff development activities. Failure to participate in at least some of these activities conveys the impression that administrators consider themselves elitist "know-it-alls" who have no further need for training. Furthermore, such non-participation can be seen as an unwillingness to take part in activities designed to improve services. Staff may well question why they should be concerned with improved service delivery if administrators do not demonstrate a similar commitment. Training activities which are perceived as "busy-work" for line staff quickly lose credibility.

Administrators with clinical experience who cannot find the time to lend their expertise to case conferences will find their commitment to the clinical process questioned. Administrators who do not possess clinical expertise have an even greater need to sit in on case conferences, so that they can become familiar with the agency's services. Similarly, administrators who cannot find time to participate in seminars dealing with new techniques raise questions about their commitment to program improvement through clinical and procedural change. This issue will be discussed in the next section.

While debate exists in regard to who should administer social service programs, one cogent argument favors social workers because of their knowledge and skills in interpersonal relationships. Social work administrators who are unwilling to use these interpersonal skills within their own program need to re-examine their professional priorities.

Administrators also need to be aware of role-modeling behavior, for their relationships with staff can set the tone for staff-client interaction. If administrative interaction with staff is characterized by an aloof, elitist attitude, staff may demonstrate similar attitudes in their relationships with clients. In such a setting, clients may have little to say about their personal preferences in regard to service options.

It has been suggested that social work administrators and clinicians have different temperaments and skills (Patti and Austin, 1977). While this may be true, a common element for both clinicians and administrators should be their skill and knowledge in the area of human relationships. The interpersonal aspects of staff development activities will be further discussed in the section which describes the program model.

Since the primary intent of staff development is to upgrade staff skill and knowledge through exposure to new techniques and ideas, administrators should be prepared for the logical next step: requests for changes in service delivery content and/or format. Administrative issues involved in dealing with suggestions for change will be discussed in the next section.

Conflict versus Creative Change

How the administrator responds to requests for change represents the true test of her commitment to staff development. The issue here is whether the administrator has the vision to encourage growth and change, and be a part of this process, rather than limit himself to an administrative role that maintains the status quo.

Administrators err to the extent that they demonstrate an unwillingness to enter into a give-and-take dialogue with staff in regard to program improvement. Administrators should acknowledge the potential for creative change inherent in a process which involves shared concern and mutual respect between administrative and line staff. Such situations also represent an excellent opportunity for administrators to demonstrate behaviors and attitudes which, through the phenomenon of role modeling, can be transmitted to staff. As noted previously, evidence of lack of concern for staff input is likely to result in a similar lack of concern in regard to client input.

Although staff participation in decision making should be encouraged, there are several important caveats. In the final analysis, it is the administrator who must answer for the success or failure of programmatic change. Though she may delegate a certain amount of authority to others in the organization, the administrator cannot delegate ultimate responsibility for the functioning of the program. Therefore, the administrator should feel comfortable with changes which are to be introduced, rather than accept something he feels is inappropriate. There will be times when the administrator needs firmly to say "No."

Also, there are situations in which regulations, funding realities, personal confidences, or political considerations preclude certain actions or changes. Although administrators should try, whenever possible, to share information with staff in regard to the reasons behind decisions, there are times when such sharing is impossible. Hopefully, there will be enough residual trust between administration and line staff so that friction and paranoia can be minimized when this occurs.

In the best of all possible worlds, all men and women are created with equal education, training, judgment, and administrative responsibility. In the real world of social agencies, these qualities are distributed unequally among staff. While staff consensus is desireable, it is not always attainable. Administrators charged with responsibility for program operations should be prepared for occasions when they have to abandon staff consensus and make decisions based on their own best judgment.

Importance of Regular Communication

Staff meetings, case conferences, formal staff development training seminars, and supervisory conferences are examples of mechanisms generally employed to ensure regular staff communication. While less formal means of communication exist, information may not reach all staff, or it may be intentionally or unintentionally distorted.

Poor communication practices within a program can lead to poor staff morale, which will be reflected ultimately in poor services to clients.

Staff Meetings

The purpose of staff meetings is to provide a forum for the exchange of relevant program information. The frequency of staff meetings, and their length, will vary according to program size, number of program units, and the administrative staff's judgment regarding the need for this type of staff communication.

Staff meetings should not be used to air individual grievances or complaints; these should be reserved for supervisory conferences. Similarly, staff meetings should not be used by administrators and supervisors to reprimand publicly individual staff members; issues that require reprimand should also be reserved for supervisory conferences.

Case Conferences

Case conferences provide the opportunity for program staff to forge a common treatment philosophy. In a drug abuse program, such conferences allow discussion of some of the common frustrations that stem from working with a population where relapse is common, even after lengthy periods of stability and progress (Weiner, 1975).

Case conferences should be chaired by senior staff clinicians. As an example of format, clinical staff can present cases on a rotating basis, with all staff who work with a specific client sharing in the presentation. After the presentation of specific treatment issues, all staff should be encouraged to volunteer suggestions about treatment options. Specific treatment plans should be formulated and noted in the client's chart. In addition to providing the opportunity to formulate a treatment plan for specific clients, cases can be used didactically to illustrate characteristic treatment issues, and to help staff gain insight into their own clients by generalizing from a discussion of others. Case conferences can also assist in identifying areas of clinical interest that can be pursued further in formal staff development training seminars.

Staff Development Training Seminars

Staff development training seminars help to upgrade staff skills by providing the opportunity for focused discussion on clinical issues and specific therapeutic techniques. Group and family therapy, vocational rehabilitation, Gestalt therapy, and psychodrama are specific therapeutic techniques that can serve as topics for staff development seminars in a drug abuse program.

In drug programs, seminars focusing on the medical and legal aspects of abuse can provide specific knowledge that can contribute to a better understanding of problems frequently associated with addiction. The seminars can also be used to acquaint staff with health facilities, vocational training programs, social service agencies, and legal resources which can be used for referral purposes.

Personnel Management Issues

While it is beyond the scope and intent of this chapter to present an extensive analysis of personnel management, the importance of such issues for overall staff development should be recognized. Agency policies in regard to staff recruitment and hiring, employee pay classification, performance evaluations, affirmative action, promotion, and salary increases are subjects which represent valid content for in-service training sessions. Lack of adequate information or the presence of misinformation can result in poor morale and needless conflict if these conditions cause individual staff members to feel that they are being treated unfairly, so staff development time should be devoted to a thorough discussion of these issues. Special care should be taken to discuss these matters with new staff as a part of their orientation, so that agency policy will be clear from the onset.

UNION-MANAGEMENT RELATIONS

Since unionization is increasingly common in human service institutions, administrators need to be prepared for coping with changes that result from labor management contracts. By introducing added structure into the employer-employee relationship, such contracts sometimes decrease the latitude of supervisors and administrators in that certain management decisions are clearly proscribed. For example, the union contract may prohibit changing an employee's work hours or switching staff between units, even if these changes would result in improved services.

While the social work profession has traditionally supported unionization, it is important to recognize that unionization can lead to negative as well as positive consequences for all levels of staff. The author would like to cite two examples of the kinds of management issues which are sometimes unanticipated by administrators who have not had previous experience with a staff composed of unionized workers.

In an urban child care center where professional employees had recently become unionized under the local school district contract, administrators were chagrined to find that social workers were leaving at the exact departure time stipulated in the contract, even though some of the children had not been called for by their mothers. Prior to unionization, the social workers would remain on the premises at the end of the day to provide supervision for these children and talk with the mothers about the importance of punctuality. Once these workers joined the union and had a contract which specified a definite work day, the unattended children were defined as a problem for management to resolve, and the union supported the right of the workers to leave at the specified time.

The second example relates to the fact that certain workers are union officials. A staff member who is a union shop steward, for example, has a dual role as both worker and union official, and sometimes she must be consulted as a representative of the union when worker-supervisor disagreements touch on personnel management issues covered by the contract. In one instance, a program director in a newly unionized facility was surprised to learn that the union shop steward had to be a party to a contested supervisory reprimand of a fellow employee. Prior to unionization, the appeal for such a disagreement would have only involved the employee and the program director.

The subtle and not so subtle political considerations involved in relating to an employee who is both a worker and a union representative should be recognized. Also, since employees sometimes view career advancement and promotion possibilities along the lines of union positions, administrators need to be aware of the fact that advancement in the union often requires a worker to demonstrate that he can "stand up" to administration.

Where staff are unionized, they need to understand clearly how the union contract affects the conditions of their employment. It is incorrect to assume that all union members are thoroughly briefed in regard to specific details of the contract, even though the union may have attempted to accomplish this through mailings and meetings. In-service training sessions should be set aside for a discussion of these issues to prevent needless misunderstanding. This becomes especially important after a new contract has been negotiated and signed.

JOB DESCRIPTIONS

It is the responsibility of administration to make certain that current, accurate, and concise job descriptions exist for each staff position. By outlining the purpose of each job and the specific functions to be performed by staff members in each position, job descriptions become the basis for recruiting and hiring the staff needed for program operation.

A job description should begin with a general statement about the purpose of the position. This is followed by a listing of the specific responsibilities of the job and the authority delegated to the person, for responsibilities require corresponding authority to enable the person to complete the job. The section on responsibilities and authority should contain a clear statement of the supervisory relationships, upward and downward, that relate to the position. Since responsibilities relate to broad, general areas of concern, it is also necessary to specify the standards of performance that will be used to evaluate the person.

STANDARDS OF PERFORMANCE

Standards of performance specify the expectations for a particular job. Standards of performance can serve as a guide to management's productivity expectations. The performance standards for a particular job should be mutually agreed upon by the staff member and her supervisor. This enables the staff member to evaluate on a continuing basis his own performance, and to determine when things are going according to plan. Performance standards are subject to change, and they should be revised periodically to correspond with the current realities of the job. Job descriptions and performance standards serve as the basis for supervision and the periodic evaluations of a person's job performance.

PERIODIC EVALUATIONS

In addition to ongoing supervision, good administration requires a mechanism for periodic evaluation of all staff. These evaluations should be an outgrowth of the supervisory process, and summarize a supervisor's satisfaction or dissatisfaction with a staff member's performance.

Evaluations should occur at least annually, and they should always involve a written statement documenting the supervisor's appraisal in various areas; they should also comment on the employee's potential for promotion and advancement within the program. The appraisals should not contain any "surprises," negative statements about performance that have not been previously discussed as part of the supervisory process. Such "surprises" reflect poor staff relationships and a breakdown in the supervisory process.

Supervisory Conferences

Supervision is the process by which each staff member is connected to the program's administrative hierarchy (American Management Association, 1970). It is a mechanism for communicating staff concerns to higher levels of administration for consideration and a mechanism for communicating administrative concerns about the performance of specific staff members.

The specific purposes of supervisory conferences with staff include monitoring client progress, clinical planning, discussion of special problems, in-service training, administrative planning, discussion of staff strengths and problems, and staff motivation.

Monitoring Client Progress. Supervisory conferences allow the unit director to review each staff member's caseload to determine the progress clients are making toward specific treatment goals.

Clinical Planning. Based on the assessment of client progress toward specific treatment goals, plans are formulated for further treatment. Plans for continuing treatment could include the introduction of group and/or family therapy, for example, or vocational evaluation and training. Referral for health care, legal services, or financial assistance could also be discussed.

Discussion of Special Problems. Clients who present special therapeutic, administrative, or case management problems are discussed, and plans formulated. As noted above, planning might involve referral to other health care or social service facilities.

In-service Training. Supervisory conferences allow the unit director to work individually with staff to upgrade skills and knowledge. This training supplements formal training seminars that are organized for all staff.

Administrative Planning. Staff members are encouraged to share their suggestions for changes that would improve the quality and effectiveness of services. For example, a staff member might discuss the formation of a new group that she feels would be of interest to clients.

Discussion of Staff Strengths and Problems. Supervisory conferences provide an opportunity for the unit director to discuss with each staff member areas of specific concern related to inadequate performance. Areas of strength should also be noted, and mutually agreed upon performance objectives should be established.

Motivating Staff. One of the functions of program administrators is to motivate staff. People sometimes get discouraged, or they may doubt the value of their contribution because of personal insecurity. Everyone needs a "pep talk" once in a while, and supervisory conferences provide the opportunity for unit directors to motivate staff to do their best.

Informal supervision should occur daily as a part of the ongoing work routine. It usually involves issues that do not require extensive discussion or deliberation.

Design and Evaluation of Staff Development Activities

As noted earlier, staff development is concerned with enhancing staff skills and knowledge to facilitate the achievement of program objectives. Mention has also been made of the importance of involving all staff in the design and implementation of staff development activities to ensure relevance and enhance work group cohesion. In the program model presented in the following section, staff were involved in the design of staff development activities through individual interviews and meetings. Other methods of involving staff in the design and evaluation of staff development activities require the use of written input which is then collated to determine needs and interests. Various types of pre- and post-test materials can also be used to evaluate the effectiveness of staff development, and to determine if knowledge and skills have improved.

A cautionery note should be added in regard to the use of the more sophisticated written evaluation techniques in multidisciplinary settings which employ paraprofessionals. The author has found that paraprofessionals sometimes find it difficult and embarassing to express themselves in writing because of poor writing skills. For example, a frequent topic of discussion in supervisory conferences with paraprofessionals involves their reluctance to enter adequate progress notes in clients' charts. It has been the experience of the author that this reluctance often stems from embarrassment in regard to poor writing skills rather than insufficient knowledge of client progress. Similar reluctance may be encountered where staff development evaluation requires written input.

While the more sophisticated written evaluative techniques may yield information which can be analyzed in greater detail, the use of such techniques diminishes the staff interaction which can occur as a part of the evaluation process. Therefore, care must be exercised to make certain that sophistication of technique does not occur at the expense of the benefits to be derived from the interpersonal processes which lead to improved staff communication. If, as recommended earlier, all staff participate as "consumers" in staff development activities, all staff should similarly be involved in evaluating the effectiveness of such activities.

The program model presented in the following section illustrates how the design and ongoing evaluation of staff development activities involves all levels of staff through meetings and individual interviews arranged for this purpose. The focus of the program model presentation will be on in-service training activities, since extra-curricular and case conference requirements will vary greatly from program to program.

Program Model

As noted earlier, staff training helps develop a consensus treatment philosophy among clinicians, and reasserts the primary service goals of the agency. The problem of "burn-out" among staff members, or the erosion of empathy and motivation when working for extended periods in stressful interpersonal counseling (Maslach, 1976), can be diminished by the supportive effects of staff training. Also, staff development updates and enhances counselors' therapeutic skills and resources, which is particularly important in drug abuse treatment because clients' limited resources and severe psychosocial impairment are a constant reality.

Finally, drug program staff are vulnerable to feelings of isolation and lack of appreciation from the community. Staff training which illustrates the complex web of interactions and interdependencies between drug treatment, other types of treatment agencies, and the community helps staff members to understand realistically their relationship to the community.

The program is a multimodality drug treatment agency, employing over fifty staff and serving more than six hundred clients. It is part of a large, inner-city community mental health center. Staff include social workers (master's and bachelor's level), psychologists, psychiatrists, internists, teachers, nurses, vocational specialists, ex-addicts, ex-ministers, pharmacists, research and evaluation specialists, and clerical support staff. Treatment modalities include two methadone maintenance clinics, an ambulatory detoxification program, an educational and vocational rehabilitation program, and a network of drug counselors working in neighborhood mental health facilities. The program's large size, diversity, and heterogeneous staff provide a rich resource pool for in-service training based upon staff members training each other. However, small agencies or programs restricted to a single treatment modality may still benefit from a modification of a training model presented below.

The basic operation of the in-service training program is as follows:

1. Staff training is scheduled weekly for one and one half hours. All clinic and administrative-clerical activities are closed at that time, so that all staff members can attend training meetings. A central location, accessible to all staff, has been chosen for the meetings.

2. All staff receive a monthly training newsletter, describing each training session's content. Included in the same newsletter are messages concerning training available outside of the agency.

3. Special training seminars, which respond to the special needs of staff members, are developed and provided at other times. Special needs refer, for example, to paraprofessional staff members needs, off-site training for nurses, and the like.

Four parameters of the in-service training program are discussed in the following sections: administration, resource development, special needs, and examples of training activities.

ADMINISTRATION OF THE TRAINING PROGRAM

The program director designated the family therapist, already involved in a specific training task, to design and administer the system-wide in-service training program. The director of training reports weekly to administrative and managerial staff concerning current plans and objectives of the training program. At these meetings, supervisory staff have the opportunity to discuss staff development needs specific to their treatment modality. Short-/and long-range goals result from this collaboration.

The director of training is responsible for informing all administrative staff about activities which will include part or all of the staff. Quarterly and annual reports, summarizing training efforts and results, are shared with all program administrators.

Effective in-service training is dependent upon accurate assessment of each staff member's previous training, current work demands, and ideas concerning what he needs to learn to function more effectively. Much of this data is collected by supervisory staff and shared with the director of training. Also, every three months all staff members discuss the content of the previous training and make recommendations for future training content.

The director of training keeps appropriate records, contracts, and arranges for staff members to present training material, pursues potential training speakers outside of the agency, and administers other staff development activities. A thorough and comprehensive guide to the design and administration of an in-service training program for drug abuse treatment agencies is provided by the Accreditation Council for Psychiatric Facilities (1975).

DEVELOPMENT OF TRAINING RESOURCES

Possibly the most crucial task of the director of training is the search for the human resources needed for an in-service training program. He must get to know each staff member well enough to tap her knowledge, skills, and enthusiasm. Support must be given to staff members who are anxious about offering presentations to their peers. The director of training must also pursue leads into the professional community surrounding the treatment agency, to discover and utilize their knowledge and specialized skills for presentation to program staff. The director of training is searching for the maximum amount of useful information at the least possible cost, and he must be alert and open-minded so that all possibilities are explored.

Equally important to the success of this training model is the program staff's awareness that they are able to teach each other and are mutually responsible for the success of their professional development. They learn that they will not be treated as passive receipients of someone else's idea of what they need to learn. Staff are involved in diagnosing their own needs, presenting their own needs, and, insofar as is possible, responding to each other's needs. This approach assumes that every staff member has something to contribute, something to teach his fellow workers.

Data concerning training needs derives from individual interviews with staff members and from group meetings. Often, the information gained from individual interviews tends to be thoughtful and unique to the individual. Data from group meetings tends to be a "shopping list" of needs, requiring review and modification prior to implementation.

Staff members and visitors to training sessions are asked for information concerning other treatment systems within the community. If the drug treatment agency is part of a larger mental health or social service organization, other treatment and prevention specialists are available for staff development activities.

The director of training must pursue these possibilities constantly. He collects a list of potential speakers who have the interest and time to meet with the drug program staff. The results of these exploratory efforts are often quite gratifying, in that representatives of these special interests and activities are usually eager to present their message. In turn, drug program staff may be invited to give their message to a community group or institution.

SPECIAL STAFF DEVELOPMENT TRAINING NEEDS

The training efforts described thus far focused on the general needs of the total program staff. Within the larger staff group, however, individual staff members and small sub-groups of the program staff have special training needs.

1. Paraprofessionals were found to need training in the rudiments of counseling, with a focus on theories and techniques. The training format includes lectures and presentations by seminar participants.

2. A similar seminar, composed of nurses interested in counseling and a vocational teacher interested in a better understanding of her students, is held once a week.

3. A third seminar, held bi-weekly, teaches the theory and techniques of family therapy to several community-based drug abuse social workers who are well versed in community outreach, but unprepared for direct intervention in family problems involving adolescent drug abuse.

4. A weekly meeting of all field placement students provides a forum for the sharing of training experiences. The multidisciplinary aspect of this meeting enlivens clinical and case management discussions, while a social work administration student provides an additional perspective on agency functioning.

5. Another format is the cotherapist relationship in which students and less experienced staff sit in as cotherapist with senior clinicians. Long-term training in family and marital therapy is facilitated by the use of videotape and two-way mirror facilities.

6. Staff members who have no academic credentials are urged to take advantage of formal educational programs. The agency supports such efforts by reducing the work hours of staff members seeking undergraduate credits.

7. Finally, opportunities for relatively brief, extramural training relevant to drug abuse treatment are sought and offered to staff. Other community agencies and special interest groups offer one-time meetings, or weekend workshops, often at little or no cost to participants. Once a staff

member participates in such training, he is asked to share this experience with the total staff at an in-service training meeting.

WEEKLY TRAINING MEETINGS

As noted above, all staff meet weekly for one and one half hours. Below are some examples of the content of the meetings.

1. Several staff members, including a psychiatrist, social workers, and psychologists, planned a series of training sessions focused upon interviewing techniques. Similarities and differences among these disciplines, and the relationship of diagnosis to effective treatment, were analyzed.

2. A staff member outlined the theoretical concepts of Gestalt therapy, and discussed its applicability to drug treatment.

3. The team of community drug abuse social workers presented the differences between community-based treatment and the more structured, clinical activities of methadone maintenance treatment. Staff members became reacquainted with the social, racial, and economic characteristics of the communities served by the program.

4. The program's family therapist, in consultation with the program's legal counsel, analyzed a new state law concerning child abuse and neglect, and staff responsibility in regard to reporting requirements. Similarly, a psychiatrist was invited to explain a new state law concerning voluntary and involuntary psychiatric commitment procedures.

5. A worker in the mental health center's alcoholism program described screening and referral procedures for clients suspected of alcohol abuse.

6. The program director and clinical coordinator discussed the program's finances and means of support. The relationship between grant writing and program functioning was analyzed.

7. The program director and clinical coordinator discussed the state and federal regulations which pertain to drug abuse treatment. A lively discussion ensued in regard to the ways in which regulations limit clinical and administrative options.

8. A worker in the drug program's research and evaluation unit met with the staff to describe the current psychosocial and demographic characteristics of the client population. Also included were data concerning effects of treatment, such as drop out rates and readmissions.

9. Contact was made with a community legal services center. In a series of meetings, the operations and goals of the legal services program were described. Such issues as job discrimination towards drug clients, housing problems, domestic and marital conflicts, and clients' rights were defined by the law center's attorneys.

10. A social worker trained in yoga visited the staff, described the basic tenets and goals of meditative yoga, and demonstrated some of its practices. He also discussed efforts to implement this approach with psychologically impaired clients.

11. A staff nurse, trained in neurology, discussed the basic dynamics and symptoms of seizure disorders of the brain and presented emergency treatment techniques.

12. The job developer of the vocational program met with the staff to review current opportunities in the job market. He offered specific criteria for evaluating client job readiness.

These are some examples of the material presented in the staff development training program during the course of a year.

Summary

This chapter presented a discussion of administrative issues related to staff development. Emphasis has been placed on the importance of staff development as an area of administrative responsibility, and suggestions have been given in regard to the structural, financial, and interpersonal commitments necessary for an effective program.

Staff development activities facilitate the achievement of program objectives, and the importance of these activities in multidisciplinary settings was noted. Specifically, staff development presents an opportunity to improve morale and motivation while fostering a consensus treatment philosophy and enhancing work group cohension.

Particular emphasis has been placed on the interpersonal elements of staff development, as these relate to administrative functioning. Participation was noted to be a crucial ingredient: the participation of all staff in planning for staff development activities, and the participation of all levels of staff (including administrators) in these activities. New ideas and requests for programmatic change are a natural consequence of the stimulation and professional growth which accompany staff development, and administrators are encouraged to enter into a creative give-and-take process with staff to discuss requests for changes in program content and/or format. Several important caveats were noted in regard to the limits of consensus decision making, and a special section discussed supervision as a part of the staff development continuum. In the concluding section, a drug program model was presented to illustrate the planning and implementation of staff development activities in a multidisciplinary setting.

Administrators need to be cognizant of the way in which their interactions with staff set the tone for staff interaction with clients. If administrators demonstrate that they are sensitive to the fact that staff have personal needs for recognition as well as professional needs for growth, morale and motivation will be high. Staff development represents an excellent opportunity to improve morale and motivation while enhancing skills and knowledge. Ultimately, each of these elements are essential for effective service delivery.

References

Accreditation Council for Psychiatric Facilities. *Standards for Drug Abuse Treatment and Rehabilitation Programs*. Chicago: Joint Commission on Accreditation of Hospitals, 1975.

American Management Association. *How To Improve Individual Manager Performance*. 1970.

Churden, Herbert, and Arthur Sherman. *Personnel Management*. Cincinnati: South-Western, 1976.

Cohen, Gertrude. "Staff Development in Social Work." *The Encyclopedia of Social Work*. Washington: National Association of Social Workers, 1977.

Kaslow, Florence, ed. *Issues in Human Services*. San Francisco: Jossey-Bass, 1972.

Kaslow, Florence, ed. *Supervision, Consultation and Staff Training in the Helping Professions*. San Francisco: Jossey-Bass, 1977.

Maslach, Christina. "Burned Out." *Human Behavior* 5, no. 9 Sept. 1976, pp. 17–21.

Patti, Rino, and Michael Austin. "Socializing the Direct Service Practitioner in the Ways of Supervisory Management." *Administration in Social Work* 1, no. 3 (Fall 1977): 267–280.

Smalley, Ruth. *Theory for Social Work Practice*. New York: Columbia University Press, 1967.

Weiner, Harvey. "Methadone Counseling: A Social Work Challenge." *Journal of Psychedelic Drugs* 7, no. 4 (Oct.-Dec. 1975): 381–387.

Weiner, Harvey, and Jacob Schut. "Management in a Drug Abuse Unit: A Primer for Masochists". *Journal of Psychedelic Drugs* 8, no. 2 (April-June 1976): 129–134.

Weiner, Harvey, and Herbert Kleber. *Basic Administration Priniciples for Drug Abuse Treatment Programs*. Medical Monograph Series, 1, no. 3. Arlington, Va.: National Drug Abuse Center, Aug. 1977.

INDEX